The Princess Cas (Volume

Henry James

Alpha Editions

This edition published in 2024

ISBN 9789362096265

Design and Setting By

Alpha Editions

www.alphaedis.com

Email - info@alphaedis.com

Contents

BOOK THIRD

<u>3</u>

XXII

Hyacinth got up early—an operation attended with very little effort, as he had scarce closed his eyes all night. What he saw from his window made him dress as quickly as a young man might who desired more than ever that his appearance shouldn't give strange ideas about him: an old garden with parterres in curious figures and little intervals of lawn that seemed to our hero's cockney vision fantastically green. At one end of the garden was a parapet of mossy brick which looked down on the other side into a canal, a moat, a quaint old pond (he hardly knew what to call it) and from the same standpoint showed a considerable part of the main body of the house— Hyacinth's room belonging to a wing that commanded the extensive irregular back—which was richly grey wherever clear of the ivy and the other dense creepers, and everywhere infinitely a picture: with a high-piled ancient russet roof broken by huge chimneys and queer peep-holes and all manner of odd gables and windows on different lines, with all manner of antique patches and protrusions and with a particularly fascinating architectural excrescence where a wonderful clock-face was lodged, a clock-face covered with gilding and blazonry but showing many traces of the years and the weather. He had never in his life been in the country—the real country, as he called it, the country which was not the mere 4 ravelled fringe of London—and there entered through his open casement the breath of a world enchantingly new and after his recent feverish hours unspeakably refreshing; a sense of sweet sunny air and mingled odours, all strangely pure and agreeable, and of a musical silence that consisted for the greater part of the voices of many birds. There were tall quiet trees near by and afar off and everywhere; and the group of objects that greeted his eyes evidently formed only a corner of larger spaces and of a more complicated scene. There was a world to be revealed to him: it lay waiting with the dew on it under his windows, and he must go down and take of it such possession as he might.

On his arrival at ten o'clock the night before he had only got the impression of a mile-long stretch of park, after turning in at a gate; of the cracking of gravel under the wheels of the fly and of the glow of several windows, suggesting indoor cheer, in a front that lifted a range of vague grand effects into the starlight. It was much of a relief to him then to be informed that the Princess, in consideration of the lateness of the hour, begged to be excused till the morrow: the delay would give him time to recover his balance and look about him. This latter opportunity was offered first as he sat at supper in a vast high hall with the butler, whose acquaintance he had made in South Street, behind his chair. He had not exactly wondered how he should be treated: too blank for that his conception of the way in which, at a country-house, invidious distinctions might be made and shades of importance marked; but it was plain the best had been ordered for him. He was at all events abundantly content with his reception and more and more excited by it. The repast was delicate— though his other senses were so awake that hunger dropped out and he ate, as it were, without 5 eating—and the grave automatic servant filled his glass with a liquor that reminded him of some lines of Keats in the "Ode to a Nightingale." He wondered if he should hear a nightingale at Medley (he was vague about the seasons of this vocalist) and also if the butler would attempt to talk to him, had ideas about him, knew or suspected who he was and what: which after all there was no reason for his doing save perhaps the aspect of the scant luggage attending the visitor from Lomax Place. Mr. Withers, however (it was this name Hyacinth heard used by the driver of his fly), had given no further symptom of sociability than to ask him at what time he would be called in the morning; to which our young man replied that he preferred not to be called at all—he would get up by himself. The butler rejoined, "Very good, sir," while Hyacinth thought it probable he puzzled him a good deal and even considered the question of giving him a precautionary glimpse of an identity that might be later on less fortunately betrayed. The object of this diplomacy was that he should not be oppressed and embarrassed with attentions to which he was unused; but the idea came to nothing for the simple reason that before he spoke he found himself liking what he had feared. His impulse to deprecate services departed, he was already aware there were none he should care to miss or was not quite prepared for. He knew he had probably thanked Mr. Withers too much, but he couldn't help this—it was an irrepressible tendency and an error he should doubtless always commit.

He had lain in a bed constituted in a manner so perfect to ensure rest that it was naturally responsible in some degree for his want of ease, and in a large high room where long dressing-glasses emitted ghostly glances even after the light was extinguished. Suspended on the walls were many prints, mezzotints 6 and old engravings which he supposed, possibly without reason, to be of the finest and rarest. He got up several times in the night, lighted his candle and walked about looking at them. He looked at himself in one of the long glasses, and in a place where everything was on such a scale it seemed to him more than ever that Mademoiselle Vivier's son, lacking all the social dimensions, was scarce a perceptible person at all. As he came downstairs he encountered housemaids with dusters and brooms, or perceived them through open doors on their knees before fireplaces; and it was his belief that they regarded him more boldly than if he had been a guest of the usual kind. Such a reflexion as that, however, ceased to trouble him after he had passed out of doors and begun to roam through the park, into which he let himself loose at first, and then, in narrowing circles, through the nearer grounds. He rambled an hour in breathless ecstasy, brushing the dew from the deep fern and bracken and the rich borders of the garden, tasting the fragrant air and stopping everywhere, in murmuring rapture, at the touch of some exquisite impression. His whole walk was peopled with recognitions; he had been dreaming all his life of just such a place and such objects, such a morning and such a chance. It was the last of April and everything was fresh and vivid; the great trees, in the early air, were a blur of tender shoots. Round the admirable house he revolved repeatedly, catching every aspect and feeling every value, feasting on the whole expression and wondering if the Princess would observe his proceedings from a window and if they would be offensive to her. The house was not hers, but only hired for three months, and it could flatter no princely pride that he should be struck with it. There was something in the way the grey walls rose from the green lawn that brought tears to his eyes; 7 the spectacle of long duration unassociated with some sordid infirmity or poverty was new to him; he had lived with people among whom old age meant for the most part a grudged and degraded survival. In the favoured resistance of Medley was a serenity of success, an accumulation of dignity and honour.

A footman sought him out in the garden to tell him breakfast was served. He had never thought of breakfast, and as he walked back to the house attended by the inscrutable flunkey this offer appeared a free extravagant gift, unexpected and romantic. He found he was to breakfast alone and asked no questions, but when he had finished the butler came in to say that the Princess would see him after luncheon but that in the meanwhile she wished him to understand the library to be all at his service. "After luncheon"—that threw the hour he had come for very far into the future, and it caused him some bewilderment that she should think it worth while to invite him to stay with her from Saturday evening to Monday morning only to let so much of his visit elapse without their meeting. But he felt neither slighted nor impatient; the impressions already crowding on him were in themselves a sufficient reward, and what could one do better precisely in such a house as that than wait for a wonderful lady? Mr. Withers conducted him to the library and left him planted in the middle of it and staring at the treasures he quickly and widely took in. It was an old brown room of great extent—even the ceiling was brown, though there were figures in it dimly gilt—where row upon row of finely-lettered backs consciously appealed for recognition. A fire of logs crackled in a great chimney, and there were alcoves with deep window-seats, and arm-chairs such as he had never seen, luxurious, leather-covered, with an adjustment for holding one's volume; and a vast 8 writing-table before one of the windows, furnished with a perfect magazine of paper and pens, inkstands and blotters, seals, stamps, candlesticks, reels of twine, paper-weights, book-knives. He had never imagined so many aids to correspondence and before he turned away had written a note to Millicent in a hand even nobler than usual—his penmanship was very minute, but at the same time wonderfully free and fair—largely for the pleasure of seeing "Medley Hall" stamped in heraldic-looking red characters at the top of his paper. In the course of an hour he had ravaged the collection, taken down almost every book, wishing he could keep it a week, and then put it back as quickly as his eye caught the next, which glowed with a sharper challenge. He came upon rare bindings and extracted precious hints—hints by which he felt himself perfectly capable of profiting. Altogether his vision of true happiness at this moment was that for a month or two he should be locked into the treasure-house of Medley. He forgot the outer world and the morning waned—the beautiful vernal Sunday—while he lingered there.

He was on the top of a ladder when he heard a voice remark, "I'm afraid they're very dusty; in this house, you know, it's the dust of centuries," and, looking down, saw Madame Grandoni posted in the middle of the room. He instantly prepared to descend and greet her, but she exclaimed: "Stay, stay, if you're not giddy; we can talk from here! I only came in to show you we *are* in the house and to tell you to keep up your patience. The Princess will probably see you in a few hours."

"I really hope so," he returned from his perch, rather dismayed at the "probably."

"*Natürlich*," said the old lady; "but people have come sometimes and gone away without seeing her. It all depends on her mood." 9

"Do you mean even when she has sent for them?"

"Oh, who can tell whether she has sent for them or not?"

"But she sent for me, you know," Hyacinth declared, staring down and struck with the odd effect of Madame Grandoni's wig in that bird's-eye view.

"Oh yes, she sent for you, poor young man!" The old lady looked up at him with a smile and they communicated a little in silence. Then she added: "Captain Sholto has come like that more than once and has gone away no better off."

"Captain Sholto?" Hyacinth repeated.

"Very true, if we talk at this distance I must shut the door." She retraced her course while he watched her, and pushed it to, then advanced into the room again with her superannuated, shuffling step, walking as if her shoes were too big for her. Hyacinth, moreover, descended the ladder. "There it is. She's a *capricciosa*."

"I don't understand how you speak of her," Hyacinth remarked gravely. "You seem her friend, yet you say things not favourable to her."

"Dear young man, I say much worse to her about herself than I should ever say to you. I'm rude, oh yes—even to you, to whom, no doubt, I ought to be particularly kind. But I'm not false. That's not our German nature. You'll hear me some day. I *am* the friend of the Princess; it would be well enough if she never had a worse one! But I should like to be yours too—what will you have? Perhaps it's of no use. At any rate here you are."

"Yes, here I am decidedly!" Hyacinth uneasily laughed.

"And how long shall you stay? Pardon me if I ask that; it's part of my rudeness."

"I shall stay till to-morrow morning. I must be at my work by noon."

"That will do very well. Don't you remember, the other time, how I told you to remain faithful?"

"That was very good advice. But I think you exaggerate my danger."

"So much the better," said Madame Grandoni; "though now that I look at you well I doubt it a little. I see you're one of those types that ladies like. I can be sure of that—I like you myself. At my age—a hundred and twenty—can't I say that? If the Princess were to do so it would be different; remember that—that any flattery she may ever offer you will be on her lips much less discreet. But perhaps she will never have the chance; you may never come again. There are people who have come only once. *Vedremo bene.* I must tell you that I'm not in the least against a young man's taking a holiday, a little quiet recreation, once in a while," Madame Grandoni continued in her disconnected, discursive, confidential way. "In Rome they take one every five days; that's no doubt too often. In Germany less often. In this country I can't understand if it's an increase of effort: the English Sunday's so difficult! This one will in any case have been beautiful for you. Be happy, make yourself comfortable; but go home to-morrow!" And with this injunction Madame Grandoni took her way again to the door while he went to open it for her. "I can say that because it's not my house. I'm only here like you. And sometimes I think I also shall go to-morrow!"

"I imagine you've not, like me, your living to get every day. That's reason enough for me," said Hyacinth.

She paused in the doorway with her expressive, ugly, kindly little eyes on his face. "I believe I'm nearly as poor as you. And I've not, like you, the 11 appearance of nobility. Yet I'm noble," said the old lady, shaking her wig.

"And I'm not!" Hyacinth deeply smiled.

"It's better not to be lifted up high like our friend. It doesn't give happiness."

"Not to one's self possibly; but to others!" From where they stood he looked out into the great panelled and decorated hall, lighted from above and roofed with a far-away dim fresco, and the reflexion of this grandeur came into his appreciative eyes.

"Do you admire everything here very much—do you receive great pleasure?" asked Madame Grandoni.

"Oh, so much—so much!"

She considered him a moment longer. "*Poverino!*" she murmured as she turned away.

A couple of hours later the Princess sent for him and he was conducted upstairs, through corridors carpeted with crimson and hung with pictures, and ushered into a large bright saloon which he afterwards learned that his hostess used as a boudoir. The sound of music had come to him outside the door, so that he was prepared to find her seated at the piano, if not to see her continue to play after he appeared. Her face was turned in the direction from which he entered, and she smiled at him without lifting her hands from the keys while the servant, as if he had just arrived, formally pronounced his name. The room, placed in an angle of the house and lighted from two sides, was large and sunny, upholstered in fresh gay chintz, furnished with all sorts of sofas and low familiar seats and convenient little tables, most of these holding great bowls of early flowers; littered over with books, newspapers, magazines, photographs of celebrities slashed across by signatures, and full of the marks of luxurious and rather indolent habitation. Hyacinth stood 12 there, not advancing very far, and the Princess, still playing and smiling, nodded toward a seat near the piano. "Put yourself there and listen to me." He did so and she played a long time without glancing at him. This left him the more free to rest his eyes on her own face and person while she looked about the room, vaguely, absently, but with an expression of quiet happiness, as if lost in her music, soothed and pacified by it. A window near her was half-open and the soft clearness of the day and all the odour of the spring diffused themselves and made the place cheerful and pure. The Princess struck him as extraordinarily young and fair, and she seemed so slim and simple, and so friendly too, in spite of having neither abandoned her occupation nor offered him her hand, that he at last sank back in his seat with the sense that all his uneasiness, his nervous tension, was leaving him, and that he was safe in her kindness, in the free original way with which she evidently would always treat him. This peculiar manner, half consideration, half fellowship, seemed to him to have already so mild and wise an intention. She played ever so movingly, with different pieces succeeding each other; he had never listened to music nor to a talent of that order. Two or three times she turned her eyes on him, and then they shone with the wonderful expression which was the essence of her beauty; that profuse mingled light which seemed to belong to some everlasting summer and yet to suggest seasons that were past and gone, some experience that was only an exquisite memory. She asked him if he cared for music and then added, laughing, that she ought to have made sure of this before; while he answered—he had already told her so in South Street, but she appeared to have forgotten—that he was awfully fond of it. 13

The sense of the beauty of women had been given to our young man in a high degree; it was a faculty that made him conscious to adoration of all the forces of that power and depths of that mystery; of every element of loveliness, every delicacy of feature, every shade and tone that contributed to charm. Therefore even if he had appreciated less the strange harmonies the Princess drew from her instrument and her genius there would have been no lack of interest in his situation, in such an opportunity to watch her admirable outline and movement, the noble form of her head and face, the gathered-up glories of her hair, the living flower-like freshness which had no need to turn from the light. She was dressed in fair colours and as simply as a young girl. Before she ceased playing she asked him what he would like to do in the afternoon: would he have any objection to taking a drive with her? It was very possible he might enjoy the country. She seemed not to attend to his answer, which was covered by the sound of the piano; but if she had done so it would have left her very little doubt as to the reality of his inclination. She remained gazing at the cornice of the room while her hands wandered to and fro; then suddenly she stopped, got up and came toward him. "It's probable that's the most I shall ever bore you. You know the worst. Would you very kindly close the piano?" He complied with her request and she went to another part of the room and sank into an arm-chair. When he approached her again she said: "Is it really true that you've never seen a park nor a garden nor any of the beauties of nature and that sort of thing?" The allusion was to something gravely stated in his letter when he answered the note by which she proposed to him to run down to Medley, and after he had assured her it was perfectly true she exclaimed: 14 "I'm so glad—I'm so glad! I've never been able to show any one anything new and have always felt I should like it—especially with a fine sensitive mind. Then you *will* come and drive with me?" She spoke as if this would be a great favour.

That was the beginning of the communion—so strange considering their respective positions—which he had come to Medley to enjoy, and it passed into some singular phases. The Princess had an extraordinary way of taking things for granted, of ignoring difficulties, of assuming that her preferences might be translated into fact. After her guest had remained with her ten minutes longer—a period mainly occupied with her exclamations of delight at his having seen so little of the sort of thing of which Medley consisted (Where should he have seen it, gracious heaven? he asked himself); after she had rested thus briefly from her exertions at the piano she proposed that they should go out-of-doors together. She was an immense walker—she wanted her regular walk. She left him for a short time, giving him the last number of the *Revue des Deux Mondes* to entertain himself withal and calling his attention in particular to a story by M. Octave Feuillet (she should be so curious to know what he thought of it); to reappear later with dark hat and clear parasol, drawing on fresh loose gloves and offering herself to our young man at that moment as a sudden incarnation of the heroine of M. Feuillet's novel, in which he had instantly become immersed. On their way downstairs it occurred to her that he had not yet seen the house and that it would be amusing for her to show it him; so she turned aside and took him through it, up and down and everywhere, even into the vast old-fashioned kitchen where they found a small red-faced man in a white jacket and apron and a white cap (he removed the latter ornament 15 to salute the little bookbinder) with whom his companion spoke Italian, which Hyacinth understood sufficiently to perceive that she addressed her cook in the second person singular, as if he had been a feudal retainer. He remembered how it was in the same way the three Musketeers spoke to their lackeys. The Princess explained that the gentleman in the white cap was a delightful creature (she couldn't endure English servants, though she was obliged to have two or three) who would make her plenty of risottos and polentas—she had quite the palate of a contadina. She showed Hyacinth everything: the queer transmogrified corner that had once been a chapel; the secret stairway which had served in the persecutions of the Catholics (the owners of Medley were, like the Princess herself, of the old persuasion); the musicians' gallery over the hall; the tapestried room which people came from a distance to see; and the haunted chamber (the two, sometimes confounded, were quite distinct) where a horrible figure at certain times made its appearance—a dwarfish ghost with an enormous head, a dispossessed eldest brother of long ago who had passed for an idiot, which he wasn't, and had somehow been made away with. The Princess offered her visitor the privilege of sleeping in this apartment, declaring however that nothing would induce her even to enter it alone, she being a benighted creature, consumed with abject superstitions. "I don't know if I'm religious or whether if I were my religion would be superstitious, but my superstitions are what I'm faithful to." She made her young friend pass through the drawing-room very cursorily, remarking that they should see it again: it was rather stupid—drawing-rooms in English country-houses were always stupid; indeed if it would amuse him they would sit there after dinner. Madame Grandoni and she usually sat <u>16</u> upstairs, but they would do anything he should find more comfortable.

At last they came out of the house together and while they went she explained, to justify herself against the imputation of extravagance, that, though the place doubtless struck him as absurdly large for a couple of quiet women and the whole thing was not in the least what she would have preferred, yet it was all far cheaper than he probably imagined; she would never have looked at it if it hadn't been cheap. It must appear to him so preposterous for a woman to associate herself with the great uprising of the poor and yet live in palatial halls—a place with forty or fifty rooms. This was one of her only two allusions as yet to her infatuation with the "cause"; but it fell very happily, for Hyacinth had not been unconscious of the anomaly she mentioned. It had been present to him all day; it added much to the way life practised on his sense of the tragi-comical to think of the Princess's having retired to a private paradise to think out the problem of the slums. He listened therefore with great attention while she made all conscientiously the point that she had taken the house only for three months in any case, because she wanted to rest after a winter of visiting and living in public (as the English spent their lives, with all their celebrated worship of the "home") and yet didn't wish too soon to return to town; though she was obliged to confess that she had still the place in South Street on her hands, thanks to her deciding unexpectedly to go on with it rather than move out her things. One had to keep one's things somewhere, and why wasn't that as good a *dépôt* as another? Medley was not what she would have chosen if she had been left to herself; but she had not been left to herself—she never was; she had been bullied into taking it by the owners, whom she had met <u>17</u> somewhere and who had made up to her immensely, persuading her that she might really have it for nothing, for no more than she would give for the little honeysuckle cottage, the old parsonage embowered in clematis, which were really what she had been looking for. Besides, it was one of those old musty mansions, ever so far from town, which it was always difficult to let or to get a price for; and then it was a wretched house for any convenience. Hyacinth, for whom his three hours in the train had been a series of happy throbs, had not been struck with its geographic remoteness, and he asked the Princess what she meant in such a connexion by her use of the word "wretched." To this she replied that the place was tumbling to pieces, impossible in every respect, full of ghosts and bad smells. "That's the only reason I come to have it. I don't want you to think me so sunk in luxury or that I throw away money. Never, never!" Hyacinth had no standard by which he could measure the importance his opinion would have for her, and he saw that though she judged him as a creature still open to every initiation, whose *naïveté* would entertain her, it was also her fancy to treat him as an old friend, a person to whom she might have had the habit of referring her difficulties. Her performance of the part she had undertaken to play was certainly complete, and everything lay before him but the reason she might have for playing it.

One of the gardens at Medley took the young man's heart beyond the others; it had high brick walls, on the sunny sides of which was a great training of apricots and plums; it had straight walks bordered with old-fashioned homely flowers and enclosing immense squares where other fruit-trees stood upright and mint and lavender floated in the air. In the southern quarter it overhung a small disused 18 canal, and here a high embankment had been raised, which was also long and broad and covered with fine turf; so that the top of it, looking down at the canal, made a magnificent grassy terrace, than which on a summer's day there could be no more delightful place for strolling up and down with a companion—all the more that at either end was a curious pavilion, in the manner of a tea-house, which crowned the scene in an old-world sense and offered rest and privacy, a refuge from sun or shower. One of these pavilions was an asylum for gardeners' tools and superfluous flower-pots; the other was covered inside with a queer Chinese paper representing ever so many times over a group of people with faces like blind kittens, groups who drank tea while they sat on the floor. It also contained a straddling inlaid cabinet in which cups and saucers showed valuably through doors of greenish glass, together with a carved cocoanut and a pair of outlandish idols. On a shelf over a sofa which was not very comfortable, though it had cushions of faded tapestry that resembled samplers, stood a row of novels out of date and out of print—novels that one couldn't have found any more and that were only there. On the chimney-piece was a bowl of dried rose-leaves mixed with some aromatic spice, and the whole place suggested a certain dampness.

On the terrace Hyacinth paced to and fro with the Princess till she all ruefully remembered he had not had his luncheon. He protested that this was the last thing he wished to think of, but she declared she hadn't dragged him down to Medley to starve him and that he must go back and be fed. They went back, but by a very roundabout way, through the park, so that they really had half an hour's more talk. She explained to him that she herself breakfasted at twelve o'clock, in the foreign fashion, and 19 had tea in the afternoon; as he too was so foreign he might like that better, and in this case on the morrow they would breakfast together. He could have coffee and anything else he wanted brought to his room at his waking. When he had sufficiently composed himself in the presence of this latter image—he thought he saw a footman arranging a silver service at his bedside—he mentioned that really, as regarded the morrow, he should have to be back in London. There was a train at nine o'clock—he hoped she didn't mind his taking it. She looked at him gravely and kindly, as if considering an abstract idea, and then said: "Oh yes, I mind it very much. Not to-morrow—some other day." He made no rejoinder and the Princess spoke of something else; that is, his rejoinder was private and consisted of the reflexion that he *would* leave Medley in the morning, whatever she might say. He simply couldn't afford to stay; he couldn't be out of work. And then Madame Grandoni thought it so important; for though the old lady was obscure she was decidedly impressive. The Princess's protest, however, was to be reckoned with; he felt it might take a form less cursory than the words she had just uttered, a form that would make it embarrassing. She was less solemn, less explicit, than Madame Grandoni had been, but there was something in her light fine pressure and the particular tone of her mentioned preference that seemed to tell him his liberty was going—the liberty he had managed to keep (till the other day when he gave Hoffendahl a mortgage on it) and the possession of which had in some degree consoled him for other forms of penury. This made him uneasy; what would become of him if he should add another servitude to the one he had undertaken at the end of that long, anxious cab-drive through the rain, in the back bedroom of a house as to whose whereabouts he was even now 20 not clear, while Muniment and Poupin and Schinkel, all visibly pale, listened and accepted the vow? Muniment and Poupin and Schinkel—how disconnected, all the same, he felt from them at the present hour; how little he was the young man who had made the pilgrimage in the cab; and how the two latter at least, if they could have a glimpse of him now, would wonder what he was up to!

As to this Hyacinth wondered sufficiently himself, while the Princess touched upon the people and places she had seen, the impressions and conclusions she had gathered since their former meeting. It was to such matters as these she directed the conversation; she seemed to wish to keep it off his own concerns, and he was surprised at her continued avoidance of the slums and the question of her intended sacrifices. She mentioned none of her friends by name, but she talked of their character, their houses, their manners, taking for granted as before that Hyacinth would always follow. So far as he followed he was edified, but he had to admit to himself that half the time he didn't know what she was talking about. He at all events, if *he* had been with the dukes—she didn't call her associates dukes, but he was sure they were of that order—would have got more satisfaction from them. She appeared on the whole to judge the English world severely; to think poorly of its wit and even worse of its morals. "You know people oughtn't to be both corrupt and dreary," she said; and Hyacinth turned this over, feeling he certainly had not yet caught the point of view of a person for whom the aristocracy was a collection of bores. He had sometimes taken great pleasure in hearing it dubbed grossly profligate, but he was rather disappointed in the bad account the Princess gave of it. She dropped the remark that she herself had no sort of conventional morality—she ought to have 21 mentioned that before—yet had never been accused of being stupid. Perhaps he wouldn't discover it, but most of the people she had had to do with thought her only too acute. The second allusion she made to their ulterior designs (Hyacinth's and hers) was when she said: "I determined to see it"—she was speaking still of English society—"to learn for myself what it really is before we blow it up. I've been here now a year and a half and, as I tell you, I feel I've seen. It's the old régime again, the rottenness and extravagance, bristling with every iniquity and every abuse, over which the French Revolution passed like a whirlwind; or perhaps even more a reproduction of the Roman world in its decadence, gouty, apoplectic, depraved, gorged and clogged with wealth and spoils, selfishness and scepticism, and waiting for the onset of the barbarians. You and I are the barbarians, you know." The Princess was pretty vague after all in her animadversions and regaled him with no anecdotes—which indeed he rather missed—that would have betrayed the hospitality she had enjoyed. She couldn't treat him absolutely as if he had been an ambassador. By way of defending the aristocracy he said to her that it couldn't be true they were all a bad lot (he used that expression because she had let him know she liked him to speak in the manner of the people) inasmuch as he had an acquaintance among them—a noble lady—who was one of the purest, kindest, most conscientious human beings it was possible to imagine. At this she stopped short and looked at him; then she asked: "Whom do you mean—a noble lady?"

"I suppose there's no harm saying. Lady Aurora Langrish."

"I don't know her. Is she nice?"

"I like her ever so much." 22

"Is she pretty, clever?"

"She isn't pretty, but she's very uncommon," said Hyacinth.

"How did you make her acquaintance?" As he hesitated she went on: "Did you bind some books for her?"

"No. I met her in a place called Audley Court."

"Where's that?"

"In Camberwell."

"And who lives there?"

"A young woman I was calling on, who's bedridden."

"And the lady you speak of—what do you call her, Lady Lydia Languish?—goes to see her?"

"Yes, very often."

The Princess, with her eyes on him, had a pause. "Will you take me there?"

"With great pleasure. The young woman I speak of is the sister of the man—the one who works for a big firm of wholesale chemists—that you'll perhaps remember that I mentioned to you."

"Yes, I remember. It must be one of the first places we go to. I'm sorry, you know," the Princess added, walking on. Hyacinth asked what she might be sorry for, but she took no notice of his question, only soon saying: "Perhaps she goes to see *him*."

"Goes to see whom?"

"The young chemist—the brother." She said this very seriously.

"Perhaps she does," Hyacinth returned, laughing. "But she's a fine sort of woman."

The Princess repeated that she was sorry, and he again wanted to know for what—for Lady Aurora's being of that sort? To which she replied: "No; I mean for my not being the first—what is it you call them?—noble lady you've encountered."

"I don't see what difference that makes. You 23 needn't be afraid you don't make an impression on me."

"I wasn't thinking of that. I was thinking you might be less fresh than I first thought."

"Of course I don't know what you first thought," Hyacinth smiled.

"No; how should you?" the Princess strangely sighed. 24

XXIII

He was in the library after luncheon when word was brought him that the carriage was at the door for their drive; and when he entered the hall he found Madame Grandoni bonneted and cloaked and awaiting the descent of their friend. "You see I go with you. I'm always there," she remarked jovially. "The Princess has me with her to take care of her, and this is how I do it. Besides, I never miss my drive."

"You're different from me; this will be the first I've ever had in my life." He could establish that distinction without bitterness, because he was too pleased with his prospect to believe the old lady's presence could spoil it. He had nothing to say to the Princess that she mightn't hear. He didn't dislike her for coming even after she had said to him in answer to his own announcement, speaking rather more sententiously than her wont: "It doesn't surprise me that you've not spent your life in carriages. They've nothing to do with your trade."

"Fortunately not," he answered. "I should have made a ridiculous coachman."

The Princess appeared and they mounted into a great square barouche, an old-fashioned, high-hung vehicle with a green body, a faded hammer-cloth and a rumble where the footman sat (their hostess mentioned that it had been let with the house), which 25 rolled ponderously and smoothly along the winding avenue and through the gilded park-gates that were surmounted with an immense escutcheon. The progress of this apparently mismatched trio had a high respectability, and that is one of the reasons why Hyacinth felt the occasion intensely memorable. There might still be greater joys in store for him—he was by this time quite at sea and could recognise no shores—but he should never again in his life be so respectable. The drive was long and comprehensive, but little was said while it lasted. "I shall show you the whole country: it's exquisitely beautiful; it speaks to the heart." Of so much as this his entertainer had informed him at the start; and she added with all her foreignness and with a light allusive nod at the rich humanised landscape: "*Voilà ce que j'aime en Angleterre.*" For the rest she sat there fronting him in quiet fairness and under her softly-swaying lace-fringed parasol: moving her eyes to where she noticed his eyes rest; allowing them when the carriage passed anything particularly charming to meet his own; smiling as if she enjoyed the whole affair very nearly as much as he; and now and then calling his attention to some prospect, some picturesque detail, by three words of a cadence as soft as a hand-stroke. Madame Grandoni dozed most of the time, her chin resting on the rather mangy ermine tippet in which she had enveloped herself; expanding into consciousness at moments, however, to greet the scenery with comfortable confused ejaculations in the first language that came into her head. If Hyacinth was uplifted during these delightful hours he at least measured his vertiginous eminence, and it kept him quite solemnly still, as with the fear that a wrong movement of any sort would break the charm, cause the curtain to fall on the play. This was especially the case when his sensibility swung back 26 from the objects that sprang up by the way, every one of which was a rich image of something he had longed for, to the most beautiful woman in England, who sat there, well before him, as completely for his benefit as if he had been a painter engaged to paint her portrait. More than once he saw everything through a strange mist; his eyes were full of tears.

That evening they sat in the drawing-room after dinner, as the Princess had promised or, as he was inclined to consider it, threatened him. The force of the threat was in his prevision that the ladies would make themselves fine and that in contrast with the setting and company he should feel dingier than ever; having already on his back the one approach to a "cut" coat he possessed and being unable to exchange it for a garment of the pattern that civilised people (so much he knew, if he couldn't emulate them) put on about eight o'clock. The ladies when they came to dinner looked festal indeed; but he was able to make the reflexion that he was more pleased to be dressed as he was dressed, meanly and unsuitably as it was, than he should have been to present such a figure as Madame Grandoni, in whose toggery there was something comical. He was coming more and more round to the sense that if the Princess didn't mind his poorness of every sort he had no call to mind it himself. His present position wasn't of his seeking—it had been forced on him; it wasn't the fruit of a disposition to push. How little the Princess minded—how much indeed she enjoyed the consciousness that in having him about her in that manner she was playing a trick on society, the false and conventional society she had sounded and she despised—was manifest from the way she had introduced him to the group they found awaiting them in the hall on the return from their drive: four ladies, a mother and three daughters, who had 27 come over to call from Broome, a place some five miles off. Broome was also a great house, as he gathered, and Lady Marchant, the mother, was the wife of a county magnate. She explained that they had come in on the persuasion of the butler, who had represented the return of the Princess as imminent, and had then administered tea without waiting for this event. The evening had drawn in chill; there was a fire in the hall and they all sat near it, round the tea-table, under the great roof that rose to the top of the house. Hyacinth conversed mainly with one of the daughters, a very fine girl with a straight back and long arms, whose neck was encircled so tightly with a fur boa that, to look a little to one side, she was obliged to move her whole body. She had a handsome inanimate face, over which the firelight played without making it more lively, a beautiful voice and the occasional command of a few short words. She asked Hyacinth with what pack he hunted and whether he went in much for tennis, and she ate three muffins.

Our young man made out that Lady Marchant and her daughters had already been at Medley, and even guessed that their reception by the Princess, who probably thought them of a tiresome type, had not been enthusiastic; and his imagination projected itself further still, into the motives which, in spite of this tepidity, must have led them, on consideration of the rarity of princesses in that country, to come a second time. The talk in the firelight, while our youth laboured rather recklessly (for the spirit of the occasion on his hostess's part was passing into his own blood) with his muffin-eating beauty—the conversation, accompanied with the light click of delicate tea-cups, was as well-bred as could be consistent with an odd evident *parti-pris* of the Princess's to put poor Lady Marchant, as the phrase might be, <u>28</u> through her paces. With great urbanity of manner she appealed for the explanation of everything, and especially of her ladyship's own thin remarks and of the sense in which they had been meant; so that Hyacinth was scarce able to follow her, wondering what interest she could have in trying to appear dense. It was only afterwards he learned that the Marchant family produced a very peculiar and at moments almost maddening effect on her nerves. He asked himself what would happen to that member of it with whom he was engaged if it should be revealed to her that she was conversing (how little soever) with a beggarly London artisan; and though he was rather pleased at her not having discovered his station (for he didn't attribute her brevity to this idea) he entertained a little the question of its being perhaps his duty not to keep it hidden from her, not to flourish in a cowardly disguise. What did she take him for—or rather what didn't she take him for—when she asked him if he hunted and "went in"? Perhaps that was because it was rather dark; if there had been more light in the great vague hall she would have seen he was not one of themselves. He felt that by this time he had associated a good deal with swells, but they had always known what he was and had been able to choose how to treat him. This was the first time a young gentlewoman hadn't been warned, and as a consequence he appeared to pass muster. He determined not to unmask himself, on the simple ground that he should by the same stroke betray the Princess. It was quite open to *her* to lean over and say to Miss Marchant: "You know he's a wretched little bookbinder who earns a few shillings a week in a horrid street in Soho. There are all kinds of low things—and I suspect even something very horrible—

connected with his birth. It seems to me I ought to mention it." He almost 29 wished she would mention it for the sake of the strange violent sensation of the thing, a curiosity quivering within him to know what Miss Marchant would do at such a pinch and what chorus of ejaculations—or what appalled irremediable silence—would rise to the painted roof. The responsibility, however, was not his; he had entered a dim passage of his fate where responsibilities had dropped. Madame Grandoni's tea had waked her up; she came at every crisis to the rescue of the conversation and talked to the visitors about Rome, where they had once spent a winter, describing with much drollery the manner in which the English families she had seen there for nearly half a century (and had met of an evening in the Roman world) inspected the ruins and monuments and squeezed into the great ceremonies of the Church. Clearly the four ladies didn't know what to make of the Princess; but, though they perhaps wondered if she were a paid companion, they were on firm ground in the fact that the queer, familiar, fat person had been acquainted with the Millingtons, the Bunburys and the Tripps.

After dinner (during which the Princess allowed herself a considerable licence of pleasantry on the subject of her recent visitors, declaring that Hyacinth must positively go with her to return their call and must see their interior, their manner at home) Madame Grandoni sat down to the piano at Christina's request and played to her companions for an hour. The spaces were large in the big drawing-room, and our friends had placed themselves at a distance from each other. The old lady's music trickled forth discreetly into the multiplied mild candlelight; she knew dozens of Italian local airs, which sounded like the forgotten tunes of a people, and she followed them by a series of tender, plaintive German *Lieder*, rousing without violence the echoes 30 of the high pompous apartment. It was the music of an old woman and seemed to quaver a little as her lifted voice might have done. The Princess, buried in a deep chair, listened behind her fan. Hyacinth at least supposed she listened, for she never moved. At last Madame Grandoni left the piano and came to the young man. She had taken up on the way a French book in a pink cover which she nursed in the hollow of her arm as she stood looking at him.

"My poor little friend, I must bid you good-night. I shall not see you again for the present, as, to take your early train, you'll have left the house before I put on my wig—and I never show myself to gentlemen without it. I've looked after the Princess pretty well, all day, to keep her from harm, and now I give her up to you for a little. Take the same care, I earnestly beg you. I must put myself into my dressing-gown; at my age, at this hour, it's the only thing. What will you have? I hate to be tight," pursued Madame Grandoni, who appeared even in her ceremonial garment to have evaded this discomfort successfully enough. "Don't sit up late," she added, "and don't keep him, Christina. Remember that for an active young man like Mr. Robinson, going every day to his work, there's nothing more exhausting than such an unoccupied life as ours. For what do we do after all? His eyes are very heavy. *Basta!*"

During this little address the Princess, who made no rejoinder to that part of it which concerned herself, remained hidden behind her fan; but after Madame Grandoni had wandered away she lowered this emblazoned shield and rested her eyes a while on Hyacinth. At last she said: "Don't sit half a mile off. Come nearer to me. I want to say something to you that I can't shout across the room." He immediately got up, but at the same moment 31 she also rose; so that, approaching each other, they met halfway and before the great marble chimney-piece. She stood opening and closing her fan, then she began: "You must be surprised at my not having yet spoken to you about our great interest."

"No indeed: I'm not now surprised at anything."

"When you take that tone I feel as if we should never, after all, become friends," said the Princess.

"I hoped we were already. Certainly after the kindness you've shown me there's no service of friendship you might ask of me———!"

"That you wouldn't gladly perform? I know what you're going to say, and have no doubt you speak truly. But what good would your service do me if all the while you think of me as a hollow-headed, hollow-hearted trifler, behaving in the worst possible taste and oppressing you with clumsy attentions? Perhaps you believe me a bad, bold, ravening flirt."

"Capable of wanting to flirt with *me?*" Hyacinth demurred. "I should be very conceited."

"Surely you've the right to be as conceited as you please after the advances I've made you! Pray who has a better one? But you persist in remaining humble, and that's very provoking."

"It's not I who am provoking; it's life and society and all the difficulties that surround us."

"I'm precisely of that opinion—that they're exasperating; that when I appeal to you frankly, candidly, disinterestedly—simply because I like you, for no other reason in the world—to help me to disregard and surmount these conventions and absurdities, to treat them with the contempt they deserve, you drop your eyes, you even blush a little and make yourself small and try to edge out of the situation by pleading general devotion and insignificance. Please remember this: you cease to be 32 insignificant from the moment I've anything to do with you. My dear fellow," the Princess went on in her free, audacious, fraternising way, to which her beauty and simplicity gave nobleness, "there are people who would be very glad to enjoy, in your place, that form of obscurity."

"What do you wish me then to do?" Hyacinth asked as quietly as he could.

If he had had an idea that this question, to which, as coming from his lips and even as being uttered with perceptible impatience, a certain unexpectedness might attach, would cause her a momentary embarrassment, he was completely out in his calculation. She answered on the instant: "I want you to give me time! That's all I ask of my friends in general—all I ever asked of the best I've ever had. But none of them ever did it; none of them, that is, save the excellent creature who has just left us. She understood me long ago."

"That's all I on my side ask of you," said Hyacinth with a smile, as to attest presence of mind, that might have come from some flushed young captive under cross-examination for his life. "Give *me* time, give *me* time," he murmured, looking up at her splendour.

"Dear Mr. Hyacinth, I've given you months!—months since our first meeting. And at present haven't I given you the whole day? It has been intentional, my not speaking to you of our plans. Yes, our plans—I know what I'm saying. Don't try to look stupid; with your beautiful intelligent face you'll never succeed. I wished to leave you free to amuse yourself."

"Oh, I've amused myself," said Hyacinth.

"You'd have been very fastidious if you hadn't. However, that's precisely in the first place what I wished you to come here for. To observe the impression made by such a house as this on such a nature as <u>33</u> yours introduced to it for the first time, has been, I assure you, quite worth my while. I've already given you a hint of how extraordinary I think it that you should be what you are without having seen—what shall I call them?— beautiful, delightful old things. I've been watching you; I'm frank enough to tell you that. I want you to see more—more—more!" the Princess exclaimed with a sudden emphasis that, had he heard her use it to another, he would have taken for a passion of tenderness. "And I want to talk with you about this matter as well as others. That will be for to-morrow."

"To-morrow?"

"I noticed Madame Grandoni took for granted just now that you're going. But that has nothing to do with the business. She has so little imagination!"

He shook his head with a pale grin and had an idea his mind was made up. "I can't stay."

She returned his smile, but there was something strangely touching—it was so sad, yet as a rebuke so gentle—in the tone in which she replied: "You oughtn't make me too abject. It isn't nice."

He had reckoned without that tone; all his reasons suddenly seemed to fall from under him and crumble. He remained a moment looking on the ground. "Princess," he then said, "you've no idea—how should you have?—into the midst of what abject, pitiful preoccupations you thrust yourself. I've no money—I've no clothes."

"What do you want of money? This isn't an hotel."

"Every day I stay here I lose a day's wages. I live on my wages from day to day."

"Let me then give you wages. You'll work for me."

"What do you mean—work for you?" 34

"You'll bind all my books. I've ever so many foreign ones in paper."

"You speak as if I had brought my tools!"

"No, I don't imagine that. I'll give you the wages now, and you can do the work, at your leisure and convenience, afterwards. Then if you want anything you can go over to Bonchester and buy it. There are very good shops; I've used them." Hyacinth thought of a great many things at this juncture; she had that quickening effect on him. Among others he thought of these two: first that it was indelicate (though such an opinion was not very strongly held either in Pentonville or in Soho) to accept money from a woman; and second that it was still more indelicate to make such a woman as that go down on her knees to him. But it took more than a minute for one of these convictions to prevail over the other, and before that he had heard his friend continue in the tone of mild, disinterested argument: "If we believe in the coming democracy, if it seems to us right and just and we hold that in sweeping over the world the great wave will wash away a myriad iniquities and cruelties, why not make some attempt with our own poor means—for one must begin somewhere—to carry out the spirit of it in our lives and our manners? I want to do that. I try to do it—in my relations with you for instance. But you hang ridiculously back. You're really not a bit democratic!"

Her accusing him of a patrician offishness was a very fine stroke; nevertheless it left him lucidity (though he still hesitated an instant, wondering if the words wouldn't offend her) to say straightforwardly enough: "I've been strongly warned against you."

The offence seemed not to touch her. "I can easily understand that. Of course my proceedings—though 35 after all I've done little enough as yet—must appear most unnatural. *Che vuole?* as Madame Grandoni says."

A certain knot of light blue ribbon which formed part of the trimming of her dress hung down at her side in the folds of it. On these glossy loops Hyacinth's eyes happened for a moment to have rested, and he now took up one of them and carried it to his lips. "I'll do all the work for you that you'll give me. If you give it on purpose and by way of munificence that's your own affair. I myself will estimate the price. What decides me is that I shall do the job so well; certainly it shall be better than any one else can do—so that if you employ me there will have been at least that reason. I've brought you a book—so you can see. I did it for you last year and went to South Street to give it to you, but you had already gone."

"Give it to me to-morrow." These words appeared to express so exclusively the calmness of relief at finding he could be reasonable, as well as a friendly desire to see the proof of his talent, that he was surprised when in the next breath she said irrelevantly: "Who was it warned you against me?"

He feared she might suppose he meant Madame Grandoni, so he made the plainest answer, having no desire to betray the old lady and reflecting how, as the likelihood was small that his friend in Camberwell would ever consent to meet the Princess (in spite of her plan of going there) no one would be hurt by it. "A friend of mine in London—Paul Muniment."

"Paul Muniment?"

"I think I mentioned him to you the first time we met."

"The person who said something good? I forget what it was." 36

"It was sure to be something good if he said it. He's awfully wise."

"That makes his warning very flattering to me! What does he know about me?"

"Oh nothing of course but the little I could tell him. He only spoke on general grounds."

"I like his odd name—Paul Muniment," the Princess said. "If he resembles it I think I should like him."

"You'd like him much better than me."

"How do you know how much—or how little—I like you? I'm determined to keep hold of you simply for what you can show me." She paused a moment with her beautiful deep eyes lighted as by possibilities that half dazzled and half defied him; then again her wondrous words took it up. "On general grounds, *bien entendu*, your friend was quite right to warn you. Now those general grounds are just what I've undertaken to make as small as possible. It's to reduce them to nothing that I talk to you, that I conduct myself with regard to you as I've done. What in the world is it I'm trying to do but by every clever trick I can think of fill up the inconvenient gulf that yawns between my position and yours? You know what I make of 'positions'—I told you in London. For heaven's sake let me feel that I've—a little—succeeded!" He satisfied her sufficiently to enable her five minutes later apparently to entertain no further doubt on the question of his staying over. On the contrary she burst into a sudden explosion of laughter, replacing her argumentative pressure by one of her singular sallies. "You must absolutely go with me to call on the Marchants. It will be lovely to see you there!"

As he walked up and down the empty drawing-room after she had a trifle abruptly and, as struck him, almost unceremoniously and inconsequently left 37 him, it occurred to him to wonder if that was mainly what she was keeping him for—so that he might help her to play one of her tricks on the good people at Broome. He paced there in the still candlelight for a longer time than he measured; until the butler came and stood in the doorway, looking at him silently and fixedly as to let him know that he interfered with the custom of the house. He had told the Princess that what determined him was the thought of the manner in which he might exercise his craft in her service; but this was only half the influence that pressed him into forgetfulness of what he had most said to himself when, in Lomax Place, in an hour of unprecedented introspection, he wrote the letter by which he accepted the invitation to Medley. He would go there, he reasoned, because a man must be gallant, especially if he be a poor little bookbinder; but after he should be there he would insist at every step on knowing what he was in for. The change that had taken place in him now, from one moment to another, was that he had simply ceased to wonder what that mystery might be. All warnings, reflexions, considerations of verisimilitude, of the delicate, the natural and the possible, of the value of his independence, had become as nothing to him. The cup of an exquisite experience—a week in that enchanted palace, a week of such immunity from Lomax Place and old Crook as he had never dreamed of—was at his lips; it was purple with the wine of romance, of reality, of civilisation, and he couldn't push it aside without drinking. He might go home ashamed, but he would have for evermore in his mouth the taste of nectar. He went upstairs under the eye of the butler and on his way to his room, at the turning of a corridor, found himself face to face with Madame Grandoni. She had apparently just issued from her own apartment, 38 the door of which stood open near her; she might have been hovering there at watch for his footstep. She had donned her dressing-gown, which seemed to give her all respiratory and other ease, but had not yet parted with her wig. She still had her pink French book under her arm, and her fat little hands, tightly locked together in front of her, formed the clasp of her generous girdle.

"Do tell me it's positive, Mr. Robinson!" she said as she stopped short.

"What's positive, Madame Grandoni?"

"That you take the train in the morning."

"I can't tell you that, because it wouldn't be true. On the contrary it has been settled I shall stay over. I'm very sorry if it distresses you—but *che vuole?*" he heard himself almost "cheekily" risk.

Madame Grandoni was a humorous woman, but she gave him no smile in return; she only looked at him hard a moment and then, shrugging her shoulders silently but expressively, shuffled back to her room. 39

XXIV

"I can give you your friend's name—in a single guess. He's Diedrich Hoffendahl!" They had been strolling more and more slowly the next morning, and as she made this announcement the Princess stopped altogether, standing there under a great beech with her eyes on Hyacinth's and her hands full of primroses. He had breakfasted at noon with his hostess and Madame Grandoni, but the old lady had fortunately not joined them when the Princess afterwards proposed he should accompany her on her walk in the park. She told him how her venerable friend had, while the day was still very young, pronounced it in the worst possible taste that she shouldn't let their companion yet depart in peace; to which she had replied that about tastes there was no disputing and that they had disagreed on such matters before without any one's being the worse. Hyacinth expressed the hope that they wouldn't dispute about *him*—of all thankless subjects in the world; and the Princess assured him that she never disputed about anything. She held that there were other ways than this of arranging one's relations with people; and he guessed how thoroughly she meant that when a difference became sharp she broke off altogether. On her side then there was as little possibility as on his that they should ever quarrel: their acquaintance would be a grand friendship 40 or would be nothing at all. The Princess gave it from hour to hour more of this quality, and it may be figured how safe her guest felt by the time he began to tell her that something had happened to him in London three months before, one night, or rather in the small hours of the morning, that had altered his life altogether—had indeed as he might say changed the terms on which he held it. He was aware that he didn't know exactly what he meant by this last phrase; but it expressed sufficiently well the new feeling that had come over him since that interminable, tantalising cab-drive in the rain.

The Princess had led to this almost as soon as they left the house; making up for her avoidance of such topics the day before by saying suddenly: "Now tell me what's going on among your friends. I don't mean your worldly acquaintances, but your colleagues, your brothers. *Où en êtes-vous* at the present time? Is there anything new, is anything going to be done? I'm afraid you're always simply dawdling and muddling." Hyacinth felt as if of late he had by no means either dawdled or muddled; but before he had committed himself so far as to refute the imputation she broke out with a different effect: "How annoying it is that I can't ask you anything without giving you the right to say to yourself, 'After all what do I know? Mayn't she be in the pay of the police—?'"

"Oh that doesn't occur to me," Hyacinth gallantly protested.

"It might at all events; by which I mean it may at any moment. Indeed I think it ought."

"If you were in the pay of the police you wouldn't trouble your head about me."

"I should make you think that certainly! That would be my first care. However, if you've no tiresome suspicions so much the better," said the 41 Princess; and she pressed him again for some news from behind the scenes.

In spite of his absence of doubt on the subject of her honesty—he was sure he should never again entertain any such trumpery idea as that she might be an agent on the wrong side—he didn't open himself immediately; but at the end of half an hour he let her know that the most important event of his life had taken place, scarcely more than the other day, in the most unexpected manner. And to explain in what it had consisted he said: "I pledged myself by everything that's sacred."

"To what did you pledge yourself?"

"I took a vow—a tremendous solemn vow—in the presence of four witnesses," Hyacinth went on.

"And what was it about, your vow?"

"I gave my life away," he consciously smiled.

She looked at him askance as if to see how he would indeed carry off such a statement as that; but she betrayed no levity of criticism—her face was politely grave. They moved together a moment, exchanging a glance in silence, and then she said: "Ah well then I'm all the more glad you stayed!"

"That was one of the reasons."

"I wish you had waited—till after you had been here," it occurred to her, however, to remark.

"Why till after I had been here?"

"Perhaps then you wouldn't have given away your life. You might have seen reasons for keeping it." With which, like Hyacinth, she sacrificed to the brighter bravery. He replied that he had not the least doubt that on the whole her influence was relaxing; but without heeding this she went on: "Be so good as to tell me what you're talking about."

"I'm not afraid of you, but I'll give you no names," said Hyacinth; and he related what had 42 happened at the place known to him in Bloomsbury and during that night of which I have given some account. The Princess listened intently while they strolled under the budding trees with a more interrupted step. Never had the old oaks and beeches, renewing themselves in the sunshine as they did to-day or naked in some grey November, witnessed such an extraordinary series of confidences since the first pair that sought isolation wandered over the grassy slopes and ferny dells beneath them. Among other things our young man mentioned that he didn't go to the "Sun and Moon" any more; he now perceived, what he ought to have perceived long before, that this particular temple of their faith, with everything that pretended to get hatched there, was a hopeless sham. He had been a rare muff from the first to take it seriously. He had done so mainly because a friend of his in whom he had confidence appeared to set him the example; but now it turned out that this friend (it was Paul Muniment again by the way) had always thought the men who went there a pack of shufflers and was trying them only to try everything. There was nobody you could begin to call a first-rate man, putting aside another friend of his, a Frenchman named Poupin—and Poupin was magnificent but wasn't first-rate. Hyacinth had a standard now that he had seen a man who was the very incarnation of a strong plan. You felt *him* a big chap the very moment you came into his presence.

"Into whose presence, Mr. Robinson?" the Princess demanded.

"I don't know that I ought to tell you, much as I believe in you! I'm speaking of the extraordinary man with whom I entered into that engagement."

"To give away your life?"

"To do something that in a certain contingency 43 he'll require of me. He'll require my poor little carcass."

"Those 'strong' plans have a way of failing—unfortunately," the Princess murmured, adding the last word more quickly.

"Is that a consolation or a regret?" Hyacinth asked. "This one shan't fail—so far as depends on me. They wanted an obliging young man. Well, the place was vacant and I stepped in."

"I've no doubt you're right. We must pay for all we do." She noted this hard law calmly and coldly and then said: "I think I know the person in whose power you've placed yourself."

"Possibly, but I doubt it."

"You can't believe I've already gone so far? Why not? I've given you a certain amount of proof that I don't hang back."

"Well, if you know my friend you've gone very far indeed."

The Princess appeared on the point of pronouncing a name; but she checked herself and said instead, suddenly eager: "Don't they also want by chance an obliging young woman?"

"I happen to know he doesn't think much of women, my first-rate man. He doesn't trust them."

"Is that why you call him first-rate? You've very nearly betrayed him to me."

"Do you imagine there's only one of that opinion?" Hyacinth returned.

"Only one who, having it, still remains a superior man. That's a very difficult opinion to reconcile with others it's important to have."

"Schopenhauer did so, successfully," said Hyacinth.

"How delightful you should know old Schopenhauer!" the Princess exclaimed. "The gentleman I have in my eye is also German." Hyacinth let this 44 pass, not challenging her, because he wished not to be challenged in return, and she went on: "Of course such an engagement as you speak of must make a tremendous difference in everything."

"It has made this difference, that I've now a far other sense from any I had before of the reality, the solidity, of what's being prepared. I was hanging about outside, on the steps of the temple, among the loafers and the gossips, but now I've been in the innermost sanctuary. Yes, I've seen the holy of holies."

"And it's very dazzling?"

"Ah Princess!" the young man strangely sighed.

"Then it *is* real, it *is* solid?" she pursued. "That's exactly what I've been trying to make up my mind about so long."

"It's beyond anything I can say. Nothing of it appears above the surface; but there's an immense underworld peopled with a thousand forms of revolutionary passion and devotion. The manner in which it's organised is what astonished me. I knew that, or thought I knew it, in a general way, but the reality was a revelation. And on top of it all society lives. People go and come, and buy and sell, and drink and dance, and make money and make love, and seem to know nothing and suspect nothing and think of nothing; and iniquities flourish, and the misery of half the world is prated about as a 'necessary evil,' and generations rot away and starve in the midst of it, and day follows day, and everything is for the best in the best of possible worlds. All that's one half of it; the other half is that everything's doomed! In silence, in darkness, but under the feet of each one of us, the revolution lives and works. It's a wonderful, immeasurable trap, on the lid of which society performs its antics. When once the machinery is complete there will be a great rehearsal. That 45 rehearsal is what they want me for. The invisible, impalpable wires are everywhere, passing through everything, attaching themselves to objects in which one would never think of looking for them. What could be more strange and incredible for instance than that they should exist just here?"

"You make me believe it," said the Princess thoughtfully.

"It matters little whether one believes it or not!"

"You've had a vision," she continued.

"*Pardieu*, I've had a vision! So would you, if you had been there."

"I wish I had!" she declared in a tone charged with such ambiguous implications that Hyacinth, catching them a moment after she had spoken, rejoined with a quick, incongruous laugh—

"No, you'd have spoiled everything. He made me see, he made me feel, he made me do, everything he wanted."

"And why should he have wanted you in particular?"

"Simply because I struck him as the right person. That's his affair: I can't tell you. When he meets the right person he chalks him. I sat on the bed. There were only two chairs in the dirty little room and by way of curtain his overcoat was hung up before the window. He himself didn't sit; he leaned against the wall straight in front of me, his hands behind him. He told me certain things and his manner was extraordinarily quiet. So was mine, I think I may say; and indeed it was only poor Poupin who made a row. It was for my sake somehow: he didn't think we were all conscious enough; he wanted to call attention to my sublimity. There was no sublimity about it—I simply couldn't help myself. He and the other German had the two chairs and Muniment sat on a queer old, battered, hair-covered 46 trunk, a most foreign-looking article." Hyacinth had taken no notice of the little ejaculation with which his companion greeted in this last sentence the word "other."

"And what did Mr. Muniment say?" she presently asked.

"Oh he said it was all right. Of course he thought so from the moment he determined to bring me. He knew what the other fellow was looking for."

"I see." Then the Princess added: "We've a curious way of being fond of you."

"Whom do you mean by 'we'?"

"Your friends. Mr. Muniment and I for instance."

"I like it as well as any other. But you don't feel alike. I've an idea you yourself are sorry."

"Sorry for what?"

"That I've put my head into a noose."

"Ah you're rather snubby—I thought I concealed it so well!" the Princess cried. He recognised that his discrimination had been invidious, as there might have been for an instant a hint of tears in her voice. She looked away from him, and it was after this that, stopping short, she remarked as I have related: "Your man's Diedrich Hoffendahl."

Hyacinth took it with a stare and parted lips. "Well, you *are* in it— more than I supposed!"

"You know he doesn't trust women," his companion smiled.

"Why in the world should you have cared for any light *I* can throw if you've ever been in relation with him?"

She hesitated a little. "Oh you're very different. I like you better," she added.

"Ah if it's for that!" murmured Hyacinth.

The Princess coloured as he had seen her colour before, and in this liability on her part there was even after repetition an unexpectedness, something 47 all too touching. "Don't try to fix my inconsistencies on me," she said with a humility that matched her blush. "Of course there are plenty of them, but it will always be kinder of you to let them pass. Besides, in this case they're not so serious as they seem. As a product of the 'people' and of that strange fermenting underworld (what you say of it's so true!) you interest me more and have more to say to me even than Hoffendahl— wonderful creature as he assuredly is."

"Would you object to telling me how and where you came to know him?" her visitor asked.

"Through a couple of friends of mine in Vienna, two of the affiliated, both passionate revolutionists and clever men. They're Neapolitans, originally *poveretti* like yourself, who emigrated years ago to seek their fortune. One of them's a teacher of singing, the wisest, most accomplished person in his line I've ever known. The other, if you please, is a confectioner! He makes the most delicious *pâtisserie fine*. It would take long to tell you how I made *their* acquaintance and how they put me into relation with the Maestro, as they called him, of whom they spoke with bated breath. It's not from yesterday—though you don't seem able to believe it— that I've had a care for these interests. I wrote to Hoffendahl and had several letters from him; the singing-master and the pastry-cook went bail for my sincerity. The next year I had an interview with him at Wiesbaden; but I can't tell you the circumstances of our meeting in that place without implicating another person to whom just now at least I've no right to give you a clue. Of course Hoffendahl made an immense impression on me; he struck me as the Master indeed, the very genius of a new social order, and I fully understand the manner in which you were affected by him. When he was in London 48 three months ago I knew it and knew where to write to him. I did so and asked him if he wouldn't see me somewhere. I said I'd meet him anywhere, in any darkness, if it should have to be, that he might designate. He answered by a charming letter which I'll show you—it has nothing in the least compromising—but declined my offer, pleading his short stay and a press of engagements. He'll write to me but won't trust me. However, he shall some day!"

Hyacinth was thrown quite off his balance by this representation of the ground the Princess had already traversed, and the explanation was still but half restorative when, on his asking her why she hadn't exhibited her titles before, she replied: "Well, I thought my being quiet was the better way to draw you out." There was but little difficulty in drawing him out now, and before their walk was over he had told her more definitely what Hoffendahl demanded. This was simply that he should hold himself ready for the next five years to do at a given moment an act which would in all probability cost him his life. The act was as yet indefinite, but one might get an idea of it from the penalty involved, which would certainly be capital. The only thing settled was that it was to be done instantly and absolutely, without a question, a condition or a scruple, in the manner that should be prescribed at the moment from headquarters. Very likely it would be to shoot some one—some blatant humbug in a high place; but whether the individual should deserve it or shouldn't deserve it was not to be one's affair. If he recognised generally Hoffendahl's wisdom—and the other night it had seemed to shine like a great cold, splendid, northern aurora—it was not in order that he might challenge it in the particular case. He had taken a vow of blind obedience, the vow as of the Jesuit fathers to the 49 head of their order. It was because the Jesuits had carried out their vows (having in the first place great administrators) that their organisation had been mighty, and this sort of mightiness was what people who felt as Hyacinth and the Princess felt should go in for. It was not certain sure he should be bagged after his *coup* any more than it was certain sure he should bring down his man; but it was much to be looked for and was what he counted on and indeed preferred. He should probably take little trouble to save his skin, and he should never enjoy the idea of dodging or hiding or disavowing. If it were a question of really placing his bullet he himself should naturally deserve what would come to him. If one did that sort of thing there was an indelicacy in not being ready to pay for it, and he at least was perfectly willing. He shouldn't judge, he should simply execute. He didn't pretend to say what good his little job might do or what *portée* it might have; he hadn't the data for appreciating it and simply took upon himself to believe that at headquarters they knew what they were about. The thing was to be part of a very large plan, of which he couldn't measure the scope—something that was to be done simultaneously in a dozen different countries. The impression was to be very much in this immense coincidence. It was to be hoped it wouldn't be spoiled by any muffing. At all events *he* wouldn't hang fire, whatever the other fellows might do. He didn't say it because Hoffendahl had done him the honour of giving him the business to do, but he believed the Master knew how to pick out his men. To be sure they had known nothing about him in advance; he had only been suggested from one day to the other by those who were always looking out. The fact remained, however, that when Hyacinth stood before him he recognised him as the sort of 50 little chap he had in his eye—one who could pass through a very small opening. Humanity, in his scheme, was classified and subdivided with a truly German thoroughness and altogether of course from the point of view of the revolution—as it might forward or obstruct that cause. Hyacinth's little job was a very small part of what Hoffendahl had come to England for; he had in his hand innumerable other threads. Hyacinth knew nothing of these and didn't much want to know, except for the portentous wonder of the way Hoffendahl kept them apart. He had exactly the same mastery of them that a great musician—that the Princess herself—had of the keyboard of the piano; he treated all things, persons, institutions, ideas, as so many notes in his great symphonic massacre. The day would come when—far down in the treble—one would feel one's self touched by the little finger of the composer, would grow generally audible (with a small sharp crack) for a second.

It was impossible that our young man shouldn't become aware at the end of ten minutes that he had charmed the Princess into the deepest, most genuine attention: she was listening to him as she had never listened before. He enjoyed that high effect on her, and his sense of the tenuity of the thread by which his future hung, renewed by his hearing himself talk about it, made him reflect that at present anything in the line of enjoyment, any scrap filched from the feast of life, was so much gained for eager young experience. The reader may judge if he had held his breath and felt his heart-beats after placing himself on his new footing of utility in the world; but that emotion had finally spent itself, through a hundred forms of restlessness, of vain conjecture—through an exaltation which alternated with despair and which, equally with the despair, he concealed more <u>51</u> successfully than he supposed. He would have detested the idea that his companion might have heard his voice tremble while he told his story; but though to-day he had really grown used to his danger and resigned, as it were, to his consecration, and though it couldn't fail to be agreeable to him to perceive that, like some famous novel, he was thrilling, he still couldn't guess how very remarkable, in such a connexion, the Princess thought his composure, his lucidity, his good humour. It is true she tried to hide her wonder, for she owed it to her self-respect to let it still appear that even such a one as she was prepared for a personal sacrifice as complete. She had the air—or she endeavoured to have it—of accepting for him everything that he accepted for himself; nevertheless there was something rather forced in the smile (lovely as it might be) with which she covered him while she said after a little: "It's very serious—it's very serious indeed, isn't it?" He replied that the serious part was to come—there was no particular grimness for him (comparatively) in strolling in that fine park and gossiping with her about the matter; and it occurred to her presently to suggest to him that perhaps Hoffendahl would never give him any sign at all, so that he might wait, all the while *sur les dents*, in a false suspense. He admitted that this would be a sell, but declared that either way he should be sold, though differently; and that at any rate he would have conformed to the great religious rule—to live each hour as if it were to be one's last.

"In holiness, you mean—in great *recueillement*?" the Princess asked.

"Oh dear no; simply in extreme thankfulness for every good minute that's added."

"Ah well, there will probably be a great many good minutes," she returned. <u>52</u>

"The more the better—if they're as good as this one."

"That won't be the case with many of them in Lomax Place."

"I assure you that since that night Lomax Place has improved." Hyacinth stood there smiling, his hands in his pockets and his hat pushed back.

The Princess appeared to consider this quaint truth, as well as the charming facts of his appearance and attitude, with an extreme intellectual curiosity. "If after all then you're not called you'll have been positively happy."

"I shall have had some fine moments. Perhaps Hoffendahl's plot is simply for that: Muniment may have put him up to it!"

"Who knows? However, with me you must go on as if nothing were changed."

"Changed from what?"

"From the time of our first meeting at the theatre."

"I'll go on in any way you like," said Hyacinth. "Only the real difference will be there, you know."

"The real difference?"

"That I shall have ceased to care for what you care for."

"I don't understand," she confessed with all the candour of her beauty.

"Isn't it enough now to give my life to the beastly cause," the young man broke out, "without giving my sympathy?"

"The beastly cause?" the Princess murmured, opening her deep eyes.

"Of course it's really just as holy as ever; only the people I find myself pitying now are the rich, the happy."

"I see. You're very remarkable. You're splendid. Perhaps you pity my husband," she added in a moment. 53

"Do you call him one of the happy?" Hyacinth inquired as they walked on again.

But she only repeated: "You're very remarkable. Yes, you're splendid."

To which he made answer: "Well, it's what I want to be!"

I have related the whole of this conversation because it supplies a highly important chapter of Hyacinth's history, but we may not take time to trace all the stages and reproduce all the passages through which the friendship of the Princess Casamassima with the young man she had constituted her bookbinder was confirmed. By the end of a week the standard of fitness she had set up in the place of exploded proprieties appeared the model of justice and convenience; and during this period, a season of strange revelations for our young man, many other things happened. One of them was that he drove over to Broome with his hostess and called on Lady Marchant and her daughters; an episode that appeared to minister in the Princess to a thorough ironic glee. When they came away he asked her why she hadn't told the ladies who he was. Otherwise where was the point? And she replied: "Simply because they wouldn't have believed me. That's your fault!" This was the same note she had struck when the third day of his stay (the weather had changed for the worse and a rainy afternoon kept them indoors) she remarked to him irrelevantly and abruptly: "It *is* most extraordinary, your knowing poor dear old 'Schop'!" He answered that she really seemed quite unable to accustom herself to his little talents; and this led to a long talk, longer than the one I have already narrated, in which he took her still further into his confidence. Never had the pleasure of conversation, the greatest he knew, been so largely opened to him. The Princess admitted 54 frankly that he would to her sense take a great deal of accounting for; she observed that he was, no doubt, pretty well used to himself, but must give stupider persons time. "I've watched you constantly since you came—in every detail of your behaviour—and I'm more and more *intriguée*. You haven't a vulgar intonation, you haven't a common gesture, you never make a mistake, you do and say everything exactly in the right way. You come out of the poor cramped hole you've described to me, and yet you might have stayed in country-houses all your life. You're much better than if you had! *Jugez donc*, from the way I talk to you! I've to make no allowances—not one little allowance. I've seen Italians with that sort of natural tact and ease, but I didn't know it was ever to be found in any Anglo-Saxon in whom it hadn't been cultivated at a vast expense; unless perhaps in certain horribly 'refined' little American women."

"Do you mean I'm a gentleman?" asked Hyacinth in a peculiar tone while he looked out into the wet garden.

She faltered and then said: "It's I who make the mistakes!" Five minutes later she broke into an exclamation which touched him almost more than anything she had ever done, giving him the highest opinion of her delicacy and sympathy, putting him before himself as vividly as if the words were a little portrait. "Fancy the strange, the bitter fate: to be constituted as you're constituted, to be conscious of the capacity you must feel, and yet to look at the good things of life only through the glass of the pastry-cook's window!"

"Every class has its pleasures," he made answer with perverse sententiousness in spite of his emotion; but the remark didn't darken their mutual intelligence, which was to expand to still greater wonders, 55 and before they separated that evening he told her the things that had never yet passed his lips—the things to which he had awoke when he made Pinnie explain to him the visit to the prison. He told her in short what he was. 56

XXV

He took several long walks by himself beyond the gates of the park and through the neighbouring country—walks during which, committed as he was to reflexion on the general "rumness" of his destiny, he had still a delighted attention to spare for the green dimness of leafy lanes, the attraction of meadow-paths that led from stile to stile and seemed a clue to some pastoral happiness, some secret of the fields; the hedges thick with flowers, bewilderingly common, for which he knew no names, the picture-making power of thatched cottages, the mystery and sweetness of blue distances, the bloom of rural complexions, the quaintness of little girls bobbing curtsies by waysides (a sort of homage he had never prefigured); the soft sense of the turf under feet that had never ached but from paving-stones. One morning as he had his face turned homeward after a long stroll he heard behind him the sound of a horse's hoofs and, looking back, perceived a gentleman who would presently pass him advancing up the road which led to the lodge-gates of Medley. He went his way and as the horse overtook him noticed that the rider slackened pace. Then he turned again and recognised in this personage his occasional florid friend Captain Sholto. The Captain pulled up alongside of him, saluting him with a smile and a movement of the whip-handle. Hyacinth stared with surprise, not 57 having heard from the Princess that she was expecting him. He gathered, however, in a moment that she was not; and meanwhile he received an impression on Sholto's part of riding-gear that was "knowing"—of gaiters and spurs and a hunting-crop and a curious waistcoat; perceiving this to be a phase of the Captain's varied nature that he had not yet had occasion to observe. He struck him as very high in the air, perched on his big lean chestnut, and Hyacinth noticed that if the horse was heated the rider was cool.

"Good-morning, my dear fellow. I thought I should find you here!" the Captain exclaimed. "It's a good job I've met you this way without having to go to the house."

"Who gave you reason to think I was here?" Hyacinth asked; partly occupied with the appositeness of this inquiry and partly thinking, as his eyes wandered over his handsome friend bestriding so handsome a beast, what a jolly thing it would be to know how to ride. He had already, during the few days he had been at Medley, had time to observe that the knowledge of luxury and the wider range of sensation begot in him a taste for still bolder pleasures.

"Why, I knew the Princess was capable of asking you," Sholto said; "and I learned at the 'Sun and Moon' that you had not been there for a long time. I knew furthermore that as a general thing you go there a good deal, don't you? So I put this and that together and judged you were out of town."

This was very clear and straightforward and might have satisfied just exactions save for that irritating reference to the Princess's being "capable of asking him." He knew as well as the Captain that it had been tremendously eccentric in her to do so, but somehow a transformation had lately taken place in him which made it unpleasant he should receive that 58 view from another, and particularly from a gentleman of whom at a certain juncture several months before he had had strong grounds for thinking unfavourably. He had not seen Sholto since the evening when a queer combination of circumstances caused him to sit more queerly still and listen to comic songs in the company of Millicent Henning and this admirer. The Captain had not concealed his admiration; Hyacinth had his own ideas about his taking that line in order to look more innocent. When he accompanied Millicent that evening to her lodgings (they parted with Sholto on coming out of the Pavilion) the situation was tense between the young lady and her childhood's friend. She let him have it, as she said; she gave him a dressing which she evidently intended should be memorable for having suspected her, for having insulted her before one of the military. The tone she took and the magnificent audacity with which she took it reduced him to an odd, gratified helplessness; he watched her at last with something of the excitement with which he would have watched a clever but uncultivated actress while she worked herself into a passion that he believed to be fictitious. He gave more credence to his jealousy and to the whole air of the case than to her loud rebuttals, enlivened though these were by tremendous head-tossings and skirt-shakings. But he felt baffled and outfaced, and had recourse to sarcasms which after all proved no more than her high gibes; seeking a final solution in one of those beastly little French shrugs, as Millicent called them, with which she had already denounced him for interlarding his conversation.

The air was never cleared, though the subject of their dispute was afterwards dropped, Hyacinth promising himself to watch his playmate as he had never done before. She let him know, as may well 59 be supposed, that she had her eye on *him*, and it must be confessed that as regards the exercise of a right of supervision he had felt himself at a disadvantage ever since the night at the theatre. It scantly mattered that she had pushed him into the Princess's box (for she herself had not been jealous beforehand; she had wanted too much to know what such a person could be "up to," desiring perhaps to borrow a hint) and it signified as little also that his relations with the great lady were all for the sake of suffering humanity. The atmosphere, however these things might be, was full of thunder for many weeks, and of what importance was the quarter from which the flash and the explosion should proceed? Hyacinth was a good deal surprised to find he could care whether Millicent deceived him or not, and even tried to persuade himself that he didn't; but it was as if he yet felt between them a personal affinity deeper than any difference, so that it would torment him more never to see her at all than to see her go into tantrums in order to cover her tracks. An inner sense told him that her mingled beauty and grossness, her vulgar vitality, the spirit of contradiction yet at the same time of attachment that was in her, had ended by making her indispensable to him. She bored as much as she irritated; but if she was full of excruciating taste she was also full of life, and her rustlings and chatterings, her wonderful stories, her bad grammar and good health, her insatiable thirst, her shrewd perceptions and grotesque opinions, her blunders and her felicities, were now all part of the familiar human sound of his little world. He could say to himself that she made up to him far more than he to her, and it helped him a little to believe, though the logic was but lame, that she was not "larking" at his expense. If she were really in with a swell he didn't see why she wished 60 to retain a bookbinder. Of late, it must be added, he had ceased to devote much consideration to Millicent's ambiguities; for although he was lingering on at Medley for the sake of suffering humanity he was quite aware that to say so (should she ask him for a reason) would have almost as low a value as some of the girl's own speeches. As regards Sholto he was in the awkward position of having let him off, as it were, by accepting his hospitality, his bounty; thus he couldn't quarrel with him save on a fresh pretext. This pretext the Captain had apparently been careful not to give, and Millicent had told him after the triple encounter in the street that he had driven him out of England, the poor gentleman he insulted by his vulgar insinuations even more (why 'even more' Hyacinth hardly could think) than he outraged herself. When he asked her what she knew about the Captain's movements she made no scruple to announce to him that the latter had come to her great shop to make a little purchase (it was a pair of silk braces, if she remembered rightly, and she acknowledged unreservedly the thinness of the pretext) and had asked her with much concern whether his gifted young friend (that's what he called him—Hyacinth could see he meant well) was still in a huff. Millicent had replied that she was afraid he was—the more shame to him; and then the Captain had declared it didn't matter, as he himself was on the point of leaving England for several weeks (Hyacinth—he called him Hyacinth this time—couldn't have ideas about a man in a foreign country, could he?) and hoped that by the time he returned the little cloud would have blown over. Sholto had added that she had better tell him frankly—recommending her at the same time to be gentle with their morbid friend—about his visit to the shop. Their candour, their humane 61 precautions, were all very well; but after this, two or three evenings, Hyacinth passed and repassed the Captain's chambers in Queen Anne Street to see if there were signs at the window of his being in London. Darkness in fact prevailed and he was forced to comfort himself a little when, at last making up his mind to ring at the door and inquire, as a test, for the occupant, he was informed by the superior valet whose acquaintance he had already made and whose air of wearing a jacket left behind by his master confirmed the statement, that the gentleman in question was at Monte Carlo.

"Have you still got your back up a little?" the Captain now demanded without rancour; and in a moment he had swung a long leg over the saddle and dismounted, walking beside his young friend and leading his horse by the bridle. Hyacinth pretended not to know what he meant, for it came over him that after all, even if he had not condoned at the time the Captain's suspected treachery, he was in no position, sitting at the feet of the Princess, to sound the note of jealousy in relation to another woman. He reflected that the Princess had originally been in a manner Sholto's property, and if he did *en fin de compte* wish to quarrel with him about Millicent he would have to cease to appear to poach on the Captain's preserves. It now occurred to him for the first time that the latter might have intended a practical exchange; though it must be added that the Princess, who on a couple of occasions had alluded slightingly to her military friend, had given him no sign of recognising this gentleman's claim. Sholto let him know at present that he was staying at Bonchester, seven miles off; he had come down from London and put up at the inn. That morning he had ridden over on a hired horse (Hyacinth had supposed this steed to be a very fine animal, but 62 Sholto spoke of it as an infernal screw); he had felt a sudden prompting to see how his young friend was coming on.

"I'm coming on very well, thank you," said Hyacinth with some shortness, not knowing exactly what business it was of the Captain's.

"Of course you understand my interest in you, don't you? I'm responsible for you—I put you forward."

"There are a great many things in the world I don't understand, but I think the thing I understand least is your interest in me. Why the devil——?" And Hyacinth paused, breathless with the force of his inquiry. Then he went on: "If I were you I shouldn't care tuppence for the sort of person I happen to be."

"That proves how different my nature is from yours! But I don't believe it, my dear boy; you're too generous for that." Sholto's imperturbability always appeared to grow with the irritation it produced, and it was proof even against the just resentment excited by his deficiency of tact. That deficiency was marked when he went on to say: "I wanted to see you here with my own eyes. I wanted to see how it looked, your domesticated state—and it *is* a rum sight! Of course you know what I mean, though you're always trying to make a fellow explain. I don't explain well in any sense, and that's why I go in only for clever people who can do without it. It's very grand, her having brought you down."

"Grand, no doubt, but hardly surprising, considering that, as you say, I was put forward by you."

"Oh that's a great thing for me, but it doesn't make any difference to her!" Sholto returned. "She may care for certain things for themselves, but it will never signify a jot to her what I may have 63 thought about them. One good turn deserves another. I wish you'd put *me* forward!"

"I don't understand you and I don't think I want to," said Hyacinth as his companion strolled beside him.

The latter put a hand on his arm, stopping him, and they stood face to face a moment. "I say, my dear Robinson, you're not spoiled already, at the end of a week—how long is it? It isn't possible you're jealous!"

"Jealous of whom?" asked Hyacinth, whose measure of the allusion was, amid the strangeness of everything, imperfect.

Sholto looked at him a moment; then with a laugh: "I don't mean Miss Henning." Hyacinth turned away and the Captain resumed his walk, now taking the young man's arm and passing his own through the bridle of the horse. "The courage of it, the insolence, the *crânerie*! There isn't another woman in Europe who could carry it off."

Hyacinth was silent a little; after which he remarked: "This is nothing, here. You should have seen me the other day over at Broome, at Lady Marchant's."

"Gad, did she take you there? I'd have given ten pounds to see it. There's no one like her!" cried the Captain gaily, enthusiastically.

"There's no one like me, I think—for going."

"Why, didn't you enjoy it?"

"Too much—too much. Such excesses are dangerous."

"Oh. I'll back you," said the Captain; then checking their pace, "Is there any chance of our meeting her?" he asked. "I won't go into the park."

"You won't go to the house?" Hyacinth demanded in wonder. 64

"Oh dear no, not while you're there."

"Well, I shall ask the Princess about you, and so have done with it once for all."

"Lucky little beggar, with your fireside talks!" the Captain lamented. "Where does she sit now in the evening? She won't tell you anything except that I'm a beastly nuisance; but even if she were willing to take the trouble to throw some light on me it wouldn't be of much use, because she doesn't understand me herself."

"You're the only thing in the world then of which that can be said," Hyacinth returned.

"I daresay I am, and I'm rather proud of it. So far as the head's concerned the Princess is all there. I told you when I presented you that she was the cleverest woman in Europe, and that's still my opinion. But there are some mysteries you can't see into unless you happen to have a little decent human feeling, what's commonly called a bit of heart. The Princess isn't troubled with that sort of thing, though doubtless just now you may think it her strong point. One of these days you'll see. I don't care a rap myself about her quantity of heart. She has hurt me already so much that she can't hurt me any more, and my interest in her is quite independent of it. To watch her, to adore her, to see her lead her life and act out her extraordinary nature, all the while she pays me no more attention than if I were the postman's knock several doors on, that's absolutely the only thing that appeals to me. It doesn't do me a scrap of good, but all the same it's my principal occupation. You may believe me or not—it doesn't in the least matter; but I'm the most disinterested human being alive. She'll tell you one's the biggest kind of donkey, and so of course one is. But that isn't all."

It was Hyacinth who stopped this time, arrested 65 by something new and natural in the tone of his companion, a simplicity of emotion he had not hitherto associated with him. He stood there a moment looking up at him and thinking again what improbable confidences it decidedly appeared to be his lot to receive from gentlefolk. To what quality in himself were they a tribute? The honour was one he could easily dispense with; though as he scrutinised Sholto he found something in his odd light eyes—a sort of wasted flatness of fidelity—which made of an accepted relation with him a less fantastic adventure. "Please go on," he said in a moment.

"Well, what I mentioned just now is my real and only motive in anything. The rest's the mere gabble of the juggler to cover up his trick and help himself do it."

"What do you mean by the rest?" asked Hyacinth, thinking of Millicent Henning.

"Oh all the straw one chews to cheat one's appetite; all the rot one dabbles in because it may lead to something which it never does lead to; all the beastly buncombe (you know) that you and I have heard together in Bloomsbury and that I myself have poured out, damme, with an assurance worthy of a better cause. Don't you remember what I've said to you—all as my own opinion—about the impending change of the relations of class with class? Impending collapse of the crust of the earth! I believe those on top of the heap are better than those under it, that they mean to stay there, and that if they're not a pack of poltroons they will."

"You don't care for the social question then?" Hyacinth inquired with an aspect of the blankness of which he was conscious.

"I only took it up because she did. It hasn't <u>66</u> helped me," Sholto smiled. "My dear Robinson," he went on, "there's only one thing I care for in life: to have a look at that woman when I can—and when I can't to approach her in the sort of way I'm doing now."

"It's a very funny sort of way."

"Indeed it is; but if it's good enough for me it ought to be good enough for you. What I want you to do is this—to induce her to ask me over to dine."

"To induce her——?" Hyacinth echoed.

"Tell her I'm staying at Bonchester and it would be an act of common humanity."

They proceeded till they reached the gates and in a moment Hyacinth said: "You took up the social question then because she did. But do you happen to know why *she* took it up?"

"Ah my dear fellow, you must worry that out for yourself. I found you the place, but I can't do your work for you!"

"I see—I see. But perhaps you'll tell me this: if you had free access to her a year ago, taking her to the theatre and that sort of thing, why shouldn't you have it now?"

This time Sholto's yellow eyes were strange again. "*You* have it now, my dear chap, but I'm afraid it doesn't follow that you'll have it a year hence. She was tired of me then, and of course she's still more tired of me now, for the simple reason that I'm more tiresome. She has sent me to Coventry and I want to come out for a few hours. See how awfully decent I am—I won't pass the gates."

"I'll tell her I met you," said Hyacinth. Then, irrelevantly, he added: "Is that what you mean by her having no heart?"

"Her treating me as she treats me? Oh dear no. Her treating *you*!" 67

This had a portentous sound, but it didn't prevent Hyacinth from turning round with his visitor—for it was the greatest part of the oddity of the present meeting that the hope of a little conversation with him, if accident were favourable, had been the motive not only of Sholto's riding over to Medley but of his coming down to stay, in the neighbourhood, at a musty inn in a dull market-town—it didn't prevent him, I say, from bearing the Captain company for a mile on his backward way. Our young man pursued this particular topic little further, but he discovered still another reason or two for admiring the light, free action with which his companion had unmasked himself, as well as the nature of his interest in the revolutionary idea, after he had asked him abruptly what he had had in his head when he travelled over that evening, the summer before—and he didn't appear to have come back as often as he promised—to Paul Muniment's place in Camberwell. What was he looking for, whom was he looking for there?

"I was looking for anything that would turn up, that might take her fancy. Don't you understand that I'm always looking? There was a time when I went in immensely for illuminated missals, and another when I collected horrible ghost-stories (she wanted to cultivate a belief in ghosts) all for her. The day I saw she was turning her attention to the rising democracy I began to collect little democrats. That's how I collected you."

"Muniment made you out exactly then. And what did you find to your purpose in Audley Court?"

"Well, I think the little woman with the popping eyes—she reminded me of a bedridden grasshopper—will do. And I made a note of the other one, the old virgin with the high nose, the aristocratic sister of mercy. I'm keeping them in reserve for my next propitiatory offering." 68

Hyacinth had a pause. "And Muniment himself—can't you do anything with him?"

"Oh my dear fellow, after you he's poor!"

"That's the first stupid thing you've said. But it doesn't matter, for he dislikes the Princess—what he knows of her—too much ever to consent to see her."

"That's his line, is it? Then he'll do!" Sholto cried. 69

XXVI

"Of course he may come, and may stay as long as he likes!" the Princess exclaimed when Hyacinth, that afternoon, told her of his encounter: she spoke with the sweet, bright surprise her face always wore when people went through the form (supererogatory she apparently meant to declare it) of asking her leave. From the manner in which she granted Sholto's petition—with a facility that made light of it, as if the question were not worth talking of one way or the other—the account he had given Hyacinth of their relations might have passed for an elaborate but none the less foolish hoax. She sent a messenger with a note over to Bonchester, and the Captain arrived just in time to dress for dinner. The Princess was always late, and Hyacinth's toilet on these occasions occupied him considerably (he was acutely conscious of its deficiencies, and yet tried to persuade himself that they were positively honourable and that the only garb of dignity for him was the costume, as it were, of his profession); therefore when the fourth member of the little party descended to the drawing-room Madame Grandoni was the only person he found there.

"*Santissima Vergine!* I'm glad to see you! What good wind has sent you?" she exclaimed as soon as Sholto came into the room.

"Didn't you know I was coming?" he asked. 70 "Has the idea of my arrival produced so little agitation?"

"I know nothing of the affairs of this house. I've given them up at last, and it was time. I remain in my room." There was nothing at present in the old lady's countenance of her usual spirit of cheer; it expressed anxiety and even a certain sternness, and the excellent woman had perhaps at this moment more than she had ever had in her life of the air of a duenna who took her duties seriously. She looked almost august. "From the moment you come it's a little better. But it's very bad."

"Very bad, dear madam?"

"Perhaps you'll be able to tell me where Christina *veut en venir.* I've always been faithful to her—I've always been loyal. But to-day I've lost patience. It has no sense."

"I'm not sure I know what you're talking about," Sholto said; "but if I understand you I must tell you I think it all magnificent."

"Yes, I know your tone; you're worse than she, because you're cynical. It passes all bounds. It's very serious. I've been thinking what I should do."

"Precisely. I know what you'll probably do."

"Oh this time I shouldn't come back!" the old lady declared. "The scandal's too great. It's intolerable. But my danger's of making it worse."

"Dear Madame Grandoni, you can't make it worse and you can't make it better," Sholto returned as he seated himself on the sofa beside her. "In point of fact no idea of scandal can possibly attach itself to our friend. She's above and outside all such considerations, such dangers. She carries everything off; she heeds so little, she cares so little. Besides, she has one great strength—she does no wrong." 71

"Pray what do you call it when a lady sends for a bookbinder to come and live with her?"

"Why not for a bookbinder as well as for a bishop? It all depends upon who the lady is and what she is."

"She had better take care of one thing first," cried Madame Grandoni—"that she shall not have been separated, with a hundred stories, from her husband!"

"The Princess can carry off even that. It's unusual, it's eccentric, it's fantastic if you will, but it isn't necessarily wicked. From her own point of view our friend goes straight. Besides, she has her opinions."

"Her opinions are perversity itself."

"What does it matter," asked Sholto, "if they keep her quiet?"

"Quiet! Do you call this quiet?"

"Surely, if you'll only be so yourself. Putting the case at the worst, moreover, who's to know he's her bookbinder? It's the last thing you'd take him for."

"Yes, for that she chose him carefully," the old woman murmured, still with a ruffled eyebrow.

"*She* chose him? It was I who chose him, dear lady!" the Captain cried with a laugh that showed how little he shared her solicitude.

"Yes, I had forgotten. At the theatre," said Madame Grandoni, gazing at him as if her ideas were confused, yet as if a certain repulsion from her interlocutor nevertheless disengaged itself. "It was a fine turn you did him there, poor young man!"

"Certainly he'll have to be sacrificed. But why was I bound to consider him so much? Haven't I been sacrificed myself?"

"Oh if he bears it like you!"—and she almost snorted with derision. 72

- 45 -

"How do you know how I bear it? One does what one can," said the Captain while he settled his shirt-front. "At any rate remember this: she won't tell people who he is for his own sake, and he won't tell them for hers. So, as he looks much more like a poet or a pianist or a painter, there won't be that sensation you fear."

"Even so it's bad enough," said Madame Grandoni. "And he's capable of bringing it out suddenly himself."

"Ah if he doesn't mind it *she* won't! But that's his affair."

"It's too terrible to spoil him for his station," the old lady went on. "How can he ever go back?"

"If you want him kept then indefinitely you're inconsistent. Besides, if he pays for it he deserves to pay. He's an abominable little conspirator against society."

Madame Grandoni was silent a time; then she looked at the Captain with a gravity which might have been impressive to him had not his accomplished jauntiness suggested an insensibility to that sort of influence. "What then does Christina deserve?" she asked with solemnity.

"Whatever she may get; whatever in the future may make her suffer. But it won't be the loss of her reputation. She's too distinguished."

"You English are strange. Is it because she's a princess?" Madame Grandoni reflected audibly.

"Oh dear no, her princedom's nothing here. We can easily beat that. But we can't beat——!" And he had a pause.

"What then?" his companion asked.

"Well, the perfection of her indifference to public opinion and the unaffectedness of her originality; the sort of thing by which she has bedevilled me."

"Oh *you*!" Madame Grandoni tossed off. 73

"If you think so poorly of me why did you say just now that you were glad to see me?" Sholto demanded in a moment.

"Because you make another person in the house, and that's more regular; the situation is by so much less—what did you call it?—eccentric. *Nun*," she presently went on, "so long as you're here I won't go off."

"Depend upon it I shall hang on tight till I'm turned out."

She rested her small troubled eyes on him, but they betrayed no particular enthusiasm at this announcement. "I don't understand how for yourself on such an occasion you should like it."

"Dear Madame Grandoni, the heart of man, without being such a hopeless labyrinth as the heart of woman, is still sufficiently complicated. Don't I know what will become of the little beggar?"

"You're very horrible," said the old woman. Then she added in a different tone: "He's much too good for his fate."

"And pray wasn't I for mine?" the Captain asked.

"By no manner of means!" Madame Grandoni returned as she rose and moved away from him.

The Princess had come into the room accompanied by Hyacinth. As it was now considerably past the dinner-hour the old lady judged that this couple, on their side, had met in the hall and had prolonged their conversation there. Hyacinth watched with extreme interest the way the Princess greeted the Captain—taking it for very simple, easy and friendly. At dinner she made no stranger of him, including him in everything as if he had been a useful familiar like Madame Grandoni, only a little less venerable, yet not giving him any attention that might cause their eyes to meet. She had told Hyacinth she didn't <u>74</u> like his eyes, nor indeed very much any part of him. Of course any admiration from almost any source couldn't fail to be in some degree grateful to an amiable woman, but of any unintended effect one might ever have produced the impression made on Godfrey Sholto in an evil hour ministered least to her vanity. He had been useful undoubtedly at times, but at others had been as a droning in her ears. He was so uninteresting in himself, so shallow, so unoccupied and futile, and really so frivolous in spite of his pretension (of which she was unspeakably weary) of being all wrapped up in a single idea. It had never by itself been sufficient to interest her in any man, the fact that he was in love with her; but indeed she could honestly say that most of the people who had liked her had had on their own side something, something in their character or conditions, that she could trouble her head about. Not so far as would do any harm save perhaps in one or two cases; but still some personal mark.

Sholto was a curious and not particularly edifying English type, as the Princess further described him; one of those odd figures produced by old societies that have run to seed, corrupt and exhausted civilisations. He was a cumberer of the earth—purely selfish for all his devoted, disinterested airs. He was nothing whatever in himself and had no character or merit save by tradition, reflexion, imitation, superstition. He had a longish pedigree—he came of some musty, mouldy "county family," people with a local reputation and an immense lack of general importance; he had taken the greatest care of his little fortune. He had travelled all over the globe several times, "for the shooting," in that murdering, ravaging way of the English, the destruction, the extirpation of creatures more beautiful, more soaring and more nimble than themselves. He had a little 75 taste, a little cleverness, a little reading, a little good furniture, a little French and Italian (he exaggerated these latter quantities), an immense deal of assurance and unmitigated leisure. That, at bottom, was all he represented—idle, trifling, luxurious, yet at the same time pretentious leisure, the sort of thing that led people to invent false, humbugging duties because they had no real ones. Sholto's great idea of himself, after his profession of being her slave, was that he was a cosmopolite and exempt from every prejudice. About the prejudices the Princess couldn't say and didn't care; but she had seen him in foreign countries, she had seen him in Italy, and she was bound to say he understood nothing of those people. It was several years before, shortly after her marriage, that she had first encountered him. He had not begun immediately to go in for adoring her—it had come little by little. It was only after she had separated from her husband that he had taken so to hanging about her—since when she had suffered much from him. She would do him one justice, however: he had never, so far as she knew, had the impudence to represent himself as anything but hopeless and helpless. It was on this he took his stand—he wanted to pass for the great model of unrewarded constancy. She couldn't imagine what he was waiting for— perhaps it was for the death of the Prince. But the Prince would never die, nor had she the least desire he should. She had no wish to be harsh, for of course that sort of thing was from any one very flattering; but really, whatever feeling poor Sholto might have, four-fifths of it were purely theatrical. He was not in the least a natural, quiet person, and had only a hundred affectations and attitudes, the result of never having been obliged to put his hand to anything, of having no serious tastes and yet being born to a little position. The Princess remarked 76 that she was so glad Hyacinth had no position, had been forced to do something else in life but amuse himself; that was the way she liked her friends now. She had said to Sholto again and again: "There are plenty of others who will be much more pleased with you; why not go to *them*? It's such a waste of time." She was sure indeed he had in some degree taken her advice, was by no means, as regards herself, the absorbed, annihilated creature he endeavoured to pass for. He had told her once he was trying to take an interest in other women—though indeed he had added that it was of no use. Of what use did he expect anything he could possibly do to be? Hyacinth, at this, didn't tell the Princess he had reason to believe the Captain's effort in that direction had not been absolutely vain; but he made the reflexion privately and with increased confidence. He recognised a further truth even when his companion said at the end that with all she had touched upon poor Sholto was a queer combination. Trifler as he was there was something sinister in him too; and she confessed she had had a vague feeling at times that some day he might do her a hurt. It was a remark that caused our young man to stop short on the threshold of the drawing-room and ask in a low voice: "Are you afraid of him?"

The Princess smiled as he had not yet seen her. "*Dio mio*, how you say that! Should you like to kill him for me?"

"I shall have to kill some one, you know. Why not him while I'm about it if he troubles you?"

"Ah my friend, if you should begin to kill every one who has troubled me!" she wonderfully wailed as they went into the room. 77

XXVII

He knew there was something out of the way as soon as he saw Lady Aurora's face look forth at him in answer to his tap while she held the door ajar. What was she doing in Pinnie's bedroom?—a very poor place, into which the dressmaker, with her reverence, would never have admitted a person of that quality unless things had got pretty bad. She was solemn too and without her usual incoherent laugh; she had removed her large hat, with its limp old-fashioned veil, and she raised her finger to her lips. Hyacinth's first alarm had been immediately after he let himself into the house with his latch-key, as he always did, and found the little room on the right of the passage, in which Pinnie had lived ever since he remembered, fireless and untenanted. As soon as he had paid the cabman who put down his portmanteau for him in the hall—he was not used to paying cabmen and was conscious he gave too much, but was too impatient in his sudden anxiety to care—he had hurried up the vile staircase that seemed viler, even through his preoccupation, than ever, and given the knock, accompanied by a call the least bit tremulous, precipitately answered by Lady Aurora. She had drawn back into the room a moment while he stared in his dismay; then she emerged again, closing the door behind her—all with the air of enjoining him to be terribly quiet. He felt suddenly so sick at the idea <u>78</u> of having lingered at Medley while there was distress in the wretched little house to which he owed so much that he scarcely found strength for an articulate question and obeyed mechanically the mute, urgent gesture by which their noble visitor appealed to him to go downstairs with her. It was only when they stood together in the deserted parlour—where he noted as for the first time what an inelegant odour prevailed—that he asked: "Is she dying—is she dead?" That was the least the strained sadness looking out of Lady Aurora's face appeared to announce.

"Dear Mr. Robinson, I'm so sorry for you. I wanted to write, but I promised her I wouldn't. She's very ill, poor dear—we're very anxious. It began ten days ago and I suppose I *must* tell you how much she has gone down." Lady Aurora spoke with more than all her usual embarrassments and precautions—eagerly, yet as if it cost her much pain: pausing a little after everything to see how he would take it, then going on with a small propitiatory rush. He learned presently what was the matter, what doctor she had sent for, and that if he would wait a little before going into the room it would be so much better; the invalid having sunk within half an hour into a doze of a less agitated kind than she had had for some time, from which it would be an immense pity to run the risk of waking her. The doctor gave her the right things, as it seemed to her ladyship, but he admitted that she had very little power of resistance. He was of course not a very large practitioner, Mr. Buffery from round the corner, yet he seemed really clever; and she herself had taken the liberty (as she confessed to this she threw off one of her odd laughs and her colour rose) of sending an elderly, respectable person—a decent nursing body known to many doctors. She was out just then, she had to 79 go once a day for the air— "only when I come of course" Lady Aurora hastened to note. Dear Miss Pynsent had had a cold hanging about her and had not taken care of it. Hyacinth would know how plucky she was about that sort of thing; she took so little interest in herself. "Of course a cold's a cold, whoever has it; isn't it?" his friend asked as if superior to the old discrimination against the power of the lowly to do justice to such visitations. Ten days previous she had taken an additional chill through falling asleep in her chair, at night, down there, and letting the fire go out. "It would have been nothing if she had been like you or me, you know," his benefactress went on; "but as she was then it made the difference. The day was horribly damp—the chill had struck into the lungs and inflammation come on. Mr. Buffery says she was impoverished, you know—so weak and low she had nothing to *go* on." The next morning she had bad pains and a good deal of fever, yet had got up. Poor Pinnie's gracious ministrant didn't make clear to Hyacinth what time had elapsed before she came to the rescue, nor by what means she had been notified, and he saw that she slurred this over, from the admirable motive of wishing him not to feel that their patient had suffered by his absence or called for him in vain. This indeed appeared not to have been the case if Pinnie had opposed successfully his being written to. "I came in very soon," Lady Aurora only said—"it was such a delightful chance. Since then she has had everything—if it wasn't so sad to see a person *need* so little. She did want you to stay where you were: she has clung to that idea. I speak the simple truth, Mr. Robinson."

"I don't know what to say to you—you're so extraordinarily good, so angelic," Hyacinth replied, bewildered and sickened by a strange, unexpected 80 shame. The episode he had just traversed, the splendour he had been living in and drinking so deep of, the unnatural alliance to which he had given himself up while his wretched little foster-mother struggled alone with her death-stroke—he could see it was that; the presentiment of it, the last stiff horror, was in all the place—this whole contrast cut him like a knife and made the ugly accident of his absence a perversity of his own. "I can never blame you when you're so kind, but I wish to God I had known!" he broke out.

Lady Aurora clasped her hands, begging him to judge her fairly. "Of course it was a great responsibility for us, but we thought it right to consider what she urged upon us. She went back to it constantly, that your visit should *not* be cut short. When you should come of yourself it would be time enough. I don't know exactly where you've been, but she said it was such a pleasant house. She kept repeating that it would do you so much good."

Hyacinth felt his eyes fill with tears. "She's dying—she's dying! How can she live when she's like that?"

He sank upon the old yellow sofa, the sofa of his lifetime and of so many years before, and buried his head on the shabby, tattered arm. A succession of sobs broke from his lips—sobs in which the accumulated emotion of months and the strange, acute conflict of feeling that had possessed him for the three weeks just past found relief and a kind of solution. Lady Aurora sat down beside him and laid her finger-tips gently on his hand. So for a minute, while his tears flowed and she said nothing, he felt her timid touch of consolation. At the end of the minute he raised his head; it came back to him that she had said "we" just before, and he asked her whom she meant. 81

"Oh Mr. Vetch, don't you know? I've made his charming acquaintance; it's impossible to be more kind." Then while for a space Hyacinth was silent, wincing, pricked with the thought that Pinnie had been beholden to the fiddler while *he* was masquerading in high life, Lady Aurora added: "He's a charming musician. She asked him once at first to bring his violin; she thought it would soothe her."

"I'm much obliged to him, but now that I'm here we needn't trouble him," said Hyacinth.

Apparently there had been a certain dryness in his tone, which was the cause of her ladyship's venturing to reply after an hesitation: "Do let him come, Mr. Robinson; let him be near you! I wonder if you know that—that he has a great affection for you."

"The more fool he; I've always treated him like a brute!" Hyacinth declared, colouring.

The way Lady Aurora spoke proved to him later that she now definitely did know his secret, or one of those mysteries rather; for at the rate things had been going for the last few months he was making a regular collection. She knew the smaller secret—not of course the greater; she had decidedly been illuminated by Pinnie's divagations. At the moment he made that reflexion, however, he was almost startled to perceive how completely he had ceased to resent such betrayals and how little it suddenly seemed to signify that the innocent source of them was about to be quenched. The sense of his larger treasure of experience swallowed up that particular anxiety, making him ask himself what it mattered, for the little time now left him, that people should exchange allusions, below their breath, to the hidden mark he now bore. The day came quickly when he believed, and yet didn't care, that it had been in that manner immensely talked about. 82

After Lady Aurora left him, promising she would call him the first moment it should seem prudent, he walked up and down the cold, stale parlour sunk in his meditations. The shock of the danger of losing Pinnie had already passed away; he had achieved so much of late in the line of accepting the idea of death that the little dressmaker, in taking her departure, seemed already to benefit by this curious discipline. What was most vivid to him in the deserted field of her unsuccessful industry was the changed vision with which he had come back to objects familiar for twenty years. The picture was the same, and all its horrid elements, wearing a kind of greasy gloss in the impure air of Lomax Place, made, through the mean window-panes, a dismal *chiaroscuro*—showed, in their polished misery, the friction of his own little life; yet the eyes with which he looked at it had new terms of comparison. He had known the scene for hideous and sordid, but its aspect to-day was pitiful to the verge of the sickening; he couldn't believe that for years he had accepted and even a little revered it. He was frightened at the sort of service his experience of grandeur had rendered him. It was all very well to have assimilated that element with a rapidity which had surprises even for himself; but with sensibilities now so improved what fresh arrangement could one come to with the very humble, which was in its nature uncompromising? Though the spring was far advanced the day was a dark drizzle and the room had the clamminess of a finished use, an ooze of dampness from the muddy street where the shallow defensive areas were a narrow slit. No wonder Pinnie had felt it at last, no wonder her small underfed organism had grown numb and ceased to act. At the thought of her limited, stinted life, the patient humdrum effort of her needle and scissors, which had ended only in a show-room where 83 there was nothing to show and a pensive reference to the cut of sleeves no longer worn, the tears again rose to his eyes; but he brushed them aside when he heard a cautious tinkle at the house-door, which was presently opened by the little besmirched slavey retained for the service of the solitary lodger—a domestic easily bewildered, who had a particularly lamentable, conscious squint and distressed Hyacinth by wearing shoes that didn't match, though of an equal antiquity and intimately emulous in the facility with which they dropped off. He had not heard Mr. Vetch's voice in the hall, apparently because he spoke in a whisper; but the young man was not surprised when, taking every precaution not to make the door creak, their neighbour came into the parlour. The fiddler said nothing to him at first; they only looked at each other for a long minute. Hyacinth saw what he most wanted to know—whether he knew the worst about Pinnie: but what was further in his eyes, which had an expression considerably different from any hitherto seen in them, defined itself to our hero only little by little.

"Don't you think you might have written me a word?" said Hyacinth at last. His anger at having been left in ignorance had quitted him, but he thought the question fair. None the less he expected a sarcastic answer, and was surprised at the mild reasonableness with which Mr. Vetch replied—

"I assure you that no responsibility, in the course of my life, ever did more to distress me. There were obvious reasons for calling you back, and yet I couldn't help wishing you might finish your visit. I balanced one thing against the other. It was very difficult."

"I can imagine nothing more simple. When people's nearest and dearest are dying they're usually sent for." 84

The visitor gave a strange argumentative smile. If Lomax Place and Miss Pynsent's select lodging-house wore a new face of vulgarity to Hyacinth it may be imagined whether the renunciation of the niceties of the toilet, the resigned seediness, which marked Mr. Vetch's old age was unlikely to lend itself to comparison. The glossy butler at Medley had had a hundred more of the signs of success in life. "My dear boy, this case was exceptional," the fiddler returned. "Your visit had a character of importance."

"I don't know what you know about it. I don't remember that I told you anything."

"No certainly, you've never told me much. But if, as is probable, you've seen that kind lady who's now upstairs you'll have learned that Pinnie made a tremendous point of your not being disturbed. She threatened us with her displeasure if we should hurry you back. You know what Pinnie's displeasure is!" As at this Hyacinth turned away with a gesture of irritation Mr. Vetch went on: "No doubt she's absurdly fanciful, poor dear thing; but don't now cast any disrespect on it. I assure you that if she had been here alone, suffering, sinking, without a creature to tend her and nothing before her but to die in a corner like a starved cat, she would still have faced that fate rather than cut short by a single hour your experience of novel scenes."

Hyacinth turned it miserably over. "Of course I know what you mean. But she spun her delusion—she always did all of them—out of nothing. I can't imagine what she knows about my 'experience' of any kind of scenes. I told her when I went out of town very little more than I told you."

"What she guessed, what she gathered, has been at any rate enough. She has made up her mind that you've formed a connexion by means of which 85 you'll come somehow or other into your own. She has done nothing but talk about your grand kindred. To her mind, you know, it's all one, the aristocracy; and nothing's simpler than that the person—very exalted, as she believes—with whom you've been to stay should undertake your business with her friends."

"Oh well," said Hyacinth, "I'm very glad not to have deprived you of that entertainment."

"I assure you the spectacle was exquisite." Then the fiddler added: "My dear fellow, please leave her the idea."

"Leave it? I'll do much more!" Hyacinth returned. "I'll tell her my great relations have adopted me and that I've come back in the character of Lord Robinson."

"She'll need nothing more to die happy," said Mr. Vetch.

Five minutes later, after Hyacinth had obtained from his old friend a confirmation of Lady Aurora's account of Miss Pynsent's condition, this worthy explaining that he came over like that to see how she was half-a-dozen times a day—five minutes later a silence had descended upon the pair while our youth awaited some sign from Lady Aurora that he might come upstairs. The fiddler, who had lighted a pipe, looked out of the window as if the view were a chart of all the grey past; and Hyacinth, making his tread discreet, walked about the room with his hands in his pockets. At last Mr. Vetch observed without taking his pipe out of his lips or looking round: "I think you might be a little more frank with me at this time of day and at such a crisis."

Hyacinth stopped in his walk, wondering for a moment all sincerely what his companion meant, for he had no consciousness at present of an effort 86 to conceal anything he could possibly tell—there were some things of course he couldn't: on the contrary his life seemed to him particularly open to the public view and exposed to invidious comment. It was at this moment he first noticed a certain difference; there was a tone in Mr. Vetch's voice he seemed never to have felt before—an absence of that note which had made him say in other days that the impenetrable old man was diverting himself at his expense. It was as if his attitude had changed, become more explicitly considerate, in consequence of some alteration or promotion on Hyacinth's part, his having grown older or more important, or even grown simply more surpassingly odd. If the first impression made upon him by Pinnie's old neighbour, as to whose place in the list of the sacrificial (his being a gentleman or one of the sovereign people) he formerly was so perplexed; if the sentiment excited by Mr. Vetch in a mind familiar now for nearly a month with forms of indubitable gentility was not favourable to the idea of fraternisation, this secret impatience in Hyacinth's breast was soon corrected by one of the sudden reactions or quick conversions of which the young man was so often the victim. In the light of the fiddler's appeal, which evidently meant more than it said, his musty antiquity, his typical look of having had for years a small, definite use and taken all the creases and contractions of it, even his visible expression of ultimate parsimony and of having ceased to care for the shape of his trousers because he cared more for something else—these things became so many reasons for turning round, going over to him, touching marks of an invincible fidelity, the humble, continuous, single-minded practice of daily duties and an art after all very charming; pursued, moreover, while persons of the species our restored prodigal had lately been consorting with 87 fidgeted from one selfish sensation to another and couldn't even live in the same place for three months together.

"What should you like me to do, to say, to tell you? Do you want to know what I've been doing in the country? I should have first to know myself," Hyacinth decently pleaded.

"Have you enjoyed it very much?"

"Yes certainly, very much—not knowing anything about Pinnie. I've been in a beautiful house with a beautiful woman."

Mr. Vetch had turned round; he looked very impartial through the smoke of his pipe. "Is she really a princess?"

"I don't know what you mean by 'really': I suppose all titles are great rot. But every one seems agreed to call her so."

"You know I've always liked to enter into your life, and to-day the wish is stronger than ever," the old man presently said, while he fixed his eyes steadily on his companion's.

Hyacinth returned his gaze a moment. "What makes you say that just now?"

The fiddler appeared to deliberate and at last replied: "Because you're in danger of losing the best friend you've ever had."

"Be sure I feel it. But if I've got *you*——!" his companion added.

"Oh me! I'm very old and very tired of life."

"I suppose that that's what one arrives at. Well, if I can help you in any way you must lean on me, you must make use of me."

"That's precisely what I was going to say to you," said Mr. Vetch. "Should you like any money?"

"Of course I should! But why should you offer it to me?" 88

"Because in saving it up little by little I've had you in mind."

"Dear Mr. Vetch," our young man returned, "you have me too much in mind. I'm not worth it, please believe that; and for all sorts of reasons. I should make money enough for any uses I have for it, or have any right to have, if I stayed quietly in London and attended to my work. As you know, I can earn a decent living."

"Yes, I can see that. But if you stayed quietly in London what would become of your princess?"

"Oh they can always manage, ladies in that position."

"Hanged if I understand her position!" cried Mr. Vetch, but without laughing. "You've been for three weeks without work and yet you look uncommonly smart."

"Well, my living, you see, has cost me nothing. When you stay with great people you don't pay your score," Hyacinth explained with great gentleness. "Moreover, the lady whose hospitality I've been enjoying has made me a very handsome offer of work."

"What kind of work?"

"The only kind I know. She's going to send me a lot of books to do up for her."

"And to pay you fancy prices?"

"Oh no; I'm to fix the prices myself."

"Are not transactions of that kind rather disagreeable—with a lady whose hospitality one has been enjoying?" Mr. Vetch inquired.

"Exceedingly! That's exactly why I shall do the books and then take no money."

"Your princess is rather clever!" the fiddler coldly laughed.

"Well, she can't force me to take it if I won't," said Hyacinth. 89

"No; you must only let *me* do that."

"You've curious ideas about me," the young man declared.

Mr. Vetch turned about to the window again, remarking that he had curious ideas about everything. Then he added after an interval: "And have you been making love to your great lady?"

He had expected a flash of impatience in reply to this appeal and was rather surprised at the manner in which Hyacinth began: "How shall I explain? It's not a question of that sort."

"Has she been making love to you then?"

"If you should ever see her you'd understand how absurd that supposition is."

"How shall I ever see her?" returned Mr. Vetch. "In the absence of that privilege I think there's something in my idea."

"She looks quite over my head," said Hyacinth simply. "It's by no means impossible you may see her. She wants to know my friends, to know the people who live in the Place. And she would take a particular interest in you on account of your opinions."

"Ah I've no opinions now—none any more!" the old man broke out sadly. "I only had them to frighten Pinnie."

"She was easily frightened," said Hyacinth.

"Yes, and easily reassured. Well, I like to know about your life," his neighbour sighed irrelevantly. "But take care the great lady doesn't lead you too far."

"How do you mean, too far?"

"Isn't she a conspiring socialist, a dabbler in plots and treasons? Doesn't she go in for a general rectification, as Eustache calls it?"

Hyacinth had a pause. "You should see the place—you should see what she wears, what she eats and drinks." 90

"Ah you mean that she's inconsistent with her theories? My dear boy, she'd be a droll woman if she weren't. At any rate I'm glad of it."

"Glad of it?" Hyacinth repeated.

"For you, I mean, when you stay with her; it's more luxurious!" Mr. Vetch exclaimed, turning round and smiling. At this moment a little rap on the floor above, given by Lady Aurora, announced that Hyacinth might at last come up and see Pinnie. Mr. Vetch listened and recognised it, and it led him to say with considerable force: "*There's* a woman whose theories and conduct do square!"

Hyacinth, on the threshold, leaving the room, stopped long enough to meet it. "Well, when the day comes for my friend to give up—you'll see."

"Yes, I've no doubt there are things she'll bring herself to sacrifice," the old man retorted. But Hyacinth was already out of hearing. 91

XXVIII

Mr. Vetch waited below till Lady Aurora should come down and give him the news he was in suspense for. His mind was pretty well made up about Pinnie. It had seemed to him the night before that death was written in her face, and he judged it on the whole a very good moment for her to lay down her earthly burden. He had reasons for believing that the future couldn't be sweet to her. As regards Hyacinth his mind was far from being at ease; for though aware in a general way that he had taken up with strange company, and though having flattered himself of old that he should be pleased to see the boy act out his life and solve the problem of his queer inheritance, he was worried by the absence of full knowledge. He put out his pipe in anticipation of Lady Aurora's reappearance and without this consoler was more accessible still to certain fears that had come to him in consequence of a recent talk, or rather an attempt at a talk, with Eustache Poupin. It was through the Frenchman that he had gathered the little he knew about the occasion of Hyacinth's strange and high "social" adventure. His vision of the matter had been wholly inferential; for Hyacinth had made a mystery of his absence to Pinnie, merely letting her know that there was a lady in the case and that the best luggage he could muster and the best way his shirts could be done up would still be far from $\underline{92}$ good enough. Poupin had seen Godfrey Sholto at the "Sun and Moon," and it had come to him, through Hyacinth, that a remarkable feminine influence in the Captain's life was conducive in some way to his presence in Bloomsbury—an influence, moreover, by which Hyacinth himself, for good or for evil, was in peril of being touched. Sholto was the young man's visible link with a society for which Lisson Grove could have no importance in the scheme of the universe save as a short cut (too disagreeable to be frequently used) out of Bayswater; therefore if Hyacinth left town with a new hat and a pair of kid gloves it must have been to move in the direction of that superior circle and in some degree at the solicitation of the before-mentioned feminine influence. So much as this the Frenchman suggested explicitly enough, as his manner was, to the old fiddler; but his talk had a strain of other and rarer reference which excited Mr. Vetch's curiosity rather than satisfied it. They were obscure, these deeper implications; they were evidently painful to the speaker; they were confused and embarrassed and totally wanting in that effect of high hand-polish which usually characterised the lightest allusions of M. Poupin. It was the fiddler's fancy that his friend had something on his mind which he was not at liberty to impart, and that it related to Hyacinth and might, for those who took an interest in the singular lad, give ground for no small anxiety. Mr. Vetch, on his own part, nursed this anxiety into a tolerably definite shape: he persuaded himself that the Frenchman had been leading the boy too far in the line of social criticism, had given him a push on some crooked path where a slip would be a likely accident. When on a subsequent occasion, with Poupin, he indulged in a hint of this suspicion, the bookbinder flushed a good deal and declared that his 93 conscience was pure. It was one of his peculiarities that when his colour rose he looked angry, and Mr. Vetch held that his displeasure was a proof that in spite of his repudiations he had been unwise; though before they parted Eustache gave this sign of softness that he shed tears of emotion of which the source was not clear to the fiddler and which appeared in a general way to be dedicated to Hyacinth. The interview had taken place in Lisson Grove, where Madame Poupin, however, had not shown herself.

Altogether the old man was a prey to suppositions which led him to feel how much he himself had outlived the democratic glow of his prime. He had ended by accepting everything—though indeed he couldn't swallow the idea that a trick should be played upon Hyacinth; and even by taking an interest in current politics, as to which of old he had held the opinion—the opinion deep-based in the Poupins to-day—that they had been invented on purpose to throw dust in the eyes of disinterested reformers and to circumvent the social solution. He had renounced that problem some time ago; there was no way to clear it up that didn't seem to make a bigger mess than the actual muddle of human affairs, which by the time one had reached sixty-five might mostly cease to exasperate. Mr. Vetch could still feel a certain sharpness on the subject of the prayer-book and the bishops, and if at moments he was a little ashamed of having accepted this world could reflect that at all events he continued to repudiate every other. The idea of great changes, however, took its place among the dreams of his youth; for what was any possible change in the relations of men and women but a new combination of the same elements? If the elements could be made different the thing would be worth thinking of; but it was not only impossible to introduce any 94 new ones—no means had yet been discovered for getting rid of the old. The figures on the chessboard were still the passions and jealousies and superstitions and stupidities of man, and their position with regard to each other at any given moment could be of interest only to the grim, invisible fates who played the game—who sat, through the ages, bow-backed over the table. This laxity had come upon our fiddling friend with the increase of his measurement round the waist and with that of the little heap of half-crowns and half-sovereigns that had accumulated in a tin box very stiffly padlocked which he kept under his bed and the interwoven threads of sentiment and custom uniting him to the dressmaker and her foster-son. If he was no longer pressing about the demands he felt he should have a right to make of society, as he had been in the days when his conversation scandalised Pinnie, so he was now not pressing for Hyacinth either; reflecting that though indeed the constituted powers might have to "count" with him it would be in better taste for him not to be importunate about a settlement. What he had come to fear for the interesting youth was that he should be precipitated by crude agencies into depths where the deplorable might not exclude the ridiculous. It may even be said that Mr. Vetch had a secret project of settling a little on his behalf.

Lady Aurora peeped into the room, very noiselessly, nearly half an hour after Hyacinth had left it, and let the fiddler know that she was called to other duties but that the nurse had come back and the doctor had promised to look in at five o'clock. She herself would return in the evening, and meanwhile Hyacinth was with his aunt, who had recognised him without a protest; indeed seemed intensely happy that he should be near her again and lay there with closed eyes, very weak and speechless, 95 holding his hand. Her restlessness had passed and her fever abated, but she had no pulse to speak of and Lady Aurora didn't disguise the fact that by any good judgement she was rapidly sinking. Mr. Vetch had already accepted it and after her ladyship had quitted him he lighted another philosophic pipe upon it, lingering on, till the doctor came, in the dressmaker's dismal, forsaken bower, where in past years he had indulged in so many sociable droppings-in and hot tumblers. The echo of all her little simple surprises and pointless contradictions, her gasping reception of contemplative paradox, seemed still to float in the air; but the place felt as relinquished and bereft as if she were already beneath the sod. Pinnie had always been a wonderful hand at "putting away"; the litter that testified to her most elaborate efforts was often immense, but the reaction in favour of an unspeckled carpet was greater still; and on the present occasion, before taking to her bed, she had found strength to sweep and set in order as tidily as if she had been sure the room would never again know her care. Even to the old fiddler, who had not Hyacinth's sensibility to the scenery of life, it had the cold propriety of a place arranged for interment. After the doctor had seen Pinnie that afternoon there was no doubt left as to its soon being the stage of dismal preliminaries.

Miss Pynsent, however, resisted her malady for nearly a fortnight more, during which Hyacinth was constantly in her room. He never went back to old Crook's, with whose establishment, through violent causes, his relations seemed indefinitely suspended; and in fact for the rest of the time that Pinnie demanded his care absented himself but twice from Lomax Place during more than a few minutes. On one of these occasions he travelled over to Audley Court and spent an hour there; on the other he met 96 Millicent Henning by previous understanding and took a walk with her on the Embankment. He tried to find an hour to go and thank Madame

Poupin for a sympathetic offering, many times repeated, of *tisane* concocted after a receipt thought supreme by the couple in Lisson Grove (though little appreciated in the neighbourhood generally); but he was obliged to acknowledge her kindness only by a respectful letter, which he composed with some trouble, though much elation, in the French tongue, peculiarly favourable, as he believed, to little courtesies of this kind. Lady Aurora came again and again to the darkened house, where she diffused her beneficent influence in nightly watches, in the most modern sanative suggestions, in conversations with Hyacinth more ingeniously addressed than her fluttered embarrassments might have betrayed to the purpose of diverting his mind, and in tea-makings (there was a great deal of this liquid consumed on the premises during Pinnie's illness) after a system more enlightened than the usual fashion of Pentonville. She was the bearer of several messages and of a good deal of medical advice from Rose Muniment, whose interest in the dressmaker's case irritated Hyacinth by its fine courage, which even at second-hand was still extravagant: she appeared very nearly as resigned to the troubles of others as she was to her own.

Hyacinth had been seized the day after his return from Medley with a sharp desire to do something enterprising and superior on Pinnie's behalf. He felt the pressure of an angry sense that she was dying of her poor career, of her uneffaced remorse for the trick she had played him in his boyhood—as if he hadn't long ago and indeed at the time forgiven it, judging it to have been the highest wisdom!—of something basely helpless in the attitude of her acquaintance. He wanted to do something 97 that should prove to himself he had got the very best opinion about the invalid it was possible to have: so he insisted that Mr. Buffery should consult with a West End doctor if the West End doctor would consent to meet Mr. Buffery. An oracle not averse to this condescension was discovered through Lady Aurora's agency—she had not brought him of her own movement because on the one hand she hesitated to impose on the little household in Lomax Place the expense of such a visit, and on the other, with all her narrow personal economies for the sake of her charities, had not the means to meet it herself; and in prevision of the great man's fee Hyacinth applied to Mr. Vetch, as he had applied before, for a loan. The great man came and was wonderfully civil to Mr. Buffery, whose conduct of the case he pronounced judicious; he remained several minutes in the house, gazing at Hyacinth over his spectacles—he seemed rather more concerned about him than about the patient—and with almost the whole of the Place turning out to stare at his chariot. After all he consented to accept no fee. He put the question aside with a gesture full of urbanity—a course disappointing and displeasing to Hyacinth, who felt in a manner cheated of the full effect of the fine thing he had wished to do for Pinnie; though when he said as much or something like it to Mr. Vetch the caustic fiddler greeted the observation with a face of amusement which, considering the situation, verged on the unseemly.

Hyacinth at any rate had done the best he could, and the fashionable doctor had left directions which foreshadowed commerce with an expensive chemist in Bond Street—a prospect by which our young man was to some extent consoled. Poor Pinnie's decline, however, was not arrested, and one evening more than a week after his return from Medley, as 98 he sat with her alone, it struck him that her mild spirit must already have passed. The respectable nurse had moved away to supper, and by the aid of the staircase a perceptible odour of fizzling bacon indicated that a more cheerful state of things prevailed in the lower regions. Hyacinth couldn't make out if his old friend were asleep or awake; he believed she had not lost consciousness, yet for more than an hour she had given no sign of life. At last she put out her hand as if aware he was near her and wished to feel for him, and murmured: "Why did she come? I didn't want to see her." In a moment, as she went on, he perceived to whom she was alluding: her mind had travelled back through all the years to the dreadful day—she had described every incident of it to him—when Mrs. Bowerbank had invaded her quiet life and startled her sensitive conscience with a message from the prison. "She sat there so long—so long. She was so very large and I was so frightened. She moaned and moaned and cried—too dreadful. I couldn't help it—I couldn't help it!" Her thought wandered from Mrs. Bowerbank in the discomposed show-room, enthroned on the yellow sofa, to the tragic creature at Milbank, whose accents again, for the hour, lived in her ears; and mixed with this mingled vision was still the haunting sense that she herself might have acted differently. That had been cleared up in the past, so far as Hyacinth's intention was concerned; but what was most alive in Pinnie at the present hour was the passion of repentance, of still further expiation. It sickened him that she should believe these things were still necessary, and he leaned over her and talked tenderly, said everything he could think of to soothe her. He told her not to think of that dismal far-off time, which had ceased long ago to have any consequences for either of 99 them; to consider only the future, when she should be quite strong again and he would look after her and keep her all to himself and take care of her better, far better than he had ever done before. He had thought of many things while he sat with Pinnie watching the shadows made by the night-lamp—high, imposing shadows of objects low and mean—and among them he had followed with an imagination that went further in that direction than ever before the probable consequences of his not having been adopted in his babyhood by the dressmaker. The workhouse and the gutter, ignorance and cold, filth and tatters, nights of huddling under bridges and in doorways, vermin, starvation and blows, possibly even the vigorous efflorescence of an inherited disposition to crime—these things, which he saw with unprecedented vividness, suggested themselves as his natural portion. Intimacies with a princess, visits to fine old country-houses, intelligent consideration, even, of the best means of inflicting a scare on the classes of privilege, would in that case not have been within his compass; and that Pinnie should have rescued him from such a destiny and put these luxuries within his reach represented almost a grand position as opposed to a foul, if he could only have the magnanimity to take it so.

Her eyes were open and fixed on him, but the sharp ray the little dressmaker used to direct into Lomax Place as she plied her needle at the window had completely left them. "Not there—what should I do there?" she inquired very softly. "Not with the great—the great—" and her voice failed.

"The great what? What do you mean?"

"You know—you know," she went on, making another effort. "Haven't you been with them? Haven't they received you?"

"Ah they won't separate us, Pinnie; they won't 100 come between us as much as that," said Hyacinth; and he sank to his knees by her bed.

"*You* must be separate—that makes me happier. I knew they'd find you at last."

"Poor Pinnie, poor Pinnie," murmured the young man.

"It was only for that—now I'm going," she sighed.

"If you'll stay with me you needn't fear," he smiled at her.

"Oh what would *they* think?" she quavered.

"I like you best," he insisted.

"You've had me always. Now it's their turn; they've waited."

"Yes indeed they've waited!" Hyacinth said.

"But they'll make it up; they'll make up everything!" the poor woman panted. Then she added: "I couldn't, couldn't help it!"—which was the last flicker of her strength. She gave no further sign of consciousness and four days later ceased to breathe. Hyacinth was with her and Lady Aurora, but neither could recognise the moment.

Hyacinth and Mr. Vetch carried her bier with the help of Eustache Poupin and Paul Muniment. Lady Aurora was at the funeral and Madame Poupin as well and twenty neighbours from Lomax Place; but the most distinguished member—in appearance at least—of the group of mourners was Millicent Henning, the grave yet brilliant beauty of whose countenance, the high propriety of whose demeanour and the fine taste and general style of whose rich black "costume" excited no little attention. Mr. Vetch had his idea; he had been nursing it ever since Hyacinth's return from Medley, and three days after Pinnie had been consigned to the earth he broached it to his young friend. The funeral had been on a Friday and Hyacinth had mentioned that he should return to old Crook's on Monday morning. 101 This was Sunday night and he had been out for a walk neither with Millicent Henning nor with Paul Muniment, but alone, after the manner of old days. When he came in he found the fiddler waiting for him and snuffing a tallow candle in the blighted show-room. He had three or four little papers in his hand, which exhibited some jottings of his pencil, and Hyacinth guessed, what was the truth but not all the truth, that he had come to speak to him about business. Pinnie had left a little will, of which she had appointed her old friend executor; this fact had already become known to our hero, who thought such an arrangement highly natural. Mr. Vetch informed him of the purport of this simple and judicious document and mentioned that he had been looking into the dressmaker's "affairs." They consisted, poor Pinnie's affairs, of the furniture of the house in Lomax Place, of the obligation to pay the remainder of a quarter's rent and of a sum of money in the savings bank. Hyacinth was surprised to learn that Pinnie's economies had produced fruit at this late day (things had gone so ill with her in recent years, and there had been often such a want of money in the house) until Mr. Vetch explained to him with eager clearness that he himself had watched over the little hoard, accumulated during the period of her comparative prosperity, with the stiff determination that it should be sacrificed only in case of desperate stress. Work had become scarce with her but she could still do it when it came, and the money was to be kept for the very possible event of her turning helpless. Mercifully enough she had not lived to see that day, and the sum in the bank had survived her, though diminished by more than half. She had left no debts but the matter of the house and those incurred during her illness. Of course the fiddler had known—he hastened to give his young 102 friend this assurance—that Pinnie, had she become infirm, would have been able to count absolutely upon *him* for the equivalent, in her old age, of the protection she had given him in his youth. But what if an accident had overtaken Hyacinth? What if he had incurred some horrid penalty for his revolutionary dabblings, which, little dangerous as they might be to society, were quite capable, in a country where authority, though good-natured, liked occasionally making an example, to put him on the wrong side of a prison-wall? At any rate, for better or worse, by pinching and scraping, she had saved a little, and of that little after everything was paid off a fraction would still be left. Everything was bequeathed to Hyacinth—everything but a couple of plated candlesticks and the old "cheffonier" which had been so handsome in its day; these Pinnie begged Mr. Vetch to accept in recognition of services beyond all price. The furniture, everything he didn't want for his own use, Hyacinth could sell in a lump, and with the proceeds he could wipe out old scores. The sum of money would remain to him; it amounted in its reduced condition to about thirty-seven pounds. In mentioning this figure Mr. Vetch appeared to imply that Hyacinth would be master of a very pretty little fortune. Even to the young man himself, in spite of his recent initiations, such a windfall seemed far from contemptible; it represented sudden possibilities of still not returning to old Crook's. It represented them, that is, till he presently remembered the various advances made him by the fiddler, and till he reflected that by the time these had been repaid there would hardly be twenty pounds left. That, however, was a far larger sum than he had ever had in his pocket at once. He thanked the old man for his information and remarked—and there was no hypocrisy in the speech—that 103 he was too sorry Pinnie had not given herself the benefit of the whole of the little fund in her lifetime. To this her executor replied that it had yielded her an interest far beyond any other investment, for he was persuaded she had believed she should never live to enjoy it, and that this faith had been rich to her in pictures, visions of the effect, for her brilliant boy, of his "coming into" something handsome.

"What effect did she mean—do you mean?" Hyacinth asked. As soon as he had spoken he felt he knew what the old man would say—it would be a reference to Pinnie's belief in his reunion with his "relations" and to the facilities thirty-seven pounds would afford him for cutting a figure among them; and for a moment Mr. Vetch looked at him as if exactly that response were on his lips. At the end of the moment, however, he replied quite differently.

"She hoped you'd go abroad and see the world." The fiddler watched his young friend and then added: "She had a particular wish you should go to Paris."

Hyacinth had turned pale at this suggestion and for a moment said nothing. "Ah Paris!" he almost wailed at last.

"She would have liked you even to take a little run down to Italy."

"Doubtless that would be jolly. But there's a limit to what one can do with twenty pounds."

"How do you mean, with twenty pounds?" the old man asked, lifting his eyebrows while the wrinkles in his forehead made deep shadows in the candlelight.

"That's about what will remain after I have settled my account with you."

"How do you mean, your account with me? I shan't take any of your money." 104

Hyacinth's eyes wandered over his interlocutor's suggestive shabbiness. "I don't want to be beastly ungracious, but suppose *you* should lose your powers."

"My dear boy, I shall have one of the resources that was open to Pinnie. I shall look to you to be the support of my old age."

"You may do so with perfect safety, except for that danger you just mentioned—of my being imprisoned or hanged."

"It's precisely because I think the danger will be less if you go abroad that I urge you to take this chance. You'll see the world and you'll like it better. You'll think society, even as it is, has some good points," said Mr. Vetch.

"I've never liked it better than the last few months."

"Ah well, wait till you see Paris!"

"Oh, Paris, Paris," Hyacinth repeated vaguely—and he stared into the turbid flame of the candle as if making out the most brilliant scenes there: an attitude, accent and expression which the fiddler interpreted both as the vibration of a latent hereditary chord and a symptom of the acute sense of opportunity. 105

BOOK FOURTH

XXIX

The Boulevard was all alive, brilliant with illuminations, with the variety and gaiety of the crowd, the dazzle of shops and cafés seen through uncovered fronts or immense lucid plates, the flamboyant porches of theatres and the flashing lamps of carriages, the far-spreading murmur of talkers and strollers, the uproar of pleasure and prosperity, the general magnificence of Paris on a perfect evening in June. Hyacinth had been walking about all day—he had walked from rising till bedtime every day of the week spent since his arrival—and now an extraordinary fatigue, a tremendous lassitude had fallen upon him, which, however, was not without its delight of sweet satiety, and he settled himself in a chair beside a little table in front of Tortoni's not so much to rest from it as to enjoy it. He had seen so much, felt so much, learnt so much, thrilled and throbbed and laughed and sighed so much during the past several days that he was conscious at last of the danger of becoming incoherent to himself and of the need of balancing his accounts.

To-night he came to a full stop; he simply sat at the door of the most dandified café in Paris and felt his pulse and took stock of his impressions. He had been intending to visit the Variétés Theatre, which blazed through intermediate lights and through the thin foliage of trees not favoured by the asphalt, on 108 the other side of the great avenue. But the impression of Chaumont—he relinquished that for the present; it added to the luxury of his situation to reflect that he should still have plenty of time to see the *succès du jour*. The same effect proceeded from his determination to order a *marquise* when the waiter, whose superior shirt-front and whisker emerged from the long white cylinder of an apron, came to take his commands. He knew the decoction was expensive—he had learnt as much at the moment he happened to overhear for the first time a mention of it; which had been the night before as he sat in his stall during an *entr'acte* of the Comédie Française. A gentleman beside him, a young man in evening-dress, conversing with an acquaintance in the row behind, recommended the latter to refresh himself with the luxury in question after the play: there was nothing like it, the speaker remarked, of a hot evening in the open air when one was thirsty. The waiter brought Hyacinth a tall glass of champagne in which a pineapple ice was in solution, and our hero felt he had hoped for a sensation no less intense in looking for an empty table on Tortoni's terrace. Very few tables were empty, and it was his belief that the others were occupied by high celebrities; at any rate they were just the types he had had a prevision of and had wanted most to meet when the extraordinary opportunity to come abroad with his pockets full of money (it was more extraordinary even than his original meeting with the Princess) turned real to him in Lomax Place. He knew about Tortoni's from his study of the French novel, and as he sat there he had a vague sense of fraternising with Balzac and Alfred de Musset: there were echoes and reminiscences of their works in the air, all confounded with the indefinable exhalations, the strange composite odour, half agreeable, half impure, of the Boulevard. 109 "Splendid Paris, charming Paris"—that refrain, the fragment of an invocation, a beginning without an end, hummed itself perpetually in Hyacinth's ears; the only articulate words that got themselves uttered in the hymn of praise his imagination had been addressing to the French capital from the first hour of his stay. He recognised, he greeted with a thousand palpitations, the seat of his maternal ancestors—was proud to be associated with so much of the superb, so many proofs of a civilisation that had no visible rough spots. He had his perplexities and even now and then a revulsion for which he had made no allowance, as when it came over him that the most brilliant city in the world was also the most blood-stained; but the great sense that he understood and sympathised was preponderant, and his comprehension gave him wings—appeared to transport him to still wider fields of knowledge, still higher sensations.

In other days, in London, he had thought again and again of his mother's father, the revolutionary watchmaker who had known the ecstasy of the barricade and had paid for it with his life, and his reveries had not been sensibly chilled by the fact that he knew next to nothing about him. He figured him in his mind, this mystic ancestor, had a conviction that he was very short like himself and had curly hair, an immense talent for his work and an extraordinary natural eloquence, together with many of the most attractive qualities of the French character. But he was reckless and a little cracked, also probably immoral; he had difficulties and debts and irrepressible passions; his life had been an incurable fever and its tragic termination was a matter of course. None the less it would have been a charm to hear him talk, to feel the influence of a gaiety which even political madness could never quench; for his 110 grandson had a theory that he spoke the French tongue of an earlier time, delightful and sociable in accent and phrase, exempt from the baseness of modern slang. This vague yet vivid personage became our young friend's constant companion from the day of his arrival; he roamed about with Florentine's boy hand in hand, sat opposite him at dinner, by the small table in the restaurant, finished the bottle with him, made the bill a little longer—treating him furthermore to innumerable revelations and counsels. He knew the lad's secret without being told and looked at him across the diminutive tablecloth where the great cube of bread, pushed aside a little, left room for his elbows—it puzzled Hyacinth that the people of Paris should ever have had the fierceness of hunger when the loaves were so big; gazed at him with eyes of deep, kind, glowing comprehension and with lips which seemed to murmur that when one was to die to-morrow one must eat and drink, one must gratify all one's poor senses all one could to-day. There was nothing venerable, no constraint of importance or disapproval, in this edifying and impalpable presence; the young man considered that Hyacinth Vivier was of his own time of life and could enter into his pleasures as well as his pains. Wondering repeatedly where the barricade on which his grandfather must have fallen had been erected he at last satisfied himself—though I am unable to trace the course of the induction—that it had bristled across the Rue Saint-Honoré very near to the Church of Saint-Roch. The pair had now roamed together through all the museums and gardens, through the principal churches—the republican martyr was very good-natured about this; through the passages and arcades, up and down the great avenues, across all the bridges and above all again and again along the river, where the quays were an endless 111 entertainment to Hyacinth, who lingered by the half-hour beside the boxes of old books on the parapets, stuffing his pockets with fivepenny volumes while the bright industries of the Seine flashed and glittered beneath him and on the other bank the glorious Louvre stretched either way for a league. Our young man took the same satisfaction in the Louvre as if he had been invited there, as he had been to poor obliterated Medley; he haunted the museum during all the first days, couldn't look enough at certain pictures nor sufficiently admire the high polish of the great floors in which the golden frescoed ceilings repeated themselves. All Paris struck him as tremendously artistic and decorative; he felt as if hitherto he had lived in a dusky, frowsy, Philistine world, a world in which the taste was the taste of Little Peddlington and the idea of beautiful arrangement had never had an influence. In his ancestral city it had been active from the first, and that was why his quick sensibility responded and why he murmured his constant refrain whenever the fairness of the great monuments arrested him in the pearly silvery light or he saw them take grey-blue, delicate tones at the end of stately vistas. It seemed to him the place expressed herself, and did it in the grand style, while London remained vague and blurred, inarticulate, blunt and dim. Splendid Paris, charming Paris indeed!

Eustache Poupin had given him letters to three or four democratic friends, ardent votaries of the social question, who had by a miracle either escaped the cruelty of exile or suffered the outrage of pardon and, in spite of republican *mouchards* no less infamous than the imperial and the periodical swoops of a despotism which had only changed its buttons and postage-stamps, kept alive the sacred spark which would some day become a consuming flame. 112 Hyacinth, however, had not had the thought of delivering these introductions; he had accepted them because Poupin had

had such a solemn glee in writing them, and also because he had not the courage to let the couple in Lisson Grove know how since that terrible night at Hoffendahl's a change had come over the spirit of his dream. He had not grown more concentrated, he had grown more relaxed, and it was inconsistent with relaxation that he should rummage out Poupin's friends—one of whom lived in the Batignolles and the others in the Faubourg Saint-Antoine—and make believe he cared for what they cared for in the same way as they cared for it. What was supreme in his mind to-day was not the idea of how the society that surrounded him should be destroyed; it was much more the sense of the wonderful, precious things it had produced, of the fabric of beauty and power it had raised. That destruction was waiting for it there was forcible evidence, known to himself and others, to show; but since this truth had risen before him in its magnitude he had become conscious of a transfer, partial if not complete, of his sympathies; the same revulsion of which he had given a sign to the Princess in saying that now he pitied the rich, those who were regarded as happy. While the evening passed therefore, as he kept his place at Tortoni's, the emotion that was last to visit him was compunction for not having put himself in relation with poor Poupin's friends, for having neglected to make the acquaintances of earnest people.

Who in the world, if one should come to that, was as earnest as he himself or had given such signal even though secret proofs of it? He could lay that unction to his soul in spite of his having amused himself cynically, spent all his time in theatres, galleries, walks of pleasure. The feeling had not 113 failed him with which he accepted Mr. Vetch's furtherance—the sense that since he was destined to perish in his flower he was right to make a dash at the beautiful, horrible world. That reflexion had been natural enough, but what was strange was the fiddler's own impulse, his desire to do something pleasant for him, to beguile him and ship him off. What had been most odd in this was the way Mr. Vetch appeared to overlook the fact that his young friend had already had that year such a turn of dissipation as was surely rare in the experience of London artisans. This was one of the many things Hyacinth thought of; he thought of the others in turn and out of turn; it was almost the first time he had sat still long enough to collect himself. A hundred confused reverberations of the recent past crowded on him and he saw that he had lived more intensely in the previous six months than in all the rest of his time. The succession of events finally straightened itself and he tasted over some of those rarest, strangest moments. His last week at Medley in especial had already become a far-off fable, the echo of a song; he could read it over as a romance bound in vellum and gold, gaze at it as he would have gazed at some exquisite picture. His visit there had been perfect to the end, and even the three days compromised by Sholto's sojourn had not broken the spell, for the three more that had elapsed before his own departure—when the Princess herself had given him the signal—were the most important of all. It was then she had made it clear to him that she was in earnest, was prepared for the last sacrifice. He felt her his standard of comparison, his authority, his measure, his perpetual reference; and in taking possession of his mind to this extent she had completely renewed it. She was altogether a new term, and now that he was in a foreign country he observed 114 how much her conversation, itself so foreign, had prepared him to understand it. In Paris he saw of course a great many women and noticed almost all of them, especially the actresses; inwardly confronting their movement, their speech, their manner of dressing, with that of his extraordinary friend. He judged her to be beyond them in every respect, though there were one or two actresses who had the air of trying to copy her.

The recollection of the last days he had spent with her affected him now like the touch of a tear-washed cheek. She had in the last intimacy, strangest and richest of revelations, shed tears for him, and it was his suspicion that her secret idea was to frustrate the redemption of his vow to Hoffendahl, to the immeasurable body that Hoffendahl represented. She pretended to have accepted it, and what she said was simply that when he should have played his part she would engage to save him—to fling a cloud about him as the goddess-mother of the Trojan hero used in Virgil's poem to *escamoter* Æneas. What she meant was in his view to prevent him from playing his part at all. She was in earnest for herself, not for him. The main result of his closest commerce with her, in which somehow, all without herself stooping, she had only raised him higher and higher and absolutely highest, had been to make him feel that he was good enough for anything. When he had asked her the last day if he might write to her she said Yes, after two or three weeks. He had written about Pinnie's death, and again just before coming abroad, and in doing so had taken account of something else she had said in regard to their correspondence—that she didn't wish vague phrases, protestations or compliments; she wanted the realities of his life, the smallest, the "dearest," the most personal details. Therefore he had treated her to the whole business of the break-up in Lomax Place, 115 including the sale of the rickety furniture and similar sordid items. He had told her what that transaction brought—a beggarly sum, but sufficient to help a little to pay debts, and had informed her further that one of the ways Mr. Vetch had taken to hurry him off to Paris was to press upon him thirty pounds out of his quaint little hoard, crowning the sum already inherited from Pinnie—which, in a manner that none of Hyacinth's friends of course could possibly regard as frugal or even as respectable, was now consecrated to a mere excursion. He even mentioned that he had ended by accepting the thirty pounds, adding that he feared his peculiar situation—she would know what he meant by that—made for a failure of proper dignity: it disposed one to grab all one could get, kept one at least very tolerant of whims that took the form of offered comforts.

What he didn't mention to his shining friend was the manner in which he had been received by Paul Muniment and by Millicent Henning on his return from Medley. Millicent's reception had been of the queerest; it had been quite unexpectedly mild. She had made him no scene of violence and appeared to have given up the line of throwing a blur of recrimination over her own equivocal doings. She treated him as if she liked him for having got in with the swells; she had an appreciation of success which would lead her to handle him more tenderly now that he was really successful. She tried to make him describe the style of life that was led in a house where people were invited to stay like that without having to pay, and she surprised almost as much as she gratified him by not indulging in any of her former digs at the Princess. She was lavish of ejaculations when he answered certain of her questions—ejaculations that savoured of Pimlico, "Oh I say!" and "Oh my stars!"—and he was more than ever struck 116 with her detestable habit of saying "Aye, that's where it is" when he had made some remark to which she wished to give an intelligent and sympathetic assent. But she didn't jeer at the Princess's private character; she stayed her satire in a case where there was such an opening for it. Hyacinth reflected that this was lucky for her: he couldn't have stood it (nervous and anxious as he was about Pinnie) if she had had at such a time the bad taste to be low and abusive. Under that stress he would have broken with her completely—would have been too disgusted. She displeased him enough as it was by her vulgar tricks of speech. There were two or three little, recurrent thumb-marks of the common that smutched her more blackly for him than their size warranted—as when she said "full up" for full, "sold out" for sold, or remarked to him that she supposed he was now going to "chuck up" his work at old Crook's. It was as if he were fairly requiring of her to speak *better* than women of fashion. These phrases at any rate had fallen upon his ear many a time before, but now they seemed almost unpardonable enough to quarrel about. Not that he had any wish to quarrel, for if the question had been pushed he would have admitted that to-day his intimacy with the Princess had caused any claims he might have had upon Millicent to lapse. Millicent was all discretion, however; she only, it was evident, wished to convey to him that it was better for both parties they should respect each other's liberty. A genial understanding on this subject was what Miss Henning desired, and Hyacinth forbade himself to inquire what use she proposed to make of her freedom. During the month that elapsed between Pinnie's death and his visit to Paris he had seen her several times, since the respect for each other's freedom had somehow not implied cessation of intercourse and it was only 117 natural she should have been soft to him in his bereaved condition. Hyacinth's sentiment about Pinnie was deep, and Millicent was clever enough to guess it; the consequence of which was that on these occasions she was very soft indeed. She talked to him almost as if she had been his mother and he a convalescent child; called him her dearest dear and a precious young rascal and her own old boy; moralised a good deal, abstained from beer (till she learnt he had inherited a fortune), and when he remarked once (moralising a little too) that after the death of a person we have loved we are haunted by the memory of our failures of kindness, of generosity, rejoined with a dignity that made the words almost a contribution to the philosophic view, "Yes, that's where it is!"

Something in her behaviour at this period had even made Hyacinth wonder if there were not some mystical sign in his appearance, some fine betrayal in the very expression of his face, of the predicament in which he had been placed by Diedrich Hoffendahl; he began to suspect anew the operation of that "beastly *attendrissement*" he had detected of old in people who had the benefit of Miss Pynsent's innuendoes. The compassion Millicent felt for him had never been one of the reasons why he liked her; it had fortunately been corrected, moreover, by his power to make her furious. This evening, on the Boulevard, as he watched the endless facial successions, one of the ideas that came to him was that it was odd he should like her even yet; for heaven knew he liked the Princess better, and he had hitherto supposed that when a sentiment of this kind had the energy of a possession it made a clean sweep of all minor predilections. But it was clear to him that she still existed for him as a loud-breathing feminine fact, that he couldn't feel he had quite done with 118 her or she with him, and that in spite of his having now so many other things to admire there was still a comfort in the recollection of her robust beauty and her primitive passions. Hyacinth thought of her as some clever young barbarian who in ancient days should have made a pilgrimage to Rome might have thought of a Dacian or Iberian mistress awaiting his return on the rough provincial shore. If Millicent judged his visit at a "hall" a proof of the sort of success that was to attend him—how he reconciled this with the supposition that she perceived as a ghostly crown intermingled with his curly hair the lurid light of destiny, the aureola of martyrdom, he would have had some difficulty in explaining—if Miss Henning considered, on his return from Medley, that he had taken his place on the winning side it was only consistent of her to borrow a grandeur from the fact of his course of travel; and indeed by the time he was ready to start she spoke of his participation in this privilege of the upper classes as if she had invented it herself and had even contributed materially to the funds required. It had been her theory from the first that she only liked people of spirit; and Hyacinth certainly had never had so much spirit as when he went "abroad," after the fashion of Mr. Vetch of old, with a hat-box. He could say to himself quite without bitterness that of course she would profit by his absence to put her relations with Sholto on a comfortable footing; yet somehow, after all, at this moment, as her distant English face out-blossomed the nearer, the livid Parisian, it had not that gentleman's romantic shadow across it. It was the general brightness of Paris perhaps that made him see things sharp; at any rate he remembered with kindness something she had said to him the last time he saw her and that it touched him exceedingly at the moment. He had happened to 119 observe to her in a friendly way that now Miss Pynsent had gone she was, with the exception of Mr. Vetch, the person in his whole circle who had known him longest. To this Millicent had replied that Mr. Vetch wouldn't live for ever and that she should then have the satisfaction of being his very oldest friend. "Oh well, I shan't live for ever either," said Hyacinth; which led her to ask if by chance he had a weakness of the chest. "Not that I know of, but I might get smashed in a row"; and when she broke out into scorn of his silly notion of turning everything up—as if any one wanted to know what a costermonger would like, or any of that low sort at the East End!—he amused himself with inquiring if she were satisfied with the condition of society and thought nothing ought to be done for people who at the end of a lifetime of starvation wages had only the reward of the hideous workhouse and a pauper's grave.

"I shouldn't be satisfied with anything if ever *you* was to slip up," she had answered simply, looking at him with her beautiful boldness. Then she had added: "There's one thing I can tell you, Mr. Robinson: that if ever any one was to do you a turn——!" And she had paused again, tossing back the head she carried as if it were surmounted by the plumes of a chieftainess, while Hyacinth asked what would occur in that contingency. "Well, there'd be *one* left behind who would take it up!" she had announced; and in the tone of the declaration there had been something clear and brave. It struck Hyacinth as a strange fate—though not stranger after all than his native circumstances—that one's memory should come to be represented by a shop-girl overladen with bracelets of imitation silver; but he was reminded that Millicent was a fine specimen of a woman of a type opposed to the whining, and that in her large, free temperament many disparities were reconciled. 120

XXX

On the other hand the intensity of Paris had not much power to transfigure the impression made upon him by such intercourse with Paul Muniment as he had enjoyed during the weeks that followed Pinnie's death—an impression considerably more severe than any idea of renunciation or oblivion that could connect itself with Millicent. Why it should have had the taste of sadness was not altogether clear, for Muniment's voice was as distinct as any in the chorus of approbation excited by the news that the youth was about to cultivate the most characteristic of the pleasures of gentility—an applausive unanimity the effect of which was to place his journey to Paris in a light almost ridiculous. What had got into them all—did they think he was good for nothing but to amuse himself? Mr. Vetch had been the most zealous, but the others clapped him on the back almost exactly in the same manner he had seen his mates in Soho bring their palms down on one of their number when it was disclosed to them that his "missus" had made him yet once again a father. That had been Poupin's tone, and his wife's as well; and even poor Schinkel, with his everlasting bandage, whom he had met in Lisson Grove, appeared to feel it necessary to remark that a little run across the Rhine while he was about it would open his eyes to a great many wonders. The Poupins shed 121 tears of joy, and the letters which have already been mentioned and which lay day after day on the mantel-shelf of the little room our hero occupied at an *hôtel garni* tremendously tall and somewhat lopsided in the Rue Jacob (that recommendation proceeded also from Lisson Grove, the garni being kept by a second cousin of Madame Eustache) these valuable documents had been prepared by the obliging exile many days before his young friend was ready to start. It was almost refreshing to Hyacinth when old Crook, the sole outspoken dissentient, told him he was a blockhead to waste his money on the bloody French. This worthy employer of labour was evidently disgusted at such an innovation; if he wanted a little recreation why couldn't he take it as it had been taken in Soho from the beginning of time, in the shape of a trip to Brighton or two or three days of alcoholic torpor? Old Crook was right. Hyacinth conceded freely that he was a blockhead, and was only a little uncomfortable that he couldn't explain why he didn't pretend not to be and had a kind of right to that compensatory ease.

Paul guessed why, of course, and smiled approval with a candour which gave Hyacinth a strange inexpressible heartache. He already knew his friend's view of him as mainly ornamental, as adapted only to the softer forms of the subversive energy, as constituted in short to show that the revolution was not necessarily brutal and illiterate; but in the light of the cheerful stoicism with which Muniment faced the sacrifice our hero was committed to, the latter had found it necessary to remodel a good deal his original conception of his sturdy friend's character. The result of this process was not that he admired it less but that he felt almost awe-stricken in presence of it. There had been an element of that sort in his appreciation of Muniment from the first, but the 122 weight now to carry was the sense of such a sublime consistency. Hyacinth felt that he himself could never have risen so high. He was competent to take the stiff engagement to Hoffendahl and was equally competent to keep it; but he couldn't have had the same fortitude for another, couldn't have detached himself from personal prejudice so effectually as to put forward in that manner for the terrible "job" a little chap he to all appearance really liked. That Muniment did like him it never occurred to the little chap to doubt. He had quite all the air of it to-day; he had never been more good-humoured, more placidly talkative; he was like an elder brother who knew that the "youngster" was clever and felt rather proud of it even when there was no one there to see. That temporary look of suspending their partnership which had usually marked him at the "Sun and Moon" was never visible in other places; in Audley Court he only chaffed his young friend occasionally for taking him too seriously. To-day that devotee hardly knew just how to take him; the episode of which Hoffendahl was the central figure had, as far as one could see, made so little change in his attitude. For a loyal servant, an effective agent, he was so extraordinarily candid—bitterness and denunciation so rarely sat on his lips. The criticism of everything—since everything was wrong—took so little of his time. It was as if he had been ashamed to complain; and indeed for himself as the months went on he had nothing particular to complain of. He had had a rise at the chemical works and a plan of getting a bigger room for Rosy was under serious consideration. On behalf of others he never sounded the pathetic note—he thought that sort of thing unbusiness-like; and the most that he did in the way of expatiation on the woes of humanity was occasionally to allude to 123 certain statistics, certain "returns," in regard to the remuneration of industries, applications for employment and the discharge of hands. In such matters as these he was deeply versed, moving ever in a dry, statistical and scientific air in which it cost Hyacinth an effort of respiration to accompany him. Simple and kindly as he was, and thoughtful of the sufferings of beasts, attentive and merciful to small insects and addicted even to kissing dirty babies in Audley Court, he sometimes emitted a short, satiric gleam which showed that his esteem for the poor was small and that if he had no illusions about the people who had got everything into their hands he had as few about those who had egregiously failed to do so. He was tremendously reasonable, which was largely why Hyacinth admired him, having a desire to be so himself but finding it terribly difficult.

Muniment's absence of passion, his fresh-coloured coolness, his easy, exact knowledge, the way he kept himself clean (save for fine chemical stains on his hands) in circumstances of foul contact, constituted a group of qualities that had always appeared to his admirer singularly enviable. Most enviable of all was the force that enabled him to sink personal sentiment where a great public good was to be attempted and yet keep up the form of caring for that minor interest. It seemed to our friend that if *he* had introduced a young fellow to Hoffendahl for his purposes, and Hoffendahl had accepted him on such a recommendation and everything had been settled, he would have preferred never to look at the young fellow again. That was his weakness and Paul carried it off far otherwise. It must be added that he had never made an allusion to their visit to the great taskmaster; so that Hyacinth also, out of pride, held his tongue on the subject. If his friend didn't propose expressly to yearn over him he wasn't 124 going to beg for it (especially as he didn't want it) by restless references. It had originally been a surprise to him that Muniment should be willing to countenance a possible assassination; but after all none of his ideas were narrow (one had such a sense that they ripened all the while) and if a pistol-shot would do any good he was not the man to raise pedantic objections. It is true that as regards his quiet acceptance of the predicament in which Hyacinth might be placed by it our young man had given him the benefit of a certain amount of doubt; it had occurred to him that perhaps Muniment had his own good grounds for believing that imperative sign would never really arrive, so that he might only be treating himself to the entertainment of judging of a little bookbinder's nerve. But in this case why did he take an interest in the little bookbinder's going to Paris? That was a thing he wouldn't have cared for had he held that in fact there was nothing to fear. He despised the sight of idleness, and in spite of the indulgence he had more than once been good enough to express on the subject of his young friend's sneaking love of ease what he would have been most likely to say at present was: "Go to Paris? Go to the dickens! Haven't you been out at grass long enough for one while, didn't you lark enough in the country there with the noble lady, and hadn't you better take up your tools again before you forget how to handle them?" Rosy had said something of that sort in her free, familiar way—whatever her intention she had been in effect only a little less caustic than old Crook: that Mr. Robinson was going in for a life of leisure, a life of luxury, like herself; she must congratulate him on having the means and the time. Oh the time—that was the great thing! She could speak with knowledge, having always enjoyed these advantages herself. And she intimated—or 125 was she mistaken?—that his good fortune emulated hers also in the matter of his having a high-born and beneficent friend (such a blessing now he had lost dear Miss Pynsent) who covered him with little attentions. Rose Muniment in short had been more exasperating than ever.

The Boulevard became even more brilliant as the evening went on and Hyacinth wondered whether he had a right to occupy the same table for so many hours. The theatre on the other side discharged its multitude; the crowd thickened on the wide asphalt, on the terrace of the café; gentlemen accompanied by ladies of whom he knew already how to characterise the type—*des femmes très-chic*—passed into the portals of Tortoni. The nightly emanation of Paris seemed to rise more richly, to float and hang in the air, to mingle with the universal light and the many-voiced sound, to resolve itself into a thousand solicitations and opportunities, addressed, however, mainly to those in whose pockets the chink of a little loose gold might respond. Hyacinth's retrospections had not made him drowsy, but quite the reverse; he grew restless and excited and a kind of pleasant terror of the place and hour entered into his blood. But it was nearly midnight and he got up to walk home, taking the line of the Boulevard toward the Madeleine. He passed down the Rue Royale, where comparative stillness reigned; and when he reached the Place de la Concorde, to cross the bridge which faces the Corps Législatif, he found himself almost isolated. He had left the human swarm and the obstructed pavements behind, and the wide spaces of the splendid square lay quiet under the summer stars. The plash of the great fountains was audible and he could almost hear the wind-stirred murmur of the little wood of the Tuileries on one side and of the vague expanse of the Champs Elysées on the 126 other. The place itself—the Place Louis Quinze, the Place de la Révolution—had given him a sensible emotion from the day of his arrival; he had recognised so quickly its tremendous historic character. He had seen in a rapid vision the guillotine in the middle, on the site of the inscrutable obelisk, and the tumbrils, with waiting victims, were stationed round the circle now made majestic by the monuments of the cities of France. The great legend of the French Revolution, a sunrise out of a sea of blood, was more real to him here than anywhere else; and, strangely, what was most present was not its turpitude and horror, but its magnificent energy, the spirit of creation that had been in it, not the spirit of destruction. That shadow was effaced by the modern fairness of fountain and statue, the stately perspective and composition; and as he lingered before crossing the Seine a sudden sense overtook him, making his heart falter to anguish—a sense of everything that might hold one to the world, of the sweetness of not dying, the fascination of great cities, the charm of travel and discovery, the generosity of admiration. The tears rose to his eyes as they had done more than once in the past six months, and a question, low but poignant, broke from his lips, to end in nothing. "How could he—how *could* he——?" It may be explained that "he" was a reference to Paul Muniment; for Hyacinth had dreamed of the religion of friendship.

Three weeks after this he found himself in Venice, whence he addressed to the Princess Casamassima a letter of which I reproduce the principal passages.

"This is probably the last time I shall write you before I return to London. Of course you've been in this place and you'll easily understand why here, especially here, the spirit should move me. Dear Princess, what an enchanted city, what ineffable impressions, what a revelation of the exquisite! I 127 have a room in a little campo opposite a small old church which has cracked marble slabs let into the front; and in the cracks grow little, wild, delicate flowers of which I don't know the name. Over the door of the church hangs an old battered leather curtain, polished and tawny, as thick as a mattress and with buttons in it like a sofa; and it flops to and fro laboriously as women and girls, with shawls on their heads and their feet in little wooden shoes which have nothing but toes, pass in and out. In the middle of the campo is a fountain that looks still older than the church; it has a primitive, barbaric air, and I've an idea it was put there by the first settlers—those who came to Venice from the mainland, from Aquileia. Observe how much historical information I've already absorbed; it won't surprise you, however, for you never wondered at anything after you discovered I knew something of Schopenhauer. I assure you I don't think of that musty misogynist in the least to-day, for I bend a genial eye on the women and girls I just spoke of as they glide with a small clatter and with their old copper water-jars to the fountain. The Venetian girl-face is wonderfully sweet and the effect is charming when its pale, sad oval (they all look underfed) is framed in the old faded shawl. They have also the most engaging hair, which never has done curling, and they slip along together, in couples or threes, interlinked by the arms and never meeting one's eye—so that its geniality doesn't matter—dressed in thin, cheap cotton gowns whose limp folds make the same delightful line that everything else in Italy makes. The weather is splendid and I roast—but I like it; apparently I was made to be spitted and 'done,' and I discover that I've been cold all my life even when I thought I was warm. I've seen none of the beautiful patricians who sat for the great painters—the gorgeous beings whose 128 golden hair was intertwined with pearls; but I'm studying Italian in order to talk with the shuffling, clicking maidens who work in the bead-factories—I'm determined to make one or two of them look at me. When they've filled their old water-pots at the fountain it's jolly to see them perch them on their heads and patter away over the polished Venetian stones. It's a charm to be in a country where the women don't wear the hideous British bonnet. Even in my own class—forgive the expression, I remember it used to offend you—I've never known a young female in London to put her nose out of the door without it; and if you had frequented such young females as much as I have you would have learnt of what degradation that dreary imposition is the source. The floor of my room is composed of little brick tiles, and to freshen the air in this temperature one sprinkles it, as you no doubt know, with water. Before long if I keep on sprinkling I shall be able to swim about; the green shutters are closed and the place makes a very good tank. Through the chinks the hot light of the campo comes in. I smoke cigarettes and in the pauses of this composition recline on a faded magenta divan in the corner. Convenient to my hand in that attitude are the works of Leopardi and a second-hand dictionary. I'm very happy—happier than I have ever been in my life save at Medley—and I don't care for anything but the present hour. It won't last long, for I'm spending all my money. When I've finished this I shall go forth and wander about in the splendid Venetian afternoon; and I shall spend the evening in that enchanted square of Saint Mark's which resembles an immense open-air drawing-room, listening to music and feeling the sea-breeze blow in between those two strange old columns of the piazzetta which seem to make a doorway for it. I can scarcely believe <u>129</u> that it's of myself I'm telling you these fine things; I say to myself a dozen times a day that Hyacinth Robinson isn't in it—I pinch my leg to see if I'm not dreaming. But a short time hence, when I've resumed the exercise of my profession in sweet Soho, I shall have proof enough that it has been my very self: I shall know this by the terrible grind of the life and the penance to come.

"That will mean, no doubt, that I'm deeply demoralised. It won't be for you, however, in this case, to cast the stone at me; for my demoralisation began from the moment I first approached you. Dear Princess, I may have done you good, but you haven't done me much. I trust you'll understand what I mean by that speech and not think it flippant or impertinent. I may have helped you to understand and enter into the misery of the people—though I protest I don't know much about it; but you've led my imagination into quite another train. Nevertheless I'm not wholly pretending it's all your fault if I've lost sight of the sacred cause almost altogether in my recent adventures. It's not that it hasn't been there to see, for that perhaps is the clearest result of extending one's horizon— the sense, increasing as we go, that want and toil and suffering are the constant lot of the immense majority of the human race. I've found them everywhere but haven't minded them. Forgive the cynical confession. What has struck me is the great achievements of which man has been capable in spite of them—the splendid accumulations of the happier few, to which doubtless the miserable many have also in their degree contributed. The face of Europe appears to be covered with them and they've had much the greater part of my attention. They seem to me inestimably precious and beautiful and I've become conscious more than ever before of how little I understand <u>130</u> what in the great rectification you and Poupin propose to do with them. Dear Princess, there are things I shall be too sorry to see you touch, even you with your hands divine; and—shall I tell you *le fond de ma pensée*, as you used to say?—I feel myself capable of fighting for them. You can't call me a traitor, for you know the obligation I supremely, I immutably recognise. The monuments and treasures of art, the great palaces and properties, the conquests of learning and taste, the general fabric of civilisation as we know it, based if you will upon all the despotisms, the cruelties, the exclusions, the monopolies and the rapacities of the past, but thanks to which, all the same, the world is less of a 'bloody sell' and life more of a lark—our friend Hoffendahl seems to me to hold them too cheap and to wish to substitute for them something in which I can't somehow believe as I do in things with which the yearnings and the tears of generations have been mixed. You know how extraordinary I think our Hoffendahl—to speak only of him; but if there's one thing that's more clear about him than another, it's that he wouldn't have the least feeling for this incomparable, abominable old Venice. He would cut up the ceilings of the Veronese into strips, so that every one might have a little piece. I don't want every one to have a little piece of anything and I've a great horror of that kind of invidious jealousy which is at the bottom of the idea of a redistribution. You'll say I talk of it all at my ease while in a delicious capital I smoke cigarettes on a magenta divan; and I give you leave to scoff at me if it turns out that when I come back to London without a penny in my pocket I don't hold the same language. I don't know what it comes from, but during the last three months there has crept over me a deep mistrust of that same grudging attitude—the intolerance of positions and fortunes <u>131</u> that are higher and brighter than one's own; a fear, moreover, that I may in the past have been actuated by such motives, and a devout hope that if I'm to pass away while I'm yet young it may not be with that odious stain upon my soul." <u>132</u>

XXXI

He spent the first days after his return to London in a process supposed by him to be the quest of a lodging; but in reality he was pulling himself together for the business of his livelihood, an effort he found by no means easy or agreeable. As he had told the Princess, he was demoralised, and the perspective of old Crook's dirty staircase had never seemed so steep. He lingered on the brink before he plunged again into Soho: he wished not to go back to the shop till he should be settled and delayed to get settled in order not to go back to the shop. He saw no one during this interval, not even Mr. Vetch; he waited to call on the fiddler till he should have the appearance of not coming as a beggar or a borrower—have recovered his employment and be able to give an address, as he had heard Captain Sholto say. He went to South Street—not meaning to go in at once but wishing to look at the house—and there he had the surprise of seeing the advertisement of an auctioneer in the window of the Princess's late residence. He had not expected to find her in town—having heard from her the last time three weeks before, when she had said nothing about her prospects; but he was puzzled by this indication that she had moved away altogether. There was something in it all, however, that he felt he had at bottom been expecting; it appeared 133 to prove the justice of a suspicion attached to all the steps of any intercourse with the Princess—a vague apprehension that one might suddenly stretch out one's hand and miss her altogether from one's side. He decided to ring at the door and ask for news of her; but there was no response to his summons: the stillness of an August afternoon—the year had come round again from his first visit—hung over the place, the blinds were down and the caretaker appeared to be absent. Before these facts he was much at a loss; unless indeed he should address a letter to his wonderful friend at Medley. It would doubtless be forwarded, though her short lease of the country-house had terminated, as he knew, several weeks before. Captain Sholto was of course a possible agent, a probable source of light; but nothing would have induced Hyacinth to ask such a service of him.

He turned away from South Street with a strange sinking of the heart; his state of ignorance struck inward, as it were—had the force of a deeply disquieting portent. He went to old Crook's only when he had arrived at his last penny. This, however, was very promptly the case. He had disembarked at London Bridge with only seventeen pence in his pocket and had lived on that sum for three days. The old fiddler in Lomax Place was having a chop before he went to the theatre, and he invited Hyacinth to share his repast, sending out at the same time for another pot of beer. He took the youth with him to the play, where, as at that season there were very few spectators, he had no difficulty in finding him a place. He seemed to wish to keep hold of him and peered strangely over his spectacles—Mr. Vetch wore the homely double glass in these latter years—when he learned that Hyacinth had found a retreat not in their old familiar quarter but in the unexplored 134 purlieus of Westminster. What had determined our young man was the fact that from this part of the town the journey was comparatively a short one to Camberwell; he had suffered so much, before Pinnie's death, from being separated by such a distance from his best friends. There was a pang in his heart connected with the image of Paul Muniment, but none the less the prospect of an evening hour from time to time in Audley Court struck him as one of the few nameable beguilements of his odd future. He could have gone straight to Camberwell to live, but that would carry him too far from the scene of his profession, and in Westminster he was nearer to old Crook's than he had been in Lomax Place. He said to Mr. Vetch that if it would give *him* pleasure he would abandon his lodging and take another in Pentonville. But the old man replied after a moment that he should be sorry to put that constraint upon him; if he were to make such an exaction Hyacinth would think he wanted to watch him.

"How do you mean, to watch me?"

Mr. Vetch had begun to tune his fiddle and he scraped it a little before answering. "I mean it as I've always meant it. Surely you know that in Lomax Place I had my eyes on you. I watched you as a child on the edge of a pond watches the little boat he has constructed and set afloat."

"You couldn't discover much. You saw, after all, very little of me," Hyacinth said.

"I made what I could of that little. It was better than nothing."

Hyacinth laid his hand gently on the old man's arm; he had never felt so acute a kindness for him, not even when accepting his thirty pounds before going abroad. "Certainly I'll come to see you."

"I was much obliged to you for your letters," Mr. Vetch observed without heeding these words but 135 continuing to scrape. He had always, even into the shabbiness of his old age, kept that mark of English good-breeding (which is composed of some such odd elements) that there was a shyness, an aversion to possible phrase-making, in his manner of expressing gratitude for favours, and that in spite of this cursory tone his acknowledgment had ever the accent of sincerity.

Hyacinth took little interest in the piece, which was an inanimate revival; he had been at the Théâtre Français and the tradition of that house was still sufficiently present to him to make any other style of interpretation of comedy appear at the best but a confident form of horseplay. He sat in one of the front stalls, close to the orchestra; and while the thing went forward—or backward, ever backward, as it seemed to him—his thoughts wandered far from the shabby scene and the dusty boards, revolving round a question which had come up immensely during the last few hours. The Princess was a *capricciosa*—this at least had been Madame Grandoni's account of her; and was that blank, expressionless house in South Street a sign that an end had come to the particular caprice in which he had happened to be involved? On his return to London the desire to be with her again on the same terms as at Medley had begun to ache in him like a sorrow or a dreaded wrong—so sharp was his sense that if he mightn't absolutely count upon her she had been all cruelly, all abominably dishonest. Yet the wonder of the other time remained, in the great silence that had come, altogether a wonder. Circumstances had favoured in an extraordinary degree his visit to her, and it was by no means clear that they would again be so accommodating or that what had been possible for a few days should be possible with continuity and in the midst of the ceremonies 136 and complications of London. Hyacinth felt poorer than he had ever felt before, inasmuch as he had had money and spent it, whereas in previous times he had never had it to spend. He never for an instant regretted his squandered wealth, for he said to himself that he had made a good bargain and become master of a precious equivalent. The equivalent was a rich experience—an experience that would grow richer still as he should talk it over, in the right conditions that *she* would find again, with the one person in the world to whom he was now interesting. His poverty would be no obstacle to their friendship so long as he should have a pair of legs to carry him to her door; for she liked him better shabby than furbished up, and she had given him too many pledges, they had taken together too many appointments, worked out too many ideas, to be disconcerted on either side by obstacles that were merely a part of the general conventionality. He was to go with her into the slums, to introduce her to the worst that London contained—he should have precisely to make acquaintance with it first—to show her the reality of the horrors of which she dreamed the world might be purged. He had ceased himself to care for the slums and had reasons for not wishing to spend his remnant in the study of foul things; but he would go through with his part of the engagement. He might be detached and mechanical, but any dreariness would have a gilding that should involve an association with her. What indeed if she should have changed, have availed herself of that great right of unapologetic inconsequence which he believed to be, at least in their relation with nobodies, the highest luxury of the happy? What if, from a high insolence which he thought of as lurking somewhere in the side-scenes of her nature, though he had really not once seen it step to the 137 front, she should toss back her perfect head with a movement signifying that he was too basely literal and that she knew him no more? His imagination represented her this evening in places where a barrier of dazzling light shut her out from access or even from any appeal. He saw her with other people, in splendid rooms where "the dukes" had possession of her, smiling, satisfied, surrounded, covered with jewels. When this vision grew intense he found a reassurance in reflecting that after all she would be unlikely to throw him personally over so long as she should remain as deeply compromised, subterraneously speaking, as she had—successfully it seemed—tried to become, and that it would not be easy for her to liberate herself from that entanglement. She had of course told him more, at Medley, of the manner in which she had already committed herself, and he remembered with a strange perverse elation that she had gone very far indeed.

In the intervals of the foolish play Mr. Vetch, who lingered in his place in the orchestra while his mates descended into the little hole under the stage, leaned over the rail and asked his young friend occasional questions, carrying his eyes at the same time about the dingy house at whose smoky ceiling and tarnished galleries he had been staring for so many a year. He came back to Hyacinth's letters and said: "Of course you know they were clever; they entertained me immensely. But as I read them I thought of poor Pinnie: I wished she could have listened to them; they would have made her so happy."

"Yes, poor Pinnie," Hyacinth murmured while his friend went on:

"I was in Paris in 1846; I stayed at a small hotel in the Rue Mogador. I judge from your letters that everything's changed. Does the Rue Mogador still exist? Yes, everything's changed. I daresay it's 138 all much finer, but I liked it very much as it was then. At all events I'm right in supposing—am I not?—that it cheered you up considerably, made you really happy."

"Why should I have wanted any cheering? I was happy enough," Hyacinth replied.

The fiddler projected his old, white, conscious face; it had the stale smoothness that betrays a sedentary occupation, thirty years spent in a close crowd, amid the smoke of lamps and the odour of stage-paint. "I thought you were sad about Pinnie."

"When I jumped with that avidity at your proposing I should take a tour? Poor old Pinnie!" Hyacinth added.

"Well, I hope you think a little better of the world. We mustn't make up our minds too early in life."

"Oh I've made up mine: the world's an awfully jolly place."

"Awfully jolly, no; but I like it as I like an old pair of shoes—I like so much less the idea of putting on the new ones."

"Why should I complain?" Hyacinth asked. "What have I known but kindness? People have done such a lot for me."

"Oh well, of course they've liked you. But that's all right," murmured Mr. Vetch, beginning to scrape again. What remained in Hyacinth's mind from their colloquy was the fact that this veteran, whom he regarded distinctly as cultivated, had thought his letters clever. He only wished he had made them cleverer still; he had no doubt of his ability to have done so.

It may be imagined whether the first hours he spent at old Crook's after he took up work again were altogether to his taste, and what was the nature of the reception given him by his former comrades, 139 whom he found exactly in the same attitudes and the same clothes (he knew and hated every article they wore) and with the same primitive pleasantries on their lips. Our young man's feelings were mingled; the place and the people affected him as loathsome, but there was something delightful in handling his tools. He gave a little private groan of relief when he discovered that he still liked his work and that the shining swarm of his ideas in the matter of sides and backs returned to him. They came in still brighter, more suggestive form, and he had the satisfaction of feeling that his taste had improved, that it had been purified by experience, and that the covers of a book might be made to express an astonishing number of high conceptions. Strange enough it was, and a proof surely of our little hero's being a true artist, that the impressions he had accumulated during the last few months appeared to mingle and confound themselves with the very sources of his craft and to lie open to technical "rendering." He had quite determined by this time to carry on his life as if nothing were hanging over him and he had no intention of remaining a little bookbinder to the end of his days; for that medium would after all translate only some of his conceptions. Yet his trade was a resource, an undiminished resource, for the present, and he had a particular as well as a general motive in attempting new flights—the prevision of the exquisite work he was to do during the coming year for the Princess, work it was so definite to him he owed her. When that debt should have been paid and his other arrears made up he proposed to himself to write something. He was far from having decided as yet what it should be; the only point settled was that it should be very remarkable and should not, at least on the face of it, have anything to do with a fresh deal of the social pack. 140 That was to be his transition—into literature: to bind the book, charming as the process might be, was after all much less fundamental than to write it. It had occurred to Hyacinth more than once that it would be a fine thing to produce a rare death-song.

It is not surprising that among such reveries as this he should have been conscious of a narrow range in the tone of his old work-fellows. They had only one idea: that he had come into a thousand pounds and had gone to spend them in France with a regular high one. He was aware in advance of the diffusion of this legend and did his best to allow for it, taking the simplest course, which was to gainsay nothing, but to catch the ball as it came and toss it still further, enlarging and embroidering humorously until Grugan and Roker and Hotchkin and all the rest, who struck him as not having washed since he left them, seemed really to begin to understand how it was he could have spent such a rare sum in so short a time. The impressiveness of this achievement helped him greatly to slip into his place; he could see that, though the treatment it received was superficially irreverent, the sense that he was very sharp and that the springs of his sharpness were somehow secret gained a good deal of strength from it. Hyacinth was not incapable of being rather pleased that it *should* be supposed, even by Grugan, Roker and Hotchkin, that he could get rid of a thousand pounds in less than five months, especially as to his own conscience the fact had altogether yet to be proved. He got off on the whole easily enough to feel a little ashamed, and he reflected that the men at old Crook's showed at any rate no symptoms of the social jealousy lying at the bottom of the desire for a fresh deal. This was doubtless an accident and not inherent in the fact that they were highly 141 skilled workmen— old Crook had no others—and therefore sure of constant employment; for it was impossible to be more skilled in a special line than Paul Muniment, who yet—though not out of jealousy of course—went in for the great grim restitution. What struck him most, after he had got used again to the sense of his apron and bent his back a while over his battered table, was the simple, synthetic patience of the others who had bent *their* backs and felt the rub of that dirty drapery all the while he was lounging in the halls of Medley, dawdling through boulevards and museums and admiring the purity of the Venetian girl-face. With Poupin, to be sure, his relations were all particular; but the explanations he owed the sensitive Frenchman were not such as could make him very unhappy, once he had determined to resist as much as possible the friction of a consciousness as galling at times as a misfitting harness. There was, moreover, more sorrow than anger in Poupin's face when he learned that his young friend and pupil had failed to cultivate in Paris the rich opportunities he had offered him. "You're cooling off, my child; there's something about you! Have you the weakness to flatter yourself that anything has been done or that humanity suffers a particle less? *Enfin* it's between you and your conscience."

"Do you think I want to get out of it?" Hyacinth grimaced; this expositor's phrases about humanity, which used to thrill him so, having grown of late strangely hollow and rococo.

"You owe me no explanations; the conscience of the individual is absolute, except of course in those classes in which, from the very nature of the infamies on which they're founded, no conscience can exist. Speak to me, however, of my City; *she* is always divine," Poupin went on, though showing 142 signs of irritation when Hyacinth began to praise to him the magnificent creations of the arch-fiend of December. In the presence of this picture he was in a terrible dilemma—gratified as a Parisian and a patriot but all disconcerted as a lover of liberty: it cost him a pang to admit that anything amid the *seuils sacrés* was defective, yet he saw still less his way to concede that it could owe any charm to the perjured monster of the Second Empire or even to the hypocritical, mendacious republicanism of the régime before which the inspired Commune had gone down in blood and fire. "Ah yes, it's very fine, no doubt," he remarked at last, "but it will be finer still when it's ours!"—a speech which caused Hyacinth to turn back to his work with a feeling of sickness. Everywhere, everywhere he saw the ulcer of envy—the greed of a party hanging together only that it might despoil another to its advantage. In old Eustache, one of the "pure," this was especially disenchanting. 143

XXXII

The landing at the top of the stairs in Audley Court was always dark; but it seemed darker than ever to Hyacinth while he fumbled for the door-latch after he had heard Rose Muniment's penetrating voice bid him come in. During that instant his ear caught the sound, if it could trust itself, of another voice, which prepared him a little for the spectacle fully presented as soon as the door—his attempt to reach the handle in his sudden agitation proving fruitless—was opened to him by Paul. His friend stood there tall and hospitable, saying something loud and jovial that he didn't distinguish. His eyes had crossed the threshold in a flash, but his step faltered a moment, only to obey, however, the vigour of Muniment's outstretched hand. Hyacinth's glance had gone straight, and though with four persons in it Rosy's little apartment looked crowded he saw no one but the object of his quick preconception—no one but the Princess Casamassima seated beside the low sofa, the grand feature introduced during his absence from London, on which, arrayed in the famous pink dressing-gown, Miss Muniment now received her visitors. He wondered afterwards why he should have been so startled; for he had said often enough both to himself and to his wonderful lady that so far as she was concerned he was proof against astonishment: it was so evident that the 144 note of her conduct would always be a sort of splendour of freedom. In fact now that he perceived she had made her way to Camberwell without his assistance the feeling in possession of him was a refined embarrassment; he blushed a little as he entered the circle, the fourth member of which was inevitably Lady Aurora Langrish. Was it that his intimacy with the Princess gave him a certain sense of responsibility for her course in respect to people who knew her as yet so scantly, and that there was something too little explained in the confidence with which she had practised a descent upon them? It indeed came over our young man that by this time perhaps they knew her a good deal; and moreover a woman's behaviour spoke for itself when she could sit looking in that fashion like a radiant angel dressed in a simple bonnet and mantle and immensely interested in an appealing corner of the earth. It took Hyacinth but an instant to infer that her character was in a different phase from any yet exhibited to him. There had been a glory of gentleness about her the night he made her acquaintance, and she had never ceased at any moment since to strike him as full of the imagination of sympathy and pity, unless perforce in relation to her husband, against whom—for reasons after all doubtless very sufficient— her heart appeared absolutely steeled. Now at any rate this high mildness had deepened to a rapture of active, ministering charity. She had put off her splendour, but her beauty was unquenchably bright; she had made herself humble for her pious excursion; she had, beside Rosy (who in the pink dressing-gown looked much the more luxurious of the two), almost the attitude of an hospital nurse; and it was easy to see from the meagre line of her garments that she was tremendously in earnest. If Hyacinth was flurried her own countenance expressed no confusion; 145 for her evidently this queer little bower of poverty and pain was a place in which it was perfectly natural that *he* should turn up. The sweet, still greeting her eyes offered him might exquisitely have conveyed that she had been waiting for him, that she knew he would come and that there had been a tacit appointment for that very moment. They said other things besides in their beautiful friendliness; they said: "Don't notice me too much or make any kind of scene. I've an immense deal to say to you, but remember that I've the rest of our life before me to say it in. Consider only what will be easiest and kindest to these people, these delightful people, whom I find enchanting (why didn't you ever tell me more—I mean really more—about them?). It won't be particularly complimentary to them if you've the air of seeing a miracle in my presence here. I'm very glad of your return. The quavering, fidgety 'ladyship' is as striking as the others."

Hyacinth's reception at the hands of his old friends was cordial enough quite to obliterate the element of irony that had lurked, fifteen weeks before, in their godspeed; their welcome was not boisterous, but it seemed to express the idea that the occasion, already so rare and agreeable, needed but his arrival to make it perfect. By the time he had been three minutes in the room he was able to measure the impression produced by the Princess, who, it was clear, had cast the charm of the worshipful over the little company. This was in the air, in the face of each, in their smiling, their excited eyes and heightened colour; even Rosy's wan grimace, at all times screwed up to ecstasy, had the supreme glitter of great occasions. Lady Aurora looked more than ever dishevelled with interest and wonder; the long strands of her silky hair floated like gossamer while, 146 in her extraordinary, religious attention, with her hands raised and clasped to her bosom as if she were praying, her respiration rose and fell. She had never seen any one like the Princess; but Hyacinth's apprehension of some months before had been groundless—she evidently didn't think her "flashy." She thought her divine and a revelation of beauty and benignity; and the illuminated, amplified room could contain no dissentient opinion. It was her beauty primarily that "fetched" them, Hyacinth could easily see, and it was not hidden from him that the impression had been made as much on Paul Muniment as on his companions. It was not in Paul's nature to be jerkily demonstrative and he had not lost his head on the present occasion; but he had already appreciated the difference between a plain, suspicious man's preconception of a meretricious, factitious, fine lady and the actual influence of such a personage. She was gentler, fairer, wiser than even a chemical expert could have guessed in advance. In short she held the trio in her hand, having reduced Lady Aurora to exactly the same simplicity as the others, and she performed admirably and artistically for their benefit. Almost before Hyacinth had had time to wonder how she had found the Muniments out—he had no recollection of giving her specific directions— she mentioned that Captain Sholto had been so good as to introduce her; doing so as if she owed him that explanation and were a woman who would be scrupulous in such a case. It was rather a blow to him to learn she had been accepting the Captain's mediation, and this was not softened by her saying she was too impatient to wait for his own return: he was apparently so pleased with the roving life that one couldn't be sure it would ever take place. The Princess might at least have been sure that to see her again very soon was still more necessary to 147 his happiness than anything the roving life could offer. No adventure was so prodigious as sticking as fast as possible to *her*.

It came out in the conversation he had with her, to which the others listened with respectful curiosity, that Captain Sholto had brought her a week before, but that she had then seen only Miss Muniment. "I took the liberty of coming again by myself to-day, because I wanted to see the whole family," she developed, looking from Paul to Lady Aurora with a bright blandness which purified the statement (as regarded her ladyship) of impertinence. The Princess added frankly that she had now been careful to arrive at an hour when she thought Mr. Muniment might be at home. "When I come to see gentlemen I like at least to find them," she continued, and she was so great a lady that there was no dowdy diffidence in her attitude: it was a simple matter for her to call on a young man employed at large chemical works if she had a reason. Hyacinth could see that the reason had already been brought forward—her immense interest in problems that Mr. Muniment had completely mastered and in particular their common acquaintance with the extraordinary man whose mission it was to solve them. He learned later that she had pronounced the name of the great, patient, powerful Hoffendahl. A part of the lustre in Rosy's eye came no doubt from the declaration she had inevitably been moved to make in respect to any sympathy with wicked theories that might be imputed to *her*; and of course the effect of this intensely individual little protest—such was always its effect—emanating from the sofa and the pink dressing-gown was to render the home of the Muniments still more quaint and original. In that spot Paul always gave the pleasantest go-by to any attempt to draw out his views; so you would have 148 thought, to hear him, that he allowed himself the reputation of having them only in order to get a "rise" out of his sister and let their visitors see with what wit and spirit she could repudiate them. This, however, would only be a reason the more for the Princess's following up her scent. She would doubtless not expect to get at the bottom of his ideas in Audley Court: the opportunity would occur rather in case of his having the civility—on which surely she might count—to come and talk them over with her in her own house.

Hyacinth mentioned to her the disappointment he had had in South Street and she replied: "Oh, I've given up that house and taken quite a different one." But she didn't say where it was, and in spite of her having given him so much the right to expect she would communicate to him a matter so nearly touching them both as a change of address he felt a great shyness about asking.

Their companions watched them as if they considered that something rather witty and showy now would be likely to come off between them; but Hyacinth was too full of regard for his beautiful friend's tacit notification to him that they must not appear too thick, which was after all more flattering than the most pressing inquiries or the most liberal announcements about herself could have been. She never asked him when he had come back; and indeed it was not long before Rose Muniment took that business on herself. Hyacinth, however, ventured to assure himself if Madame Grandoni were still at her post and even to remark—when his fellow-visitor had replied, "Oh yes, still, still. The great refusal, as Dante calls it, has not yet come off"—"You ought to bring her to see Miss Rosy. She's a person Miss Rosy would particularly appreciate."

"I'm sure I should be most happy to receive any 149 friend of the Princess Casamassima," said this young lady from the sofa; and when the Princess answered that she certainly would not fail to produce Madame Grandoni some day, Hyacinth—though he doubted if the presentation would really take place—guessed how much she wished her old friend might have heard the strange, bedizened little invalid make that speech.

There were only three other seats, for the introduction of the sofa—the question profoundly studied in advance—had rendered necessary the elimination of certain articles; so that Muniment, on his feet, hovered round the little circle with his hands in his pockets, laughing freely and sociably but not looking at the Princess; even if, as Hyacinth was sure, none the less agitated by her presence.

"You ought to tell us about foreign parts and the grand things you've seen; except that our distinguished visitor must know all about them," Muniment threw out to him. Then he added: "Surely, at any rate, you've seen nothing more worthy of your respect than Camberwell."

"Is this the worst part?" the Princess asked, looking up with her noble, interested face.

"The worst, madam? What grand ideas you must have! We admire Camberwell immensely."

"It's my brother's ideas that are grand!" cried Rose Muniment, betraying him conscientiously. "He does want everything changed, no less than you, Princess; though he's more cunning than you and won't give one a handle where one can take him up. He thinks all this part most objectionable—as if dirty people won't always make everything dirty where they live! I daresay he thinks there ought to be no dirty people, and it may be so; only if every one was clean where would be the merit? You'd get no credit for keeping yourself tidy. If it's a question 150 of soap and water, at any rate, every one can begin by himself. My brother thinks the whole place ought to be as handsome as Brompton."

"Ah yes, that's where the artists and literary people live, isn't it?" the Princess asked attentively.

"I've never seen it, but it's very well laid out," Rosy returned with her competent manner.

"Oh I like Camberwell better than that," Muniment said with due amusement.

The Princess turned to Lady Aurora and, with the air of appealing to her for her opinion, gave her a glance that travelled in a flash from the topmost bow of her large misfitting hat to the crumpled points of her substantial shoes. "I must get *you* to tell me the truth," she breathed. "I want so much to know London—the real London. It seems so difficult!"

Lady Aurora looked a little frightened, but at the same time gratified, and after a moment responded: "I believe a great many artists live in Saint John's Wood."

"I don't care about the artists!" said the Princess, shaking her head slowly and with the sad smile that sometimes made her beauty so inexpressibly touching.

"Not when they've painted you such beautiful pictures?" Rosy demanded. "We know about your pictures—we've admired them so much. Mr. Hyacinth has described to us your precious possessions."

The Princess transferred her smile to Rosy and rested it on that young lady's shrunken countenance with the same ineffable head-shake. "You do me too much honour. I've no possessions."

"Gracious, was it all a make-believe?" Rosy cried, flashing at Hyacinth an eye that was never so eloquent as when it demanded an explanation. 151

"I've nothing in the world—nothing but the clothes on my back!" the Princess repeated very gravely and without looking at their indiscreet friend.

The words struck Hyacinth as an admonition, so that, though much puzzled, he made no attempt for the moment to reconcile the contradiction. He only replied: "I meant the things in the house. Of course I didn't know to whom they belonged."

"There are no things in my house now," the Princess went on; and there was a touch of pure, high resignation in the words.

"Laws, I shouldn't like that!" Rose Muniment declared, glancing with complacency over her own decorated walls. "Everything here belongs to me."

"I shall bring Madame Grandoni to see you," said the Princess irrelevantly but kindly.

"Do you think it's not right to have a lot of things about?" Lady Aurora, with sudden courage, inquired of her distinguished companion, pointing a vague chin at her but looking into one of the upper angles of the room.

"I suppose one must always settle that for one's self. I don't like to be surrounded with objects I don't care for, and I can care only for one thing—that is for one class of things—at a time. Dear lady," the Princess pursued, "I fear I must confess to you that my heart's not in bibelots. When thousands and tens of thousands haven't bread to put in their mouths I can dispense with tapestry and old china." And her fair face, bent charmingly, conciliatingly, on Lady Aurora, appeared to argue that if she was narrow at least she was honest.

Hyacinth wondered, rather vulgarly, what strange turn she had taken and whether this singular picture of her denuded personality were not one of her famous caprices, a whimsical joke, a nervous perversity. Meanwhile he heard Lady Aurora urge 152 anxiously: "But don't you think we ought to make the world more beautiful?"

"Doesn't the Princess make it so by the mere fact of her existence?" Hyacinth interposed, his perplexity escaping in a harmless manner through this graceful hyperbole. He had observed that though the lady in question could dispense with old china and tapestry she couldn't dispense with a pair of immaculate gloves which fitted her to a charm.

"My people have a mass of things, you know, but I've really nothing myself," said Lady Aurora, as if she owed this assurance to such a representative of suffering humanity.

"The world will be beautiful enough when it becomes good enough," the Princess resumed. "Is there anything so ugly as unjust distinctions, as the privileges of the few contrasted with the degradation of the many? When we want to beautify we must begin at the right end."

"Surely there are none of us but what have our privileges!" Rose Muniment exclaimed with eagerness. "What do you say to mine, lying here between two members of the aristocracy and with Mr. Hyacinth thrown in?"

"You're certainly lucky—with Lady Aurora Langrish. I wish she would come and see *me*," the Princess genially sighed as she rose.

"Do go, my lady, and tell me if it's so poor!" Rosy went on gaily.

"I think there can't be too many pictures and statues and works of art," Hyacinth broke out. "The more the better, whether people are hungry or not. In the way of ameliorating influences are not those the most definite?"

"A piece of bread and butter's more to the purpose if your stomach's empty," the Princess declared.

"Robinson has been corrupted by foreign influences," 153 Paul Muniment suggested. "He doesn't care for bread and butter now; he likes French cookery."

"Yes, but I don't get it. And have you sent away the little man, the Italian, with the white cap and apron?" Hyacinth asked of the Princess.

She hesitated a moment but presently replied laughing and not in the least offended at his question, though it was an attempt to put her in the wrong from which Hyacinth had not been able to refrain in his astonishment at these ascetic pretensions: "I've sent him away many times!"

Lady Aurora had also got up; she stood there gazing at her beautiful fellow-visitor with a timidity that made her wonder only more apparent. "Your servants must be awfully fond of you."

"Oh my servants!" said the Princess as if it were only by a stretch of the meaning of the word that she could be said to enjoy the ministrations of menials. Her manner seemed to imply that she had a charwoman for an hour a day. Hyacinth caught the tone and determined that since she was going, as it appeared, he would break off his own visit and accompany her. He had flattered himself at the end of three weeks of Medley that he knew her in every phase, but here was a field of freshness. She turned to Paul Muniment and put out her hand to him, and while he took it in his own his face was visited by the most beautiful eyes that had ever rested there. "Will you come and see me one of these days?" she asked with a voice as pure as her glance.

Hyacinth waited for Paul's answer with an emotion that could only be accounted for by his affectionate sympathy, the manner in which he had spoken of him to the Princess and which he wished him to justify, the interest he had in his appearing completely 154 the fine fellow he believed him. Muniment neither stammered nor blushed; he held himself straight and looked back at his interlocutress with eyes at least as open as her own to everything that concerned him. Then by way of answer: "Well madam, pray what good will it do me?" And the tone of the words was so humorous and kindly, and so instinct with a plain manly sense, that though they were not gallant Hyacinth was not ashamed for him. At the same moment he observed that Lady Aurora was watching their friend as if she had at least an equal stake in what he might say.

"Ah none; only me perhaps a little." With this rejoinder and with a wonderful, sweet, indulgent dignity in which there was none of the stiffness of pride or resentment the Princess quitted him and approached Lady Aurora. She asked if *she* wouldn't do her the kindness to come. She should like so much to know her and had an idea there was a great deal they might talk about. Lady Aurora said she should be delighted, and the Princess took one of her cards out of her pocket and gave it to the noble spinster. After she had done so she stood a moment holding her hand and brought out: "It has really been such a happiness to me to meet you. Please don't think it's very clumsy if I say I *do* like you so!" Lady Aurora was evidently exceedingly moved and impressed; but Rosy, when the Princess took leave of her and the irrepressible invalid had assured her of the pleasure with which she should receive her again, uttered the further truth that in spite of this she herself could never conscientiously enter into such theories.

"If every one was equal," Rosy asked, "where would be the gratification I feel in getting a visit from a grandee? That's what I have often said to her ladyship, and I consider that I've kept her in 155 her place a little. No, no; no equality while I'm about the place!"

The company appeared to comprehend that there was a natural fitness in Hyacinth's seeing the great lady on her way, and accordingly no effort was made to detain him. He guided her, with the help of an attendant illumination from Muniment, down the dusky staircase, and at the door of the house there was a renewed, brief leave-taking with their host, who, however, showed no signs of relenting or recanting in respect to the Princess's invitation. The warm evening had by this time grown thick and the population of Audley Court appeared to be passing it for the most part in the open air. As Hyacinth assisted his companion to thread her way through groups of sprawling, chattering children, gossiping women with bare heads and babies at the breast and heavily-planted men smoking very bad pipes, it seemed to him that their project of exploring the slums was already in the way of execution. He said nothing till they gained the outer street, but then, pausing a moment, inquired how she would be conveyed. Had she a carriage somewhere or should he try and get a cab?

"A carriage, my dear fellow? For what do you take me? I won't trouble you about a cab: I walk everywhere now."

"But if I had not been here?"

"I should have gone alone"; and she smiled at him through the turbid twilight of Camberwell.

"And where, please, gracious heaven? I may at least have the honour of accompanying you."

"Certainly, if you can walk so far."

"So far as what, dear Princess?"

"As Madeira Crescent, Paddington."

"Madeira Crescent, Paddington?" Hyacinth stared. 156

"That's what I call it when I'm with people with whom I wish to be fine, as with you. I've taken a small house there."

"Then it's really true that you've given up your beautiful things?"

"I've sold everything to give to the poor."

"Ah, Princess———!" the young man almost moaned; for the memory of some of her treasures was vivid to him.

She became very grave, even stern, and with an accent of reproach that seemed to show she had been wounded where she was most sensitive demanded: "When I said I was willing to make the last sacrifice did you then believe I was lying?"

"Haven't you kept *anything*?" he went on without heeding this challenge.

She looked at him a moment. "I've kept *you*!" Then she passed her hand into his arm and they moved forward. He saw what she had done; she was living in a little ugly, bare, middle-class house and wearing simple gowns; and the energy and good faith of her behaviour, with the abruptness of the transformation, took away his breath. "I thought I should please you so much," she added after they had gone a few steps. And before he had time to reply, as they came to a part of the street where there were small shops, those of butchers, greengrocers and pork-pie men, with open fronts, flaring lamps and humble purchasers, she broke out joyously: "Ah, this is the way I like to see London!" 157

XXXIII

The house in Madeira Crescent was a low stucco-fronted edifice in a shabby, shallow semicircle, and Hyacinth could see as they approached it that the window-place in the parlour, on a level with the street-door, was ornamented by a glass case containing stuffed birds and surmounted by an alabaster Cupid. He was sufficiently versed in his London to know that the descent in the scale of the gentility was almost immeasurable for a person who should have moved into that quarter from the neighbourhood of Park Lane. The street was not squalid and was strictly residential; but it was mean and meagre and fourth-rate and had in the highest degree that petty parochial air, that absence of style and elevation, which is the stamp of whole districts of London and which Hyacinth had already more than once mentally compared with the high-piled, important look of the Parisian perspective. It was marked by the union of every quality which should have made it detestable to the Princess; it was almost as bad as Lomax Place. As they stopped before the narrow ill-painted door, on which the number of the house appeared on a piece of common porcelain cut in a fanciful shape, it struck him that he had felt in their long walk the touch of the passion persuading his companion to divest herself of her superfluities, but that it would take the romantic out of one's heroism 158 to settle one's self in such a paltry Philistine row. However, if the Princess had wished to mortify the flesh she had chosen an effective means of doing so, and of mortifying the spirit as well. The long light of the grey summer evening was still in the air and Madeira Crescent wore a soiled, dusty expression. A hand-organ droned in front of a neighbouring house and the cart of the local washerwoman, to which a donkey was harnessed, was drawn up opposite. The local children as well were dancing on the pavement to the music of the organ, and the scene was surveyed from one of the windows by a gentleman in a dirty dressing-gown, smoking a pipe, who made Hyacinth think of Mr. Micawber. The young man gave the Princess a deep look before they went into the house, and she smiled as if she guessed every comment he hadn't uttered.

The long, circuitous walk with her from the far-away south of London had been strange and delightful; it reminded him more queerly than he could have expressed of some of the rambles he had taken on summer evenings with Millicent Henning. It was impossible to resemble this young lady less than the Princess resembled her, but in her enjoyment of her unwonted situation (she had never before, on a summer's evening—to the best of Hyacinth's belief at least—lost herself in the unfashionable districts on the arm of a seedy artisan) the distinguished personage exhibited certain coincidences with the shop-girl. She stopped as Millicent had done to look into the windows of vulgar establishments and amused herself with picking out the abominable objects she should like to possess; selecting them from a new point of view, that of a reduced fortune and the domestic arrangements of the "lower middle class," and deriving extreme diversion from the idea that she now belonged to 159 that aggrieved body. She was in a state of light, fresh, sociable exhilaration which Hyacinth had hitherto not in the same degree seen in her, and before they reached Madeira Crescent it had become clear to him that her present phase was little more than a brilliant *tour de force*—which he could yet not imagine her keeping up long, for the simple reason that after the novelty and strangeness of the affair had passed away she wouldn't be able to endure the contact of so much that was common and ugly. For the moment, none the less, her discoveries in this line diverted her as all discoveries did, and she pretended to be sounding in a scientific spirit—that of the social philosopher, the student and critic of manners—the depths of the British Philistia. Hyacinth was struck more than ever with the fund of life that was in her, the energy of feeling, the high, free, reckless spirit. These things expressed themselves, as the couple proceeded, in a hundred sallies and droll proposals, kindling the young man's pulses and making him conscious of the joy with which, in any extravagance, he would bear her company to the death. She affected him at this moment as playing with life so audaciously and defiantly that the end of it all would inevitably be some violent catastrophe.

She desired exceedingly that Hyacinth should take her to a music-hall or a coffee-tavern; she even professed a curiosity to see the inside of a public-house. Since she still had self-control enough to remember that if she stayed out beyond a certain hour Madame Grandoni would begin to worry about her they were obliged to content themselves with the minor "lark," as the Princess was careful to designate their peep into an establishment, glittering with polished pewter and brass, which bore the name of the "Happy Land." He had feared she would turn 160 nervous after the narrow, befingered door had swung behind her, or that at all events she would be disgusted at what she might see and hear in such a place and would immediately wish to retreat. By good luck, however, there were only two or three convivial spirits in occupancy and the presence of the softer sex was apparently not so rare as to excite surprise. The softer sex furthermore was embodied in a big, hard, red woman, the publican's wife, who looked as if she were in the habit of dealing with all sorts and mainly interested in seeing whether even the finest put down their money before they were served. The Princess pretended to "have something" and to admire the ornamentation of the bar; and when Hyacinth asked her in a low tone what disposal they should make, when the great changes came, of such an embarrassing type as that, replied off-hand, "Oh, drown her in a barrel of beer!" She professed when they came out to have been immensely interested in the "Happy Land" and was not content until Hyacinth had fixed an evening on which they might visit a music-hall together. She talked with him largely, by fits and starts, of his adventures abroad and his impressions of France and Italy; breaking off suddenly with some irrelevant but almost extravagantly appreciative allusion to Rose Muniment and Lady Aurora and then returning with a question as to what he had seen and done—the answer to which, however, in many cases, she was not at pains to wait for. Yet it implied her having paid considerable attention to what he told her that she should be able to say toward the end, with that fraternising frankness which was always touching because it appeared to place her at one's mercy, to show how she counted on one's having an equal loyalty: "Well, my dear friend, you've not wasted your time; you know everything, you've 161 missed nothing; there are lots of things you can tell me—so that we shall have some famous talks in the winter evenings." This last reference was apparently to the coming season, and there was something in the tone of quiet friendship with which it was uttered and which seemed to involve so many delightful things, something that for Hyacinth bound them still closer together. To live out of the world with her that way, lost among the London millions in a queer little cockneyfied retreat, was a refinement of intimacy—with revelations perhaps even beyond those that had left him wonder-struck at Medley.

They found Madame Grandoni sitting alone in the twilight, very patient and peaceful and having after all, it was clear, accepted the situation too completely to fidget at such a trifle as her companion's not coming home at a ladylike hour. She had placed herself in the back part of the tawdry little drawing-room, which looked into a small smutty garden whence by the open front window the sound of the hurdy-gurdy and the voices of the children romping to its music came to her through the summer dusk. The influence of London was present in a mitigated far-away hum, and for some reason or other at that moment the place took on to our young friend the semblance of the home of an exile—a spot and an hour to be remembered with a throb of fondness in some danger or sorrow of after-years. The old lady never moved from her chair as she saw the Princess come in with the little bookbinder, and her observation rested on that member of their circle as familiarly as if she had seen him go out with her in the afternoon. The Princess stood smiling a moment before her mild monitress. "I've done a great thing. What do you think I've done?" she asked as she drew off her gloves.

"God knows! I've ceased to think!"—and 162 Madame Grandoni stared up with her fat, empty hands on the arms of her chair.

"I've come on foot from the far south of London—how many miles? four or five—and I'm not a particle tired."

"*Che forza, che forza!*" the old woman sighed. "She'll knock you up completely," she added, turning to Hyacinth with her customary compassion.

"Poor darling, *she* misses the carriage," Christina remarked, passing out of the room.

Madame Grandoni's eyes followed her and Hyacinth made out in them a considerable lassitude, a plaintive bewilderment and surrender. "Don't you like to use cabs—I mean hansoms?" he asked, wishing to be of comfort and suggestion.

"It's not true I miss anything; my life's only too full," she replied. "I lived worse than this—in my bad days." In a moment she went on: "It's because you're here—she doesn't like Assunta to come."

"Assunta—because I'm here?" Hyacinth didn't immediately catch her meaning.

"You must have seen her Italian maid at Medley. She has kept her and is ashamed of it. When we're alone Assunta comes for her hat and things. But she likes you to think she waits on herself."

"That's a weakness—when she's so strong! And what does Assunta think of it?" Hyacinth asked, looking at the stuffed birds in the window, the alabaster Cupid, the wax flowers on the chimney-piece, the florid antimacassars on the chairs, the sentimental engravings on the walls—in frames of papier-mâché and "composition," some of them enveloped in pink tissue paper—and the prismatic glass pendants attached to everything.

"She says, 'What on earth will it matter to-morrow?'" 163

"Does she mean that to-morrow the Princess will have her luxury back again? Hasn't she sold all her beautiful things?"

Madame Grandoni made up a face. "She has kept a few. They're put away."

"*A la bonne heure!*" Hyacinth cried with a laugh. He sat down with the ironical old woman; he spent nearly half an hour in desultory conversation with her before candles were brought in and while their friend was in Assunta's hands. He noticed how resolutely the Princess had withheld herself from any attempt to sweeten the dose she had taken it into her head to swallow, to mitigate the ugliness of her vulgar little house. She had respected its horrible signs and tokens, had left rigidly in their places the gimcracks finding favour in Madeira Crescent. She had flung no draperies over the pretentious furniture and disposed no rugs upon the staring carpet; and it was plainly her theory that the right way to acquaint one's self with the sensations of the wretched was to suffer the anguish of exasperated taste. Presently a female servant came in—not the sceptical Assunta, but a stunted young woman of the maid-of-all-work type, the same who had opened the door to the pair a short time before—and let him know of the Princess's wishing him to understand that he was expected to remain to tea. He learned from Madame Grandoni that the custom of an early dinner followed in the evening by the frugal repast of the lower orders was another of Christina's mortifications; and when shortly afterwards he saw the table laid in the back parlour, which was also the dining-room, and observed the nature of the crockery with which it was decorated, he noted that whether or no her earnestness were durable it was at any rate for the time intense. Madame Grandoni put before him definitely, as the Princess had done only in scraps, 164 the career of the two ladies since his departure from Medley, their relinquishment of that fine house and the sudden arrangements Christina had made to change her mode of life after they had been only ten days in South Street. At the climax of the London season, in a society which only desired to treat her as one of its brightest ornaments, she had retired to Madeira Crescent, concealing her address—with only partial success of course—from every one, and inviting a celebrated curiosity-monger to come and look at her bibelots and tell her what he would give for the lot. In this manner she had parted with them at a fearful sacrifice. She had wished to avoid the nine days' wonder of a public sale; for, to do her justice, though she liked to be original she didn't like to be notorious, an occasion of stupid chatter. What had precipitated this violent step was a remonstrance received from her husband just after she had left Medley on the subject of her excessive expenditure: he had written her that it was past a joke—as she had appeared to consider it—and that she must really pull up. Nothing could gall her more than an interference on that head—since she maintained that she knew the exact figure of the Prince's income, of which her allowance was an insignificant part—and she had pulled up with a vengeance, as Hyacinth might perceive. The young man divined on this occasion one of the eminent lady's high anxieties, of which he had never thought before—the danger of the Prince's absolutely putting on the screw, of his attempting to make her come back and live with him by withholding supplies altogether. In this case she would find herself in a very tight place, though she had a theory that if she should go to law about the matter the courts would allow her a separate maintenance. This course, however, it would scarce be in her character to adopt; she would 165 be more likely to waive her right and support herself by lessons in music and the foreign tongues supplemented by the remnant of property that had come to her from her mother. That she was capable of returning to the

Prince some day as an effect of her not daring to face the loss of luxury was an idea that couldn't occur to our youth in the midst of her assurances, uttered at various times, that she positively yearned for a sacrifice; and such an apprehension was less present to him than ever while he listened to Madame Grandoni's account of the manner in which their friend's rupture with the fashionable world had been enacted. It must be added that the old lady devoted a deep groan to her not knowing how it would all end, as some of Christina's economies were most expensive; and when Hyacinth pressed her a little she proceeded to say that it was not at present the question of complications arising from the Prince that troubled her most, but the fear that his wife was seriously compromised by her reckless, her wicked correspondences: letters arriving from foreign countries, from God knew whom (Christina never told her, nor did she desire it), all about uprisings and manifestations and liberations—of so much one could be sure—and other matters that were no concern of honest folk. Hyacinth but half knew what Madame Grandoni meant by this allusion, which seemed to show that during the last few months their hostess had considerably extended her revolutionary connexion: he only thought of Hoffendahl, whose name, however, he was careful not to pronounce, and wondered whether his friend had been writing to the Master to intercede for *him*, to beg that he might be let off. His cheeks burned at the thought, but he contented himself with remarking to his entertainer that their extraordinary companion enjoyed the sense of danger. The old 166 lady wished to know how she would enjoy the hangman's rope—with which, *du train dont elle allait*, she might easily make acquaintance; and when he expressed the hope that she didn't regard him as a counsellor of imprudence replied: "You, my poor child? Oh I saw into you at Medley. You're a simple *codino*!"

The Princess came back to tea in a very dull gown and with a bunch of keys at her girdle; and nothing could have suggested the thrifty housewife better than the manner in which she superintended the laying of the cloth and the placing on it of a little austere refreshment—a pile of bread and butter flanked by a pot of marmalade and a morsel of bacon. She filled the teapot from a shiny tin canister locked up in a cupboard, of which the key worked with difficulty, and made the tea with her own superb hands; taking pains, however, to explain to Hyacinth that she was far from imposing that régime on Madame Grandoni, who understood that the grocer had a standing order to supply her, for her private consumption, with any delicacy she might desire. For herself she had never been so well as since following a homely diet. On Sundays they had muffins and sometimes for a change a smoked haddock or even a fried sole. Hyacinth lost himself in worship of the Princess's housewifely ways and of the exquisite figure she made as a small bourgeoise; judging that if her attempt to combine plain living with high thinking were all a burlesque it was at least the most finished entertainment she had yet offered him. She talked to Madame Grandoni of Lady Aurora; described her with much drollery, even to the details of her dress; declared that she was a delightful creature and one of the most interesting persons she had seen for an age; expressed to Hyacinth the conviction that she should like her exceedingly if the poor 167 dear would only believe a little in *her*. "But I shall like her whether she does or not," the Princess all the same declared. "I always know when that's going to happen; it isn't so common. She'll begin very well with me and be 'fascinated'—isn't that the way people begin with me?—but she won't understand me at all nor make out in the least what kind of a queer fish I am, try as I may to show her. When she thinks she does at last she'll give me up in disgust and never know she has understood me quite wrong. That has been the way with most of the people I've liked; they've run away from me *à toutes jambes*. Oh I've inspired aversions!" she mirthfully wailed as she handed Hyacinth his cup of tea. He recognised it by the aroma as a mixture not inferior to that of which he had partaken at Medley. "I've never succeeded in knowing any one who would do me good, for by the time I began to improve under their influence they could put up with me no longer."

"You told me you were going to visit the poor. I don't understand what your Gräfin was doing there," said Madame Grandoni.

"She had come out of charity—in the same way as I. She evidently goes about immensely over there; I shall insist on her taking me with her."

"I thought you had promised to let *me* be your guide in those explorations," Hyacinth promptly pleaded.

The Princess looked at him a moment. "Dear Mr. Robinson, Lady Aurora knows more than you."

"There have been times surely when you've complimented me on my knowledge."

"Oh I mean more about the lower classes!" she returned; and oddly enough there was a sense in which he was unable to deny the claim made for her ladyship. He presently came back to something said by his hostess a moment before, declaring 168 that it had not been the way with Madame Grandoni and him to take to their heels, and to this she replied: "Oh you'll run away yet! Don't be afraid."

"I think that if I had been capable of quitting you I should have done it by this time: I've neglected such opportunities," the old woman sighed. Hyacinth now made out that her eye had quite lost or intermitted its fine old pleasantry: she was troubled about many things.

"It's true that if you didn't leave me when I was rich it wouldn't look well for you to leave me at present," the Princess suggested; and before Madame Grandoni could meet this speech she said to Hyacinth: "I liked that odd man, your friend Muniment, so much for saying he wouldn't come to see me. 'What good would it do him,' poor fellow? What good would it do him indeed? You were not so difficult: you held off a little and pleaded obstacles, but one easily saw you'd come down," she continued while she covered her guest with her mystifying smile. "Besides I was smarter then, more splendid; I had on gewgaws and suggested worldly lures. I must have been more attractive. But I liked him for refusing," she repeated; and of the many words she uttered that evening it was these that made most impression on our hero. He remained an hour after tea, for on rising from the table she had gone to the piano—not depriving herself of this resource she had a humble instrument of the so-called "cottage" kind—and begun to play in a manner that reminded him of her commemorative outburst, as he might have fancied it, the day of his arrival at Medley. The night had grown close and as the piano was in the front room he opened at her request the window that looked into Madeira Crescent. Beneath it assembled the youth of both sexes, the dingy 169 loiterers, who had clustered an hour before round the hurdy-gurdy. But on this occasion they didn't caper about; they leaned in silence against the area-rails and listened to the wondrous music. When Hyacinth told the player of the spell she had thrown on them she declared that it made her singularly happy; she added that she was really glad, almost proud, of her day; she felt as if she had begun to do something for the people. Just before he took leave she encountered some occasion for saying that she was certain the odd man in Audley Court wouldn't come; and he forbore to contradict her because he believed in fact he wouldn't. 170

XXXIV

How right had been her prevision that Lady Aurora would be fascinated at first was proved as soon as Hyacinth went to Belgrave Square—a visit he was promptly led to pay by a deep sense of the obligations under which her ladyship had placed him at the time of Pinnie's death. The conditions in which he found her were quite the same as those of his visit the year before; she was spending the unfashionable season in her father's empty house and amid a desert of brown holland and the dormant echoes of heavy conversation. He had seen so much of her during Pinnie's illness that he felt—or had felt then—that he knew her almost intimately, that they had become real friends, almost comrades, and might meet henceforth without reserves or ceremonies. She was in spite of this as fluttered and awkward as she had been on the other occasion: not distant, but entangled in new coils of shyness and apparently unmindful of what had happened to draw them closer. Hyacinth, however, always liked extremely to be with her, for she was the person in the world who quietly, delicately and as a matter of course treated him most as a gentleman and appeared most naturally to take him for one. She had never addressed him the handsome flattering freedoms that had fallen from the lips of the Princess, and never explained at all her view of him; but her timid, cursory, receptive 171 manner, which took all sorts of equalities and communities for granted, was a homage to the idea of his fine essence. It was in this manner that she now conversed with him on the subject of his foreign travels; he found himself discussing the political indications of Paris and the Ruskinian theories of Venice in Belgravia after the fashion of the cosmopolites bred by those wastes. It took him none the less but a few minutes to be sure Lady Aurora's heart was not in these considerations; the deferential smile she bent upon him while she sat with her head thrust forward and her long hands clasped in her lap was slightly mechanical, her attitude all perfunctory. When he gave her his views of some of the *arrière-pensées* of M. Gambetta—for he had views not altogether, as he thought, deficient in originality—she didn't interrupt, for she never interrupted; but she took advantage of his first pause to say quickly and irrelevantly: "Will the Princess Casamassima come again to Audley Court?"

"I've no doubt she'd come again if they'd particularly like her to."

"I do hope she will. She's very wonderful," Lady Aurora richly breathed.

"Oh yes, she's very wonderful. I think she gave Rosy pleasure."

"Rosy can talk of nothing else. It would really do her great good to have such an experience again. Don't you think her quite different from anybody one has ever seen?" But her ladyship added before waiting for an answer to this: "I liked her quite extraordinarily."

"She liked you just as much. I know it would give her great pleasure if you could go to see her," Hyacinth said.

"Fancy that!" his companion gasped; and she instantly obtained the Princess's address from him 172 and made a note of it in a small shabby pocket-book. She mentioned that the card the Princess had given her in Camberwell exhibited in fact no address, and he recognised that vagary— the Princess was so off-hand. Then she said, hesitating a little: "Does she really care for the poor?"

"If she doesn't," the young man replied, "I can't imagine what interest she has in pretending to."

"If she does she's very remarkable—she deserves great honour."

"You really care—so why is she more remarkable than you?" Hyacinth demanded.

"Oh it's very different—she's so wonderfully attractive!" Lady Aurora replied, making recklessly the one allusion to the oddity of her own appearance in which he was destined to hear her indulge. She became conscious of it the moment she had spoken, and said quickly, to turn it off: "I should like to talk with her, but I'm rather afraid. She's tremendously clever."

"Ah what she is—'tremendously'—you'll find out when you know her!" he could but all portentously sigh.

His hostess looked at him a little and then vaguely returned: "How very interesting!" The next moment she continued: "She might do so many other things. She might charm the world."

"She does that, whatever she does," Hyacinth smiled. "It's all by the way; it needn't interfere."

"That's what I mean, that most other people would be content— beautiful as she is. There's great merit when you give up something."

"She has known a great many bad people and she wants to know some good," he explained. "Therefore be sure to go to her soon."

"She looks as if she had known nothing bad since she was born," said Lady Aurora rapturously. "I 173 can't imagine her going into all the dreadful places she'd have to."

"You've gone into them, and it hasn't hurt you," he suggested.

"How do you know that? My family think it has."

"You make me glad then that I haven't a family," said the young man.

"And the Princess—has she no one?"

"Ah yes, she has a husband. But she doesn't live with him."

"Is he one of the bad persons?" asked Lady Aurora as earnestly as a child listening to a tale.

"Well, I don't like to abuse him—he's down."

"If I were a man I should be in love with her," said Lady Aurora. Then she added: "I wonder if we might work together."

"That's exactly what she hopes."

"I won't show her the worst places," her ladyship maliciously protested.

To which her visitor returned: "I expect you'll do what every one else has done—which is exactly what she wants!" Before he took leave he said to her: "Do you know if Paul Muniment also liked the Princess?"

She meditated a moment, apparently with some intensity. "I think she struck him as extraordinarily beautiful—as the most beautiful person he had ever seen."

"Does he still believe her a humbug?"

"Still?" asked Lady Aurora as if she didn't understand.

"I mean that that was the impression apparently made upon him last winter by my description of her."

"Oh I'm sure he thinks her tremendously plucky!" Which was all the satisfaction Hyacinth got just then as to Muniment's estimate of the Princess. 174

A few days later he returned to Madeira Crescent in the evening, the only time he was free, the Princess having given him a general invitation to take tea with her. He felt he ought to be discreet in acting on it, though he was not without reasons that would have warranted him in going early and often. He had a peculiar dread of her growing used to him and tired of him—boring herself in his society; yet at the same time he had rather a sharp vision of her boring herself without him during the dull summer evenings when even Paddington was out of town. He wondered what she did, what visitors dropped in, what pastimes she cultivated, what saved her from the sudden vagary of throwing up the whole of her present game. He remembered that there was a complete side of her life with which he was almost unacquainted—Lady Marchant and her daughters, at Medley, and three or four other persons who had called while he was there being, in his experience, the only illustrations of it—and didn't know, by the same token, to what extent she had in spite of her transformation preserved relations with her old friends; but he made out as looming the day she would discover that what she found in Madeira Crescent was less striking than what she missed. Going thither a second time he noted, for all this, that he had done her great injustice: she was full of resources, she had never been so happy, she found time to read, to write, to commune with her piano and above all to think—a delightful detachment from the invasive, vulgar, gossiping, distracting world she had known hitherto. The only interruption to her felicity was that she received quantities of notes from her former acquaintance, endless appeals to give some account of herself, to say what had become of her, to come and stay with them in the country. With these survivals of her past she took a very short 175 way, she simply burned them without answering. She told Hyacinth immediately that Lady Aurora had called two days before, at an hour when she was not in, and that she had straightway addressed her in return an invitation to come to tea any evening at eight o'clock. That was the way the people in Madeira Crescent entertained each other—the Princess knew everything about them now and was eager to impart her knowledge; and the evening, she was sure, would be much more convenient to Lady Aurora, whose days were filled with good works, with peregrinations of charity. Her ladyship arrived ten minutes after Hyacinth; she assured the Princess her invitation had been expressed in a manner so flattering that she was unwilling to wait more than a day to respond. She was introduced to Madame Grandoni and tea all bustlingly served; Hyacinth being gratefully conscious the while of the "considerate" way in which Lady Aurora forbore to appear bewildered at meeting him in such society. She knew he frequented it, having been witness of his encounter with their high personage in Audley Court; but it might have startled her to have ocular evidence of the footing on which he stood. Everything the Princess did or said at this time had for effect, whatever its purpose, to make her seem more rare and fine; and she had seldom given him greater pleasure than by the exquisite art she put forth to win Lady Aurora's confidence, to place herself under the pure and elevating influence of the noble spinster. She made herself small and simple; she spoke of her own little aspirations and efforts; she appealed and persuaded; she laid her white hand on her gentle guest's, gazing at her with an interest all visibly sincere but which yet derived half its effect from the contrast between the quality of her beauty, the whole air of her person, and the hard, dreary 176 problems of misery and crime. It was touching and Lady

Aurora was touched; that was quite clear as they sat together on the sofa after tea and the Princess protested that she only wanted to know what her new friend was doing—what she had done for years—in order that she might go and do likewise. She asked personal questions with a directness that was sometimes embarrassing to the subject—he had seen that habit in her from the first—and her yearning guest, though charmed and excited, was not quite comfortable at being so publicly probed and sounded. The public was formed of Madame Grandoni and Hyacinth; but the old lady—whose intercourse with the visitor had consisted almost wholly of watching her with a deep, speculative anxiety—presently shuffled away and was heard, through the thin partitions that prevailed in Madeira Crescent, to ascend to her own apartment. It seemed to Hyacinth that he ought also in delicacy to retire, and this was his intention from one moment to the other; to him certainly—and the very second time she met him—Lady Aurora had made as much of her confession as he had a right to look for. After that one little flash of egotism he had never again heard her refer to her own feelings or conditions.

"Do you stay in town like this, at such a season, on purpose to attend to your work?" the Princess asked; and there was something archly rueful in the tone in which she made this inquiry—as if it cost her just a pang to find that in taking such a line she herself had not been so original as she hoped. "Mr. Robinson has told me about your big house in Belgrave Square—you must let me come and see you there. Nothing would make me so happy as that you should allow me to help you a little—how little soever. Do you like to be helped or do you like to go quite alone? Are you very 177 independent or do you need to look up, to cling, to lean on some one? Pardon me if I ask impertinent questions; we speak that way—rather, you know—in Rome, where I've spent a large part of my life. That idea of your being there by yourself, in your great dull home, with all your charities and devotions, makes a kind of picture in my mind; it's quaint and touching, it's like something in some English novel. Englishwomen are so awfully accomplished, are they not? I'm really a foreigner, you know, and though I've lived here a while it takes one some time to find those things out *au juste*. Is your work for the people therefore only one of your occupations or is it everything, does it absorb your whole life? That's what I should like it to be for me. Do your family like you to throw yourself into all this or have you had to brave a certain amount of ridicule? I daresay you have; that's where you English are strong, in braving ridicule. They have to do it so often, haven't they? I don't know whether I could do it. I never tried—but with you I think I would brave anything. Are your family clever and sympathetic? No? the kind of thing that one's family generally is? Ah well, dear lady, we must make a little family together. Are you encouraged or disgusted? Do you go on doggedly or have you some faith, some great idea, that lifts you up? Are you actively religious now, *par exemple*? Do you do your work in connexion with any pious foundation or earnest movement, any missions or priests or sisters? I'm a Catholic, you know—but so little by my own doing! I shouldn't mind in the least joining hands with any one who's really producing results. I express myself awkwardly, but perhaps you know what I mean. Possibly you don't know that I'm one of those who believe that a great new deal is destined to take place 178 and that it can't make things worse than they are already. I believe, in a word, in the action of the people for themselves—the others will never act for them; and I'm all ready to act *with* them—in any intelligent or intelligible way. If that shocks you I shall be immensely disappointed, because there's something in the impression you make on me that seems to suggest you haven't the usual prejudices, so that if certain things were to happen you wouldn't be afraid. You're beautifully shy, are you not?—but you're not craven. I suppose that if you thought the inequalities and oppressions and miseries now universal were a necessary part of life and were going on for ever you wouldn't be interested in those people over the river (the bedridden girl and her brother I mean); because Mr. Robinson tells me they're advanced socialists—or at least the brother is. Perhaps you'll say you don't care for him—the sister, to your mind, being the remarkable one. She's indeed a perfect little *femme du monde*—she talks so much better than most of the people in society. I hope you don't mind my saying that, because I've an idea you're not in society. You can imagine whether I am! Haven't you judged it like me, condemned it and given it up? Aren't you sick of the egotism, the snobbery, the meanness, the frivolity, the immorality, the hypocrisy? Isn't there a great resemblance in our situations? I don't mean in our natures, for you're far better than I shall ever be. Aren't you quite divinely good? When I see a woman of your sort—not that I often do—I try to be a little less bad. You've helped hundreds, thousands of people: you must help *me*!"

These remarks, which I have strung together, didn't of course fall from the Princess's lips in an uninterrupted stream; they were arrested and interspersed by frequent, inarticulate responses and 179 embarrassed protests. Lady Aurora shrank from them even while they gratified her, blinking and fidgeting in the dazzling, direct light of her hostess's sympathy. I needn't repeat her answers, the more so as they none of them arrived at completion but passed away into nervous laughter and averted looks, the latter directed at the ceiling, the floor, the windows, and appearing to project a form of entreaty to some occult or supernatural power that the conversation should become more impersonal. In reply to the Princess's allusion to the convictions prevailing in the Muniment family she said that the brother and sister thought differently about public questions but were of the same mind with regard to the interest taken by persons of the upper class in the working people, the attempt on the part of their so-called superiors to enter into their life: they pronounced it a great mistake. At this information the Princess looked much disappointed; she wished to know if the Muniments deemed it so impossible to do them any good. "Oh I mean a mistake from *our* point of view," said Lady Aurora. "They wouldn't do it in our place; they think we had much better occupy ourselves with our own pleasures." And as her new friend stared, not comprehending, she went on: "Rosy thinks we've a right to our own pleasures under all circumstances, no matter how badly off the poor may be; and her brother takes the ground that we're not likely to have them much longer and that in view of what may happen we're great fools not to make the most of them."

"I see, I see. That's very strong," the Princess murmured in a tone of high appreciation.

"I daresay. But, all the same, whatever's going to come one *must* do something."

"You do think then that something's going to come?" said the Princess. 180

"Oh immense changes, I daresay. But I don't belong to anything, you know."

The Princess thought this over. "No more do I. But many people do. Mr. Robinson for instance." And she turned her golden light on Hyacinth.

"Oh if the changes depend on *me*——!" Mr. Robinson exclaimed with a blush.

"They won't set the Thames on fire—I quite agree to that!"

Lady Aurora had the manner of not considering she had a warrant for going into the question of Hyacinth's affiliations; so she stared abstractedly at the piano and in a moment remarked to her hostess: "I'm sure you play awfully well. I should like so much to hear you."

Hyacinth could see their friend thought this *banal*. She had not asked Lady Aurora to spend the evening with her simply that they should fall back on the resources of the vulgar. Nevertheless she replied with perfect good nature that she should be delighted to play; only there was a thing she should like much better—which was that Lady Aurora should narrate her life.

"Oh don't talk about mine; yours, yours!" her ladyship cried, colouring with eagerness and for the first time since her arrival indulging in the free gesture of laying her hand on that of the Princess.

"With so many grand confidences in the air I certainly had better take myself off," said Hyacinth; and the Princess offered no opposition to his departure. She and Lady Aurora were evidently on the point of striking up a tremendous intimacy, and as he turned this idea over walking away it made him sad for strange vague reasons that he couldn't have expressed. 181

XXXV

The Sunday following this occasion he spent almost entirely with the Muniments, with whom, since his return to his work, he had been able to have no long, fraternising talk of the kind that had marked their earlier relations. The present, however, was a happy day; it added its large measure to the esteem in which he now held the inscrutable Paul. The warm, bright, September weather enriched even the dinginess of Audley Court, and while in the morning Rosy's brother and their visitor sat beside her sofa the trio amused themselves with discussing a dozen different plans for giving a festive turn to the day. There had been moments in the last six months when Hyacinth had the conviction he should never again be able to enter into such ideas as that, and these moments had been connected with the strange conversion taking place in his mental image of the man whose hardness—of course he was obliged to be hard—he had never expected to see turned upon a passionate admirer. At present, for the hour at least, the darkness had cleared away and Paul's company become a sustaining, inspiring influence. He had never been kinder, jollier, safer, as it were; it had never appeared more desirable to hold fast to him and trust him. Less than ever would an observer have guessed at a good reason why the two young men might have winced as they looked 182 at each other. Rosy naturally took part in the question debated between her companions—the question whether they should limit their excursion to a walk in Hyde Park; should embark at Lambeth Pier on the penny steamer which would convey them to Greenwich; or should start presently for Waterloo Station and go thence by train to Hampton Court. Miss Muniment had visited none of these scenes, but she contributed largely to the discussion, for which she seemed perfectly qualified; talked about the crowd on the steamer and the inconvenience arising from drunken persons on the return quite as if she had suffered from such drawbacks; reminded the others that the view from the hill at Greenwich was terribly smoky and at that season the fashionable world—half the attraction of course—altogether absent from Hyde Park; and expressed strong views in favour of Wolsey's old palace, with whose history she appeared intimately acquainted. She threw herself into her brother's holiday with eagerness and glee, and Hyacinth marvelled again at the stoicism of the hard, bright creature, polished, as it were, by pain, whose imagination appeared never to concern itself with her own privations, so that she could lie in her close little room the whole golden afternoon without bursting into sobs as she saw the western sunbeams slant upon the shabby, ugly, familiar paper of her wall and thought of the far-off fields and gardens she should never see. She talked immensely of the

Princess, for whose beauty, grace and benevolence she could find no sufficient praise; declaring that of all the fair faces that had ever hung over her couch—and Rosy spoke as from immense opportunities for comparison—she had far the noblest and most refreshing. She seemed to make a kind of light in the room and to leave it behind after she had gone. Rosy could call up her image as she <u>183</u> could hum a tune she had heard, and she expressed in her quaint, particular way how, as she lay there in the quiet hours, she repeated over to herself the beautiful air. The Princess might be anything, she might be royal or imperial, and Rosy was well aware how little *she* should complain of the dulness of a life in which such apparitions as that could pop in any day. She made a difference in the place—it gave it a regular finish for her to have come there; if it was good enough for a princess it was good enough for the likes of *her*, and she hoped she shouldn't hear again of Paul's wishing her to move out of a room with which she should have henceforth such delightful associations. The Princess had found her way to Audley Court and perhaps wouldn't find it to another lodging, for they couldn't expect her to follow them about London at their pleasure; and at any rate she had evidently been altogether struck with the little room, so that if they were quiet and canny who could say but the fancy would take her to send them a bit of carpet or a picture, or even a mirror with a gilt frame, to make it a bit more tasteful? Rosy's transitions from pure enthusiasm to the imaginative calculation of benefits were performed with a serenity peculiar to herself. Her chatter had so much spirit and point that it always commanded attention, but to-day Hyacinth was less tolerant of it than usual, because so long as it lasted Muniment held his tongue, and what he had been anxious about was much more Paul's impression of the Princess. Rosy made no remark to him on the monopoly he had so long enjoyed of this wonderful lady: she had always had the manner of an indulgent incredulity about Hyacinth's social adventures, and he saw the hour might easily come when she would begin to talk of their grand acquaintance as if she herself had been the first to discover her. She had <u>184</u> much to say, however, about the nature of the connexion Lady Aurora had formed with her, and she was mainly occupied with the glory she had drawn upon herself by bringing two such exalted persons together. She fancied them alluding, in the great world, to the occasion on which "we first met—at Miss Muniment's, you know"; and she related how Lady Aurora, who had been in Audley Court the day before, had declared she owed her a debt she could never repay. The two ladies had liked each other more, almost, than they liked any one; and wasn't it a rare picture to think of them moving hand in hand, like great twin lilies, through the bright upper air? Muniment inquired in rather a coarse, unsympathetic way what the mischief she ever wanted of *her*; which led Hyacinth to demand in return: "What do you mean? What does who want of whom?"

"What does the beauty of beauties want of *our* poor plain lady? She has a totally different stamp. I don't know much about women, but I can see that."

"Where do you see a different stamp? They both have the stamp of their rank!" cried Rosy.

"Who can ever tell what women want, at any time?" Hyacinth asked with the off-handedness of a man of the world.

"Well, my boy, if you don't know any more than I you disappoint me! Perhaps if we wait long enough she'll tell us some day herself."

"Tell you what she wants of Lady Aurora?"

"I don't mind about Lady Aurora so much; but what in the name of long journeys she wants with *us*!"

"Don't you think you're worth a long journey?" Rosy cried gaily. "If you weren't my brother, which is handy for seeing you, and I weren't confined to my sofa, I'd go from one end of England to 185 the other to make your acquaintance! He's in love with the Princess," she went on to Hyacinth, "and he asks those senseless questions to cover it up. What does any one want of anything?"

It was decided at last that the two young men should go down to Greenwich, and after they had partaken of bread and cheese with Rosy they embarked on a penny steamer. The boat was densely crowded, and they leaned, rather squeezed together, in the fore part of it, against the rail of the deck, and watched the big black fringe of the yellow stream. The river had always for Hyacinth a deep beguilement. The ambiguous appeal he had felt as a child in all the aspects of London came back to him from the dark detail of its banks and the sordid agitation of its bosom: the great arches and pillars of the bridges, where the water rushed and the funnels tipped and sounds made an echo and there seemed an overhanging of interminable processions; the miles of ugly wharves and warehouses; the lean protrusions of chimney, mast and crane; the painted signs of grimy industries staring from shore to shore; the strange, flat, obstructive barges, straining and bumping on some business as to which everything was vague but that it was remarkably dirty; the clumsy coasters and colliers which thickened as one went down; the small loafing boats whose occupants, somehow, looking up from their oars at the steamer, as they rocked in the oily undulations of its wake, appeared profane and sarcastic; in short all the grinding, puffing, smoking, splashing activity of the turbid flood. In the good-natured crowd, amid the fumes of vile tobacco, beneath the shower of sooty particles and to the accompaniment of the bagpipe of a dingy Highlander who sketched occasionally an unconvincing reel, Hyacinth forbore to speak to his companion 186 of what he had most at heart; but later, as they lay in the brown, crushed grass on one of the slopes of Greenwich Park and saw the river stretch away and shine beyond the pompous colonnades of the Hospital, he asked him if there were any truth in what Rosy had said about his being sweet on their friend the Princess. He said "their friend" on purpose, speaking as if, now that she had been twice to Audley Court, Muniment might be regarded as knowing her almost as well as he himself did. He wished to conjure away the idea that he was jealous of Paul, and if he desired information on the point I have mentioned this was because it still made him almost as uncomfortable as it had done at first that his comrade should take the scoffing view. He didn't easily see such a fellow as Muniment wheel about from one day to the other, but he had been present at the most exquisite exhibition he had ever observed the Princess make of that divine power of conciliation which was not perhaps in social intercourse the art she chiefly exercised but was certainly the most wonderful of her secrets, and it would be remarkable indeed that a sane young man shouldn't have been affected by it. It was familiar to Hyacinth that Muniment wasn't easily reached or rubbed up by women, but this might perfectly have been the case without detriment to the Princess's ability to work a miracle. The companions had wandered through the great halls and courts of the Hospital; had gazed up at the glories of the famous painted chamber and admired the long and lurid series of the naval victories of England—Muniment remarking to his friend that he supposed he had seen the match to all that in foreign parts, offensive little travelled beggar that he was. They had not ordered a fish-dinner either at the "Trafalgar" or the "Ship"—having a frugal vision of tea and shrimps with Rosy 187 on their return—but they had laboured up and down the steep undulations of the shabby, charming park; made advances to the tame deer and seen them amble foolishly away; watched the young of both sexes, hilarious and red in the face, roll in promiscuous accouplement over the slopes; gazed at the little brick observatory, perched on one of the knolls, which sets the time to English history and in which Hyacinth could see that his companion took an expert, a technical interest; wandered out of one of the upper gates and admired the trimness of the little villas at Blackheath, where Muniment declared it his conception of supreme social success to be able to live. He pointed out two or three small semi-detached houses, faced with stucco and with "Mortimer Lodge" or "The Sycamores" inscribed on the gate-posts, and Hyacinth guessed these to be the sort of place where he would like to end his days—in high pure air, with a genteel window for Rosy's couch and a cheerful view of suburban excursions. It was when they came back into the Park that, being rather hot and a little sated, they stretched themselves under a tree and Hyacinth yielded to his curiosity.

"Sweet on her—sweet on her, my boy!" said Muniment. "I might as well be sweet on the dome of Saint Paul's, which I just make out off there."

"The dome of Saint Paul's doesn't come to see you and doesn't ask you to return the visit."

"Oh I don't return visits—I've got plenty of jobs of my own to attend to. If I don't put myself out for the Princess isn't that a sufficient answer to your question?"

"I'm by no means sure," said Hyacinth. "If you went to see her, simply and civilly, because she asked you, I shouldn't regard it as a proof you had taken a fancy to her. Your hanging off is more suspicious; 188 it may mean that you don't trust yourself—that you're in danger of falling in love if you go in for a more intimate acquaintance."

"It's a rum go, your wanting me to make up to her. I shouldn't think it would suit your book," Muniment returned while he stared at the sky with his hands clasped under his head.

"Do you suppose I'm afraid of you?" his comrade asked. "Besides," Hyacinth added in a moment, "why the devil should I care now?"

Paul made for a little no rejoinder; he turned over on his side and, with his arm resting on the ground, leaned his head on his hand. Hyacinth felt his eyes on his own face, but he also felt himself colouring and didn't meet them. He had taken a private vow never to indulge, to this companion, in certain inauspicious references, and the words just spoken had slipped out of his mouth too easily. "What do you mean by that?" Paul demanded at last; and when Hyacinth looked at him he saw nothing but the strong, fresh, irresponsible, the all so manly and sturdy face. Its owner had had time before speaking to prefigure a meaning.

Suddenly an impulse he had never known before, or rather that he had always resisted, took possession of our young man. There was a mystery which it concerned his happiness to clear up, and he became unconscious of his scruples, of his pride, of the strength he had ever believed to be in him—the strength for going through his work and passing away without a look behind. He sat forward on the grass with his arms round his knees and offered his friend a presence quickened by his difficulties. For a minute the two pairs of eyes met with extreme clearness, and then Hyacinth brought out: "What an extraordinary chap you are!"

"You've hit it there!" Paul smiled. 189

"I don't want to make a scene or work on your feelings, but how will you like it when I'm strung up on the gallows?"

"You mean for Hoffendahl's job? That's what you were alluding to just now?" Muniment lay there in the same position, chewing a long blade of dry grass which he held to his lips with his free hand.

"I didn't mean to speak of it; but after all why shouldn't it come up? Naturally I've thought of it a good deal."

"What good does that do?" Muniment returned. "I hoped you didn't—I noticed you never spoke of it. You don't like it. You'd rather chuck it up," he added.

There was not in his voice the faintest note of irony or contempt, no sign whatever that he passed judgement on such an attitude. He spoke in a quiet, human, memorising manner, as if it had originally quite entered into his thought to allow for weak regrets. Nevertheless the complete reasonableness of his tone itself cast a chill on Hyacinth's spirit; it was like the touch of a hand at once very firm and very soft, yet strangely cold. "I don't want in the least to repudiate business, but did you suppose I liked it?" our hero asked with rather a forced laugh.

"My dear fellow, how could I tell? You like a lot of things I don't. You like excitement and emotion and change, you like remarkable sensations—whereas I go in for a holy calm, for sweet repose."

"If you object, for yourself, to change, and are so fond of still waters, why have you associated yourself with a revolutionary movement?" Hyacinth demanded with a little air of making rather a good point.

"Just for that reason!" Paul blandly said. "Isn't our revolutionary movement as quiet as the grave? 190 Who knows, who suspects anything like the full extent of it?"

"I see. You take only the quiet parts!"

In speaking these words Hyacinth had had no derisive intention, but a moment later he flushed with the sense that they had a sufficiently low sound. Paul, however, appeared to see no offence in them, and it was in the gentlest, most suggestive way, as if he had been thinking over what might comfort his little mate, that he replied: "There's one thing you ought to remember—that it's quite on the cards the beastly call may never be made."

"I don't desire that reminder," Hyacinth said; "and moreover you must let me tell you I somehow don't easily fancy *you* mixed up with things that don't come off. Anything you have to do with will come off, I think."

Muniment reflected a moment, as if his little mate were charmingly ingenious. "Surely I've nothing to do with the particular job——!"

"With the execution, perhaps not; but how about the idea of it? You seemed to me to have a great deal to do with it the night you took me to see him."

Paul changed his posture, raising himself, and in a moment was seated Turk-fashion beside his friend. He put his arm over his shoulder and drew him, studying his face; and then in the kindest manner in the world he brought out: "There are three or four definite chances in your favour."

"I don't want second-rate comfort, you know," said Hyacinth with his eyes on the distant atmospheric mixture that represented London.

"What the devil *do* you want?" Paul asked, still holding him and with perfect good humour.

"Well, to get inside of *you* a little; to know how a chap feels when he's going to part with his particular pal." 191

"To part with him?" this character repeated.

"I mean putting it at the worst."

"I should think you'd know by yourself—if you're going to part with *me*."

At this Hyacinth prostrated himself, tumbled over to the grass on his face, which he buried in his hands. He remained in this attitude, saying nothing, a long time; and while he lay there he thought, with a sudden, quick flood of association, of many strange things. Most of all he had the sense of the brilliant charming day; the warm stillness, touched with cries of amusement; the sweetness of loafing there in an interval of work with a chum who was a tremendously fine fellow even if he didn't understand the inexpressible. Paul also kept the peace, and Hyacinth felt him all unaffectedly puzzled. He wanted now to relieve him, so that he pulled himself together again and turned round, saying the first thing he could think of, in relation to the general subject of their talk, that would carry them away from the personal question. "I've asked you before, and you've told me, but somehow I've never quite grasped it—so I just touch on the matter again—exactly what good you think it will do."

"The stroke of work, eh? Well, you must remember that as yet we know only very vaguely what it is. It's difficult therefore to measure closely the importance it may have, and I don't think I've ever, in talking with you, pretended to fix that importance. I don't suppose it will matter immensely whether your own engagement's carried out or not; but if it is it will have been a detail in a scheme of which the general effect will be decidedly useful. I believe, and you pretend to believe, though I'm not sure you do, in the advent of the democracy. It will help the democracy to get possession that the classes that keep them down shall be admonished from time <u>192</u> to time that they've a very definite and very determined intention of doing so. An immense deal will depend upon that. Hoffendahl's a jolly admonisher."

Hyacinth listened to this explanation with an expression of interest that was not feigned; and after a moment he returned: "When you say you believe in the democracy I take for granted you mean you positively wish for their coming into power, as I've always supposed. Now what I really have never understood is this—why you should desire to put forward a lot of people whom you regard almost without exception as rather dismal donkeys."

"Ah my dear lad," Paul laughed, "when one undertakes to meddle in human affairs one must deal with human material. The upper classes have the longest ears."

"I've heard you say you were working for an equality in human conditions—to abolish the immemorial inequality. What you want then for all mankind is the selfsame shade of asininity."

"That's very neat; did you pick it up in France? Damn the too-neat, you know; it's as bad as the too-rotten. The low tone of our fellow-mortals is a result of bad conditions; it's the conditions I want to alter. When those who have no start to speak of have a good one it's but fair to infer they'll go further. I want to try them, you know."

"But why equality?" Hyacinth asked. "Somehow that word doesn't say so much to me as it used to. Inequality—inequality! I don't know whether it's by dint of repeating it over to myself, but *that* doesn't shock me as it used."

"They didn't put you up to that in France, I'm sure!" Paul exclaimed. "Your point of view's changed. You've risen in the world."

"Risen? Good God, what have I risen to?"

"True enough; you were always a bloated little <u>193</u> swell!" And the so useful man at the great chemical works gave his young friend a sociable slap on the back. There was a momentary bitterness in its being imputed to such a one as Hyacinth, even in joke, that he had taken sides with the lucky beggars as a class, and he had it on his tongue's end to ask his friend if he had never guessed what his proud titles were—the bastard of a murderess, spawned in a gutter out of which he had been picked by a poor sewing-girl. But his lifelong reserve on this point was a habit not easily broken, and before such a challenge could burn through it Paul had gone on: "If you've ceased to believe we can do anything it will be rather awkward, you know."

"I don't know what I believe, God help me!" Hyacinth remarked in a tone of an effect so lugubrious that his mate indulged in prompt hilarity of attenuation. But our young man added: "I don't want you to think I've ceased to care for the people. What am I but one of the poorest and meanest of them?"

"You, my boy? You're a duke in disguise, and so I thought the first time I ever saw you. That night I took you to our precious 'exchange of ideas'—I liked the beggar's name for it—you had a little way with you that made me forget it; I mean that your disguise happened to be better than usual. As regards caring for the people there's surely no obligation at all," Muniment continued. "I wouldn't if I could help it—you can bet your life on that. It all depends on what you see. The way I've used my eyes in that sink of iniquity off there has led to my seeing that present arrangements won't do. They won't do," he repeated placidly.

"Yes, I see that too," said Hyacinth, with the same dolefulness that had marked his tone a moment before—a dolefulness begotten of the rather helpless 194 sense that, whatever he saw, he saw—and this was always the case—so many other things besides. He saw the immeasurable misery of the people, and yet he saw all that had been, as it were, rescued and redeemed from it: the treasures, the felicities, the splendours, the successes of the world. This quantity took the form sometimes, to his imagination, of a vast, vague, dazzling presence, an irradiation of light from objects undefined, mixed with the atmosphere of Paris and of Venice. He presently added that a hundred things Muniment had told him about the foul horrors of the worst districts of London, pictures of incredible shame and suffering that he had put before him, came back to him now with the memory of the passion they had kindled at the time.

"Oh I don't want you to go by what I've told you; I want you to go by what you've seen yourself. I remember there were things you told *me* that weren't bad in their way." And at this Paul Muniment sprang to his feet, as if their conversation had drawn to an end or they must at all events be thinking of their homeward way. Hyacinth got up too while his companion stood there. Paul was looking off toward London with a face that expressed all the healthy singleness of his vision. Suddenly he remarked, as if it occurred to him to complete, or at any rate confirm, the declaration he had made a short time before: "Yes, I don't believe in the millennium, but I do believe in the democracy with a *chance*."

He struck Hyacinth while he spoke these words as such a fine embodiment of the spirit of the people; he stood there in his powerful, sturdy newness with such an air of having learnt what he had learnt and of good nature that had purposes in it, that our hero felt the simple inrush of his old, frequent pride at having a person of that promise, a nature of that capacity, for a friend. He passed his hand into the 195 arm that was so much stronger and longer than his own and said with an imperceptible tremor of voice: "It's no use your saying I'm not to go by what you tell me. I'd go by what you tell me anywhere. There's no awkwardness to speak of. I don't know that I believe exactly what you believe, but I believe in *you*, and doesn't that come to the same thing?"

Paul evidently appreciated the cordiality and candour of this little tribute, and the way he showed it was by a motion of his elbow, to check his companion, before they started to leave the spot, and by looking down at him with a certain anxiety of friendliness. "I should never have taken you to that shop that night if I hadn't thought you'd jump at the job. It was that flaring little oration of yours, at the club, when you floored Delancey for saying you were afraid, that put me up to it."

"I did jump at it—upon my word I did; and it was just what I was looking for. That's all correct!" said Hyacinth cheerfully as they went forward. There was a strain of heroism in these words—of heroism of which the sense was not conveyed to Muniment by a vibration in their interlocked arms. Hyacinth didn't make the reflexion that he was infernally literal; he dismissed the sentimental problem that had worried him; he condoned, excused, admired—he merged himself, resting happy for the time, in the consciousness that Paul was a grand person, that friendship was a purer feeling than love, and that there was an immense deal of affection between them. He didn't even observe at that moment that it was preponderantly on his own side. 196

XXXVI

A certain Sunday in November, more than three months after she had gone to live in Madeira Crescent, was so important an occasion for the Princess as to require reporting with a certain fulness. Early in the afternoon a loud peal from her door-knocker came to her ear; it had a sound of resolution, almost of defiance, which made her look up from her book and listen. She was sitting alone by the fire, over a heavy volume on Labour and Capital. It was not yet four o'clock, but she had had candles this hour; a dense brown fog made the daylight impure without suggesting an answer to the question of whether the scheme of nature had been to veil or to deepen the sabbatical dreariness. She was not tired of Madeira Crescent, such an idea she would indignantly have repudiated; but the prospect of a visitor had a happy application—the possibility even of his being an ambassador or a cabinet minister or another of the eminent personages with whom she had conversed before embracing the ascetic life. They had not knocked at her present door hitherto in any great numbers, for more reasons than one; they were out of town and she had taken pains to diffuse the belief that she had left England. If the impression prevailed it was exactly the impression she had desired; she forgot this fact whenever she felt a certain surprise—even, it may be, a certain irritation—in 197 perceiving that people were not taking the way to Madeira Crescent. She was making the discovery, in which she had had many predecessors, that to hide in London is only too easy a game. It was very much in that fashion that Godfrey Sholto was in the habit of announcing himself when he reappeared after the intervals she explicitly imposed on him; there was a witless grace, for so world-worn a personage, in the point he made of showing that he knocked with confidence, that he had as good a right as any other. This afternoon she would have accepted his visit: she was perfectly detached from the shallow, frivolous world in which he lived, but there was still a freshness in her renunciation which coveted reminders and enjoyed comparisons—he would prove to her how right she had been to do exactly what she was doing. It didn't occur to her that Hyacinth Robinson might be at her door, for it had been understood between them that save by special appointment he was to come to her only in the evening. She heard in the hall, when the servant arrived, a voice she failed to recognise; but in a moment the door of the room was thrown open and the name of Mr. Muniment pronounced. It may be noted at once that she took pleasure in the sound, for she had both wished to see more of Hyacinth's extraordinary friend and had given him up—so little likely had it begun to appear that he would put himself out for her. She had been glad he

- 128 -

wouldn't come, as she had told Hyacinth three months before; but now that he had come she was still more glad.

Presently he was sitting before her on the other side of the fire, his big foot crossed over his big knee, his large, gloved hands fumbling with each other, drawing and smoothing in places the gloves of very red, new-looking dogskin that appeared to hurt him. So far as the size of his extremities and even 198 his attitude and movement went he might have belonged to her former circle. With the details of his dress remaining vague in the lamplight, which threw into relief mainly his powerful, important head, he might have been one of the most considerable men she had ever known. The first thing she said to him was that she wondered extremely what had brought him at last to present himself: the idea, when she proposed it, had clearly so little attracted him. She had only seen him once since then—the day she met him coming into Audley Court when she was leaving it after a visit to his sister—and, as he probably remembered, she had not on that occasion repeated her invitation.

"It wouldn't have done any good, at the time, if you had," Muniment returned with his natural laugh.

"Oh I felt that; my silence wasn't accidental!" the Princess declared with due gaiety.

"I've only come now—since you've asked me the reason—because my sister has hammered at me, week after week, dinning it into me that I ought to. Oh I've been under the lash! If she had left me alone I wouldn't have come."

The Princess blushed on hearing these words, but neither with shame nor with pain; rather with the happy excitement of being spoken to in a manner so fresh and original. She had never before had a visitor who practised so racy a frankness or who indeed had so curious a story to tell. She had never before so completely failed, and her failure greatly interested her, especially as it seemed now to be turning a little to success. She had succeeded promptly with every one, and the sign of it was that every one had rendered her a monotony of homage. Even poor little Hyacinth had tried, in the beginning, to say grand things to her. This very different type of man appeared to have his thoughts fixed on anything but flowers of 199 speech; she felt the liveliest hope that he would move further and further away from that delusion. "I remember what you asked me—what good it would do you. I couldn't tell you then; and though I now have had a long time to turn it over I haven't thought of it yet."

"Oh but I hope it will do me some," the young man said. "A fellow wants a reward when he has made a great effort."

"It does *me* some," the Princess freely answered.

"Naturally the awkward things I say amuse you. But I don't say them for that, but just to give you an idea."

"You give me a great many ideas. Besides, I know you already a good deal."

"From little Robinson, I suppose," said Muniment.

She had a pause. "More particularly from Lady Aurora."

"Oh she doesn't know much about me!" he protested.

"It's a pity you say that, because she likes you."

"Yes, she likes me," he serenely admitted.

Again his hostess hesitated. "And I hope you like her."

"Aye, she's a dear old girl!"

The Princess reflected that her visitor was not a gentleman, like Hyacinth; but this made no difference in her present attitude. The expectation that he would be a gentleman had had nothing to do with her interest in him; that had in fact rested largely on his probably finding felicity in a deep indifference to the character. "I don't know that there's any one in the world I envy so much," she observed; a statement that her visitor received in silence. "Better than any one I've ever met she has solved the problem—which if we are wise we all try to solve, don't <u>200</u> we?—of getting out of herself. She has got out of herself more perfectly than any one I've ever known. She has merged herself in the passion of doing something for others. That's why I envy her," she concluded with an explanatory smile, as if perhaps he didn't understand her.

"It's an amusement like any other," said Paul Muniment.

"Ah not like any other! It carries light into dark places; it makes a great many wretched people considerably less wretched."

"How many, eh?" asked the young man, not exactly as if he wished to dispute but as if it were always in him to enjoy discussing.

The Princess wondered why he should wish to argue at Lady Aurora's expense. "Well, one who's very near to you, to begin with."

"Oh she's kind, most kind; it's altogether wonderful. But Rosy makes *her* considerably less wretched," Muniment added.

"Very likely, of course; and so she does me."

"May I inquire what you're wretched about?" he went on.

"About nothing at all. That's the worst of it. But I'm much happier now than I've ever been."

"Is that also about nothing?"

"No, about a sort of change that has taken place in my life. I've been able to do some little things."

"For the poor, I suppose you mean. Do you refer to the presents you've made to Rosy?" the young man asked.

"The presents?" She appeared not to remember. "Oh those are trifles. It isn't anything one has been able to give. It's some talks one has had, some convictions one has arrived at."

"Convictions are a source of very innocent 201 pleasure," said the young man, smiling at his interlocutress with his bold, pleasant eyes, which seemed to project their glance further and drive it harder than any she had seen.

"Having them's nothing. It's the acting on them," the Princess replied.

"Yes; that doubtless too is good." He continued to look at her patiently, as if he liked to consider that this might be what she had asked him to come for. He said nothing more, and she went on:

"It's far better of course when one's a man."

"I don't know. Women do pretty well what they like. My sister and you have managed, between you, to bring me to this."

"It's more your sister, I suspect, than I. But why, after all, should you have disliked so much to come?"

"Well, since you ask me," said Paul Muniment, "I'll tell you frankly, though I don't mean it uncivilly, that I don't know what to make of you."

"Most people don't," returned the Princess. "But they usually take the risk."

"Ah well, I'm the most prudent of men."

"I was sure of it; that's one of the reasons I wanted to know you. I know what some of your ideas are—Hyacinth Robinson has told me; and the source of my interest in them is partly the fact that you consider very carefully what you attempt."

"That I do—I do," he agreed.

The tone in which he said this would have been almost ignoble, as regards a kind of northern canniness latent in it, had it not been corrected by the character of his face, his youth and strength, his almost military eyes. The Princess recognised both the shrewdness and the natural ease as she rejoined: "To do anything in association with you would be very safe. It would be sure to succeed." 202

"That's what poor Hyacinth thinks," he said.

She wondered a little that he could allude in that light tone to the faith their young friend had placed in him, considering the consequences such a trustfulness might yet have; but this curious mixture of qualities could only make her visitor, as a tribune of the people, more interesting to her. She abstained for the moment from touching on the subject of Hyacinth's peculiar position and only pursued: "Hasn't he told you about me? Hasn't he explained me a little?"

"Oh his explanations are grand!" Muniment laughed. "He's fine sport when he talks about you."

"Don't betray him," she said gently.

"There's nothing to betray. You'd be the first to admire it if you were there. Besides, I don't betray," he added.

"I love him very much," said the Princess; and it would have been impossible for the most impudent cynic to smile at the manner in which she made the declaration.

Her guest accepted it respectfully. "He's a sweet little lad and, putting her ladyship aside, quite the light of our humble home."

There was a short pause after this exchange of amenities, which the Princess terminated by inquiring: "Wouldn't some one else do his work quite as well?"

"His work? Why, I'm told he's a master-hand."

"Oh I don't mean his bookbinding." Then she added: "I don't know if you know it, but I'm in correspondence with a certain person. If you understand me at all you'll know whom I mean. I'm acquainted with many of our most important men."

"Yes, I know. Hyacinth has told me. Do you mention it as a guarantee, so that I may know you're sound?" 203

"Not exactly; that would be weak, wouldn't it?" the Princess asked. "My soundness must be in myself—a matter for you to appreciate as you know me better; not in my references and vouchers."

"I shall never know you better. What business is it of mine?"

"I want to help you," she said; and as she made this earnest appeal her face became transfigured: it wore an expression of the most passionate yet the purest longing. "I want to do something for the cause you represent; for the millions who are rotting under our feet—the millions whose whole life is passed on the brink of starvation, so that the smallest accident pushes them over. Try me, test me; ask me to put my hand to something, to prove that I'm as deeply in earnest as those who have already given proof. I know what I'm talking about—what one must meet and face and count with, the nature and the immensity of your organisation. I'm not trifling. No, I'm not trifling."

Paul Muniment watched her with his steady smile until this sudden outbreak had spent itself. "I was afraid you'd be like this—that you'd turn on the fountains and let off the fireworks."

"Permit me to believe you thought nothing about it. There's no reason my fireworks should disturb you."

"I have always had a fear of clever women."

"I see—that's a part of your prudence," said the Princess reflectively. "But you're the sort of man who ought to know how to use them."

He made no immediate answer to this; the way he appeared to regard her suggested that he was not following closely what she said so much as losing himself in certain matters which were beside that question—her beauty, for instance, her grace, her 204 fragrance, the spectacle of a manner and quality so new to him. After a little, however, he brought out irrelevantly: "I'm afraid I'm awfully rude."

"Of course you are, but it doesn't signify. What I mainly object to is that you don't meet my questions. Wouldn't some one else do Hyacinth Robinson's work quite as well? Is it necessary to take a nature so delicate, so intellectual? Oughtn't we to keep him for something finer?"

"Finer than what?"

"Than what he'll be called upon to do."

"And pray what's that?" the young man demanded. "You know nothing about it; no more do I," he added in a moment. "It will require whatever it will. Besides, if some one else might have done it no one else volunteered. It happened that Robinson did."

"Yes, and you nipped him up!" the Princess returned.

This expression made Muniment laugh. "I've no doubt you can easily keep him if you want him."

"I should like to do it in his place—that's what I should like," said the Princess.

"As I say, you don't even know what it is."

"It may be nothing," she went on with her grave eyes fixed on her visitor. "I daresay you think that what I wanted to see you for was to beg you to let him off. But it wasn't. Of course it's his own affair and you can do nothing. But oughtn't it to make some difference if his opinions have changed?"

"His opinions? He never had any opinions," Muniment replied. "He's not like you and me."

"Well then, his feelings, his attachments. He hasn't the passion for the popular triumph that he had when I first knew him. He's much more tepid."

"Ah well, he's quite right." 205

The Princess stared. "Do you mean that *you* are giving up——?"

"A fine, stiff conservative's a thing I perfectly understand," said Paul Muniment. "If I were on the top I'd stick."

"I see, you're not narrow," she breathed appreciatively.

"I beg your pardon, I am. I don't call that wide. One must be narrow to penetrate."

"Whatever you are you'll succeed," said the Princess. "Hyacinth won't, but you will."

"It depends upon what you call success!" the young man returned. And in a moment, before she could take it up, he added as he looked about the room: "You've got a lovely home."

"Lovely? My dear sir, it's hideous. That's what I like it for," she hastened to explain.

"Well, I like it, but perhaps I don't know the reason. I thought you had given up everything—pitched your goods out of window for a grand scramble."

"It's what I *have* done. You should have seen me before."

"I should have liked that," he quite shamelessly smiled. "I like to see solid wealth."

"Ah you're as bad as Hyacinth. I'm the only consistent one!" the Princess sighed.

"You've a great deal left, for a person who has given everything away."

"These are not mine—these abominations—or I would give them too!" Paul's hostess returned artlessly.

He got up from his chair, still looking over the scene. "I'd give my nose for such a place as this. At any rate, you're not yet reduced to poverty."

"I've a little left—to help you." 206

"I'd lay a wager you've a great deal," he declared with his north-country accent.

"I could get money—I could get money," she continued gravely. She had also risen and was standing before him.

These two remarkable persons faced each other, their eyes met again, and they exchanged a long, deep glance of mutual scrutiny. Each seemed to drop a plummet into the other's mind. Then a strange and, to the Princess, unexpected expression passed over the countenance of her guest; his lips compressed themselves as in the strain of a strong effort, his colour rose and in a moment he stood there blushing like a boy. He dropped his eyes and stared at the carpet while he repeated: "I don't trust women—I don't trust clever women!"

"I'm sorry, but after all I can understand it," she said; "therefore I won't insist on the question of your allowing me to work with you. But this appeal I *will* make: help me a little yourself—help me!"

"How do you mean, help you?" he asked as he raised his eyes, which had a new, conscious look.

"Advise me; you'll know how. I'm in trouble—I've gone very far."

"I've no doubt of that!" Paul laughed.

"I mean with some of those people abroad. I'm not frightened, but I'm worried. I want to know what to do."

"No, you're not frightened," Muniment returned after a moment.

"I'm, however, in a sad entanglement. I think you can straighten it out. I'll give you the facts, but not now, for we shall be interrupted—I hear my old lady on the stairs. For this you must come back to me." 207

As she spoke the door opened, and Madame Grandoni appeared cautiously, creeping, as if she didn't know what might be going on in the parlour. "Yes, I'll come back," said Paul quietly but clearly enough; with which he walked away, passing Madame Grandoni on the threshold and overlooking the hand-shake of farewell. In the hall he paused an instant, feeling his hostess behind him; whereby he learned that she had not come to exact from him this omitted observance, but to say once more, dropping her voice so that her companion, through the open door, might not catch: "I *could* get money—I could!"

He passed his hand through his hair and, as if he had not heard, observed: "I've not after all given you half Rosy's messages."

"Oh that doesn't matter!" she answered as she turned back into the parlour.

Madame Grandoni was in the middle of the room, wrapped in her old shawl, looking vaguely round her, and the two ladies heard the house-door close. "And pray who may that be? Isn't it a new face?" the elder one inquired.

"He's the brother of the little person I took you to see over the river—the chattering cripple with the wonderful manners."

"Ah she had a brother! That then was why you went?"

It was striking, the good humour with which the Princess received this rather coarse thrust, which could have been drawn from Madame Grandoni only by the petulance and weariness of increasing age and the antipathy she now felt to Madeira Crescent and everything it produced. Christina bent a calm, charitable smile on her ancient support and replied: "There could have been no question of our seeing him. He was of course at his work." 208

"Ah how do I know, my dear? And is he a successor?"

"A successor?"

"To the little bookbinder."

"*Mia cara*," said the Princess, "you'll see how absurd that question is when I tell you he's his greatest friend!" 209

XXXVII

Half an hour after the departure of the young chemical expert she heard another rat-tat-tat at her door; but this was a briefer, discreeter peal and was accompanied by a faint tintinnabulation. The person who had produced it was presently ushered in, without, however, causing Madame Grandoni to look round, or rather to look up, from an armchair as low as a sitz-bath and of very much the shape of such a receptacle, in which, near the fire, she had been immersed. She left this care to the Princess, who rose on hearing the name of the visitor pronounced inadequately by her maid. "Mr. Fetch," Assunta called it; but that functionary's mistress recognised without difficulty the little fat "reduced" fiddler of whom Hyacinth had talked to her, who, as Pinnie's most intimate friend, had been so mixed up with his existence, and whom she herself had always had a curiosity to see. Hyacinth had not told her he was coming, and the unexpectedness of the apparition added to its interest. Much as she liked seeing queer types and exploring out-of-the-way social corners, she never engaged in a fresh encounter nor formed a new relation of this kind without a fit of nervousness, a fear she might herself be wanting, might fail to hit the right tone. She perceived in a moment, however, that Mr. Vetch would take her as she was and require no special adjustments; he was a gentleman and a 210 man of experience and she should only have to leave the tone to him. He stood there with his large polished hat in his two hands, a hat of the fashion of ten years before, with a rusty sheen and an undulating brim— stood there without a salutation or a speech, but with a small fixed, acute, tentative smile which seemed half to interrogate and half to explain. What he explained, at all events, was that he was clever enough to be trusted and that if he had called this way, without ceremony and without an invitation, he had a reason which she would be sure to think good enough when she should hear it. There was even a certain jauntiness in his confidence—an insinuation that he knew how to present himself to a lady; and though it quickly appeared that he really did, this was the only thing about him that was inferior. It suggested a long experience of actresses at rehearsal, with whom he had formed habits of advice and compliment.

"I know who you are—I know who you are," said the Princess, though she could easily see he knew she did.

"I wonder if you also know why I've come to see you," Mr. Vetch replied, presenting the top of his hat to her as if it were a looking-glass.

"No, but it doesn't matter. I'm very glad. You might even have come before." Then she added with her characteristic honesty: "Aren't you aware of the great interest I've taken in your nephew?"

"In my nephew? Yes, my young friend Robinson. It's for his sake I've ventured to intrude on you."

She had been on the point of pushing a chair toward him, but she stopped in the act, staring with a smile. "Ah I hope you haven't come to ask me to give him up!"

"On the contrary—on the contrary!" the old man returned, lifting his hand expressively and with <u>211</u> his head on one side as if he were holding his fiddle.

"How do you mean, on the contrary?" she asked after he had seated himself and she had sunk into her former place. As if that might sound contradictious she went on: "Surely he hasn't any fear that I shall cease to be a good friend to him?"

"I don't know what he fears; I don't know what he hopes," said Mr. Vetch, looking at her now with a face in which she could see there was something more tonic than old-fashioned politeness. "It will be difficult to tell you, but at least I must try. Properly speaking, I suppose, it's no business of mine, as I'm not a blood-relation to the boy; but I've known him since he was a mite—he's not much more even now—and I can't help saying that I thank you for your great kindness to him."

"All the same I don't think you like it," the Princess declared. "To me it oughtn't to be difficult to say anything."

"He has told me very little about you; he doesn't know I've taken this step," the fiddler said, turning his eyes about the room and letting them rest on Madame Grandoni.

"Why do you speak of it as a 'step'? That's what people say when they've to do something disagreeable."

"I call very seldom on ladies. It's a long time since I've been in the house of a person like the Princess Casamassima. I remember the last time," said the old man. "It was to get my money from a lady at whose party I had been playing—for a dance."

"You must bring your fiddle some time and play to us. Of course I don't mean for money," the Princess added.

"I'll do it with pleasure, or anything else that will <u>212</u> gratify you. But my ability's very small. I only know vulgar music—things that are played at theatres."

"I don't believe that. There must be things you play for yourself—in your room alone."

Mr. Vetch had a pause. "Now that I see you, that I hear you, it helps me to understand."

"I don't think you do see me!" his hostess freely laughed; on which he desired to know if there were danger of Hyacinth's coming in while he was there. She replied that he only came, unless by prearrangement, in the evening, and her visitor made a request that she wouldn't let their young friend imagine he himself had been with her. "It doesn't matter; he'll guess it, he'll know it by instinct, as soon as he comes in. He's terribly subtle," she said; and she added that she had never been able to hide anything from him. Perhaps this served her right—for attempting to make a mystery of things not worth it.

"How well you know him!" the fiddler commented while his eyes wandered again to Madame Grandoni, who paid no attention to him as she sat staring at the fire. He delayed visibly to say what he had come for, and his hesitation could only be connected with the presence of the old lady. He considered that the Princess might have divined this from his manner; he had an idea he could trust himself to convey such an intimation with clearness and yet with delicacy. But the most she appeared to apprehend was that he desired to be presented to her companion. "You must know the most delightful of women. She also takes a particular interest in Mr. Robinson: of a different kind from mine—much more sentimental!" And then she explained to her friend, who seemed absorbed in other ideas, that Mr. Vetch was a distinguished musician, a person whom she, who had known so many in her day and 213 was so fond of that kind of thing, would like to talk with. The Princess spoke of "that kind of thing" quite as if she herself had given it up, though Madame Grandoni often heard her by the hour together improvising at the piano revolutionary battle-songs and pæans.

"I think you're laughing at me," Mr. Vetch said to her while the other figure twisted itself slowly round in its chair and regarded him. It looked at him conveniently, up and down, and then sighed out:

"Strange people—strange people!"

"It's indeed a strange world, madam," the fiddler replied; after which he inquired of the Princess if he might have a little conversation with her in private.

She looked about her, embarrassed and smiling. "My dear sir, I've only this one room to receive in. We live in a very small way."

"Yes, your excellency is laughing at me. Your ideas are very large too. However, I'd gladly come at any other time that might suit you."

"You impute to me higher spirits than I possess. Why should I be so gay?" the Princess asked. "I should be delighted to see you again. I'm extremely curious as to what you may have to say to me. I'd even meet you anywhere—in Kensington Gardens or the British Museum."

He took her deeply in before replying, and then, his white old face flushing a little, exclaimed: "Poor dear little Hyacinth!"

Madame Grandoni made an effort to rise from her chair, but she had sunk so low that at first it was not successful. Mr. Vetch gave her a hand of help, and she slowly erected herself, keeping hold of him for a moment after she stood there. "What did she tell me? That you're a great musician? Isn't that enough for any man? You ought to be content, my 214 dear gentleman. It has sufficed for people whom I don't believe you surpass."

"I don't surpass any one," said poor Mr. Vetch. "I don't know what you take me for."

"You're not a wicked revolutionary then? You're not a conspirator nor an assassin? It surprises me, but so much the better. In this house one can never know. It's not a good house, and if you're a respectable person it's a pity you should come here. Yes, she's very gay and I'm very sad. I don't know how it will end. After me, I hope. The world's not good, certainly; but God alone can make it better." And as the fiddler expressed the hope that he was not the cause of her leaving the room she went on: "*Doch, doch,* you're the cause; but why not you as well as another? I'm always leaving it for some one or for something, and I'd sooner do so for an honest man, if you *are* one—but, as I say, who can tell?—than for a destroyer. I wander about. I've no rest. I have, however, a very nice room, the best in the house. Me at least she doesn't treat ill. It looks to-day like the end of all things. If you'd turn your climate the other side up the rest would do well enough. Good-night to you, whoever you are."

The old lady shuffled away in spite of Mr. Vetch's renewed apologies, and the subject of her criticism stood before the fire watching the pair while he opened the door. "She goes away, she comes back; it doesn't matter. She thinks it a bad house, but she knows it would be worse without her. I remember about you now," the Princess added. "Mr. Robinson told me you had been a great democrat in old days, but that at present you'd ceased to care for the people."

"The people—the people? That's a silly term. Whom do you mean?"

She hesitated. "Those you used to care for, to plead for; those who are underneath every one, 215 underneath everything, and have the whole social mass crushing them."

"I see you think I'm a renegade. The way certain classes arrogate to themselves the title of the people has never pleased me. Why are some human beings the people, the people only, and others not? I'm of the people myself, I've worked all my days like a knife-grinder and I've really never changed."

"You mustn't let me make you angry," she laughed as she sat down again. "I'm sometimes very provoking, but you must stop me off. You wouldn't think it perhaps, but no one takes a snub better than I."

Mr. Vetch dropped his eyes a minute; he appeared to wish to show that he regarded such a speech as that as one of this great, perverse lady's characteristic humours and knew he should be wanting in respect to her if he took it seriously or made a personal application of it. "What I want is this," he began after a moment: "that you'll, that you'll——" But he stopped before he had got further. She was watching him, listening to him; she waited while he paused. It was a long pause and she said nothing. "Princess," the old man broke out at last, "I'd give my own life many times for that boy's!"

"I always told him you must have been fond of him!" she cried with bright exultation.

"Fond of him? Pray who can doubt it? I made him, I invented him!"

"He knows it, moreover," the Princess smiled. "It's an exquisite organisation." And as the old man gazed at her, not knowing apparently what to make of her tone, she kept it up: "It's a very interesting opportunity for me to learn certain things. Speak to me of his early years. How was he as a child? When I like people I like them altogether and want to know everything about them." 216

"I shouldn't have supposed there was much left for you to learn about our young friend. You've taken possession of his life," Mr. Vetch added gravely.

"Yes, but as I understand you, you don't complain of it? Sometimes one does so much more than one has intended. One must use one's influence for good," she went on with the noble, gentle air of accessibility to reason that sometimes lighted up her face. And then irrelevantly: "I know the terrible story of his mother. He told it me himself when he was staying with me. In the course of my life I think I've never been more affected."

"That was my fault—that he ever learnt it. I suppose he also told you that."

"Yes, but I think he understood your idea. If you had the question to determine again would you judge differently?"

"I thought it would do him good," said the old man simply and rather wearily.

"Well, I daresay it has," she returned with the manner of wishing to encourage him.

"I don't know what was in my head. I wanted him to quarrel with society. Now I want him to be reconciled to it," Mr. Vetch remarked earnestly. He appeared to desire her to understand how great a point he made of this.

"Ah, but he is!" she immediately said. "We often talk about that; he's not like me, who see all kinds of abominations. He's a bloated little aristocrat. What more would you have?"

"Those are not the opinions he expresses to *me*"—and Mr. Vetch shook his head sadly. "I'm greatly distressed and I don't make out——! I've not come here with the presumptuous wish to cross-examine you, but I should like very much to know if I *am* wrong in believing that he has gone about with you in the bad quarters—in Saint Giles's and Whitechapel." 217

"We've certainly inquired and explored together," the Princess admitted, "and in the depths of this huge, luxurious, wanton, wasteful city we've seen sights of unspeakable misery and horror. But we've been not only in the slums; we've been to a music hall and a penny-reading."

The fiddler received this information at first in silence, so that his hostess went on to mention some of the phases of life they had observed; describing with great vividness, but at the same time with a kind of argumentative moderation, several scenes which did little honour to "our boasted civilisation." "What wonder is it then that he should tell me things can't go on any longer as they are?" he asked when she had finished. "He said only the other day that he should regard himself as one of the most contemptible of human beings if he should do nothing to alter them, to better them."

"What wonder indeed? But if he said that he was in one of his bad days," the Princess replied. "He changes constantly and his impressions change. The misery of the people is by no means always on his heart. You tell me what he has told you; well, he has told me that the people may perish over and over rather than the conquests of civilisation shall be sacrificed to them. He declares at such moments that they'll be sacrificed—sacrificed utterly—if the ignorant masses get the upper hand."

"He needn't be afraid. That will never happen."

"I don't know. We can at least try," she said.

"Try what you like, madam, but for God's sake get the boy out of his muddle!"

The Princess had suddenly grown excited in speaking of the cause she believed in, and she gave for the moment no heed to this appeal, which broke from Mr. Vetch's lips with a sudden passion of anxiety. Her beautiful head raised itself higher and 218 the constant light of her fine eyes became an extraordinary radiance. "Do you know what I say to Mr. Robinson when he makes such remarks as that to me? I ask him what he means by civilisation. Let civilisation come a little, first, and then we'll talk about it. For the present, face to face with those horrors, I scorn it, I deny it!" And she laughed ineffable things, she might have been some splendid siren of the Revolution.

"The world's very sad and very hideous, and I'm happy to say that I soon shall have done with it. But before I go I want to save Hyacinth," Mr. Vetch insisted. "If he's a bloated little aristocrat, as you say, there's so much the less fitness in his being ground in your mill. If he doesn't even believe in what he pretends to do, that's a pretty situation! What's he in for, madam? What devilish folly has he undertaken?"

"He's a strange mixture of contradictory impulses," said the Princess musingly. Then as if calling herself back to the old man's question she pursued: "How can I enter into his affairs with you? How can I tell you his secrets? In the first place I don't know them, and if I did—well, fancy me!"

Her visitor gave a long, low sigh, almost a moan, of discouragement and perplexity. He had told her that now he saw her he understood how their young friend should have become her slave, but he wouldn't have been able to tell her that he understood her own motives and mysteries, that he embraced the immense anomaly of her behaviour. It came over him that she was fine and perverse, a more complicated form of the feminine mixture than any he had hitherto dealt with, and he felt helpless and baffled, foredoomed to failure. He had come prepared to flatter her without scruple, thinking this would be the expert and effective way of dealing with her; but he now recognised that these 219 primitive arts had, though it was strange, no application to such a nature, while his embarrassment was increased rather than diminished by the fact that the lady at least made the effort to be accommodating. He had put down his hat on the floor beside him and his two hands were clasped on the knob of an umbrella which had long since renounced pretensions to compactness; he collapsed a little and his chin rested on his folded hands. "Why do you take such a line? Why do you believe such things?" he asked; and he was conscious that his tone was weak and his challenge beside the question.

"My dear sir, how do you know what I believe? However, I have my reasons, which it would take too long to tell you and which after all would not particularly interest you. One must see life as one can; it comes no doubt to each of us in different ways. You think me affected of course and my behaviour a fearful *pose*; but I'm only trying to be natural. Are you not yourself a little inconsequent?" she went on with the bright, hard mildness which assured Mr. Vetch, while it chilled him, that he should extract no pledge of relief from her. "You don't want our young friend to pry into the wretchedness of London, because that excites his sense of justice. It's a strange thing to wish, for a person of whom one is fond and whom one esteems, that his sense of justice shall not be excited."

"I don't care a fig for his sense of justice—I don't care a fig for the wretchedness of London; and if I were young and beautiful and clever and brilliant and of a noble position, like you, I should care still less. In that case I should have very little to say to a poor mechanic—a youngster who earns his living with a glue-pot and scraps of old leather."

"Don't misrepresent him; don't make him out what you know he's not!" the Princess retorted 220 with her baffling smile. "You know he's one of the most civilised of little men."

The fiddler sat breathing unhappily. "I only want to keep him—to get him free." Then he added: "I don't understand you very well. If you like him because he's one of the lower orders, how can you like him because he's a swell?"

She turned her eyes on the fire as if this little problem might be worth considering, and presently she answered: "Dear Mr. Vetch, I'm very sure you don't mean to be impertinent, but some things you say have that effect. Nothing's more annoying than when one's sincerity is doubted. I'm not bound to explain myself to you. I ask of my friends to trust me and of the others to leave me alone. Moreover, anything not very nice you may have said to me—out of inevitable awkwardness—is nothing to the insults I'm perfectly prepared to see showered upon me before long. I shall do things which will produce a fine crop of them—oh I shall do things, my dear sir! But I'm determined not to mind them. Come therefore, pull yourself together. We both take such an interest in young Robinson that I can't see why in the world we should quarrel about him."

"My dear lady," the old man pleaded, "I've indeed not the least intention of failing in respect or patience, and you must excuse me if I don't look after my manners. How can I when I'm so worried, so haunted? God knows I don't want to quarrel. As I tell you, I only want to get Hyacinth free."

"Free from what?" the Princess asked.

"From some abominable secret brotherhood or international league that he belongs to, the thought of which keeps me awake at night. He's just the sort of youngster to be made a catspaw."

"Your fears seem very vague."

"I hoped you would give me chapter and verse." 221

"On what do your suspicions rest? What grounds have you?" she insisted.

"Well, a great many; none of them very definite, but all contributing something—his appearance, his manner, the way he strikes me. Dear lady, one feels those things, one guesses. Do you know that poor infatuated phrasemonger Eustache Poupin, who works at the same place as Hyacinth? He's a very old friend of mine and he's an honest man, as phrasemongers go. But he's always conspiring and corresponding and pulling strings that make a tinkle which he takes for the death-knell of society. He has nothing in life to complain of and drives a roaring trade. But he wants folk to be equal, heaven help him; and when he has made them so I suppose he's going to start a society for making the stars in the sky all of the same size. He isn't serious, though he imagines he's the only human being who never trifles; and his machinations, which I believe are for the most part very innocent, are a matter of habit and tradition with him, like his theory that Christopher Columbus, who discovered America, was a Frenchman, and his hot foot-bath on Saturday nights. He has *not* confessed to me that Hyacinth has taken some intensely private engagement to do something for the cause which may have nasty consequences, but the way he turns off the idea makes me almost as uncomfortable as if he had. He and his wife are very sweet on their young friend, but they can't make up their minds to interfere; perhaps for them indeed, as for me, there's no way in which interference can be effective. Only *I* didn't put him up to those devil's tricks—or rather I did originally! The finer the work, I suppose, the higher the privilege of doing it; yet the Poupins heave socialistic sighs over the boy, and their peace of mind evidently isn't all that it ought to be if they've given him a noble 222 opportunity. I've appealed to them in good round terms, and they've assured me every hair of his head is as precious to them as if he were their own child. That doesn't comfort me much, however, for the simple reason that I believe the old woman (whose grandmother, in Paris, in the Revolution, must certainly have carried bloody heads on a pike) would be quite capable of chopping up her own child if it would do any harm to proprietors. Besides, they say, what influence have they on Hyacinth any more? He's a deplorable little backslider; he worships false gods. In short they'll give me no information, and I daresay they themselves are tied up by some unholy vow. They may be afraid of a vengeance if they tell tales. It's all sad rubbish, but rubbish may be a strong motive."

The Princess listened attentively, following her visitor with patience. "Don't speak to me of the French; I've never cared for them."

"That's awkward if you're a socialist. You're likely to meet them."

"Why do you call me a socialist? I hate tenth-rate labels and flags," she declared. Then she added: "What is it you suppose on Mr. Robinson's part?—for you must suppose something."

"Well, that he may have drawn some accursed lot to do some idiotic thing—something in which even he himself doesn't believe."

"I haven't an idea of what sort of thing you mean. But if he doesn't believe in it he can easily let it alone."

"Do you think he's a customer who will back out of a real vow?" the fiddler asked.

The Princess freely wondered. "One can never judge of people in that way till they're tested." And the next thing: "Haven't you even taken the trouble to question him?" 223

"What would be the use? He'd tell me nothing. It would be like a man giving notice when he's going to fight a duel."

She sat for some seconds in thought; she looked up at Mr. Vetch with a pitying, indulgent smile. "I'm sure you're worrying about a mere shadow; but that never prevents, does it? I still don't see exactly how I can help you."

"Do you want him to commit some atrocity, some mad infamy?" the old man appealed.

"My dear sir, I don't want him to do anything in all the wide world. I've not had the smallest connexion with any engagement of any kind that he may have entered into. Do me the honour to trust me," the Princess went on with a certain high dryness of tone. "I don't know what I've done to deprive myself of your confidence. Trust the young man a little too. He's a gentleman and will behave as a gentleman."

The fiddler rose from his chair, smoothing his hat silently with the cuff of his coat. He stood there, whimsical and piteous, as if the sense he had still something to urge mingled with that of his having received his dismissal and as if indeed both were tinged with the oddity of another idea. "That's exactly what I'm afraid of!" he returned. Then he added, continuing to look at her: "But he *must* be very fond of life."

The Princess took no notice of the insinuation contained in these words. "Leave him to me—leave him to me. I'm sorry for your anxiety, but it was very good of you to come to see me. That has been interesting, because you've been one of our friend's influences."

"Unfortunately yes! If it hadn't been for me he wouldn't have known Poupin, and if he hadn't known Poupin he wouldn't have known his chemical friend—what's his name?—Muniment." 224

"And has that done him harm, do you think?" the Princess asked. She had risen to her feet.

"Surely: that deep fellow has been the main source of his infection."

"I lose patience with you!" she made answer, turning away.

And indeed her visitor's persistence was irritating. He went on, lingering, his head thrust forward and his short arms, out at his sides, terminating in his hat and umbrella, which he held grotesquely and as if intended for emphasis or illustration: "I've supposed for a long time that it was either Muniment or you who had got him into his scrape. It was you I suspected most—much most; but if it isn't you it must be he."

"You had better go to him then!"

"Of course I'll go to him. I scarcely know him—I've seen him but once—but I'll speak my mind."

The Princess rang for her maid to usher Mr. Vetch out, but at the moment he laid his hand on the door of the room she checked him with a quick gesture. "Now that I think of it don't go, please, to Mr. Muniment. It will be better to leave him quiet. Leave him to me," she added with a softer smile.

"Why not, why not?" he pleaded. And as she couldn't tell him on the instant why not he asked: "Doesn't he know?"

"No, he doesn't know; he has nothing to do with it." She suddenly found herself desiring to protect Paul Muniment from the imputation that was in Mr. Vetch's mind—the imputation of an ugly responsibility; and though she was not a person who took the trouble to tell fibs this repudiation on his behalf issued from her lips before she could stay it. It was a result of the same desire, though 225 also an inconsequence, that she added: "Don't do that—you'll spoil everything!" She went to him suddenly eager, she herself opened the door for him. "Leave him to me—leave him to me," she continued persuasively, while the fiddler, gazing at her, dazzled and submissive, allowed himself to be wafted away. A thought that excited her had come to her with a bound, and after she had heard the house-door close behind Mr. Vetch she walked up and down the room half an hour, all restlessly, under possession of it. 227

BOOK FIFTH

XXXVIII

Hyacinth found, that winter, considerable occupation for his odd hours, his evenings and holidays and scraps of leisure, in putting in hand the books he had promised himself at Medley to enclose in covers worthy of the high station and splendour of the lady of his life—these brilliant attributes had not then been shuffled out of sight—and of the confidence and generosity she showed him. He had determined she should receive from him something of value, and took pleasure in thinking that after he was gone they would be passed from hand to hand as specimens of rare work, connoisseurs bending charmed heads over them, smiling and murmuring, handling them delicately. His invention stirred itself and he had a hundred admirable ideas, many of which he sat up late at night to execute. He used all his skill, and by this time his skill was of a very high order. Old Crook recognised it by raising the rates at which he was paid; and though it was not among the traditions of the proprietor of the establishment in Soho, who to the end wore the apron with his workmen, to scatter sweet speeches, our young man learned accidentally that several books he had given him to do had been carried off and placed on a shelf of treasures at the villa, where they were exhibited to the members of the Crookenden circle who came to tea on Sundays. Hyacinth himself 230 indeed was included in this company on a great occasion—invited to a musical party where he made the acquaintance of half-a-dozen Miss Crookendens, an acquaintance which consisted in his standing in a corner behind several broad-backed old ladies and watching the rotation, at the piano and the harp, of three or four of his employer's thick-fingered daughters. "You know it's a tremendously musical house," said one of the old ladies to another (she called it "'ouse"); but the principal impression made upon him by the performance of the Miss Crookendens was that it was wonderfully different from the Princess's playing.

He knew he was the only young man from the shop who had been invited, not counting the foreman, who was sixty years old and wore a wig which constituted in itself a kind of social position, besides being accompanied by a little, frightened, furtive wife who closed her eyes, as if in the presence of a blinding splendour, when Mrs. Crookenden spoke to her. The Poupins were not there; which, however, was not a surprise to Hyacinth, who knew that—even if they had been asked, which they were not—they had objections of principle to putting their feet *chez les bourgeois*. They were not asked because, in spite of the place Eustache had made for himself in the prosperity of the business, it had come to be known that his wife was somehow not his wife—though she was certainly no one's else; and the evidence of this irregularity was conceived to reside vaguely in the fact that she had never been seen save in the laxity of a camisole. There had doubtless been an apprehension that if she had come to the villa she would not have come with the proper number of hooks and eyes—albeit Hyacinth, on two or three occasions, notably the night he took the pair to Mr. Vetch's theatre, had been witness of the proportions 231 to which she could reduce her figure when wishing to give the impression of a lawful tie.

It was not clear to him how the distinction conferred on him became known in Soho, where, however, it excited no sharpness of jealousy—Grugan, Roker and Hotchkin being hardly more likely to envy a person condemned to spend a genteel evening than they were to envy a monkey performing antics on a barrel-organ: both forms of effort indicated an urbanity painfully acquired. But Roker took his young comrade's breath half away with his elbow while remarking that he supposed he saw the old man had spotted him for one of the darlings at home—and while inquiring furthermore what would become in that case of the little thing he took to France, the one to whom he had stood champagne and lobster. This was the first allusion Hyacinth had heard made to the idea that he might some day marry his master's daughter, like the virtuous apprentice of tradition; but the suggestion somehow was not inspiring even when he had thought of an incident or two which gave colour to it. None of the Miss Crookendens spoke to him—they all had large faces and short legs and a comical resemblance to that elderly male with wide nostrils their father, and, unlike the Miss Marchants at Medley, they knew who he was; but their mother, who had on her head the plumage of a cockatoo mingled with a structure of glass beads, looked at him with an almost awful fixedness of charity and asked him three distinct times if he would have a glass of negus.

He had much difficulty in getting his books from the Princess; for when he reminded her of the promise she had given at Medley to make over to him as many volumes as he should require she answered that everything was changed since then, 232 that she was completely *dépouillée*, that she had now no pretension to have a library, and that in fine he had much better leave the matter alone. He was welcome to any books in the house, but, as he could see for himself, these were cheap editions, on which it would be foolish to expend such work as his. He asked Madame Grandoni to help him—to tell him at least if there were not some good volumes among the things the Princess had sent to be warehoused; it being known to him, through casual admissions of her own, that she had allowed her maid to save certain articles from the wreck and pack them away at the Pantechnicon. This had all been Assunta's work—the woman had begged so hard for a few reservations, a loaf of bread for their old days; but the

Princess herself had washed her hands of the job. "*Che, che*, there are boxes, I'm sure, in that place, with a little of everything," the old lady had said in answer to his inquiry; and Hyacinth had conferred with Assunta, who took a sympathetic, talkative, Italian interest in his undertaking and promised to fish out for him any block of printed matter that should remain. She arrived at his lodging one evening, in a cab, with an armful of pretty books, and when he asked her where they had come from waved her forefinger in front of her nose after a fashion at once evasive and expressive. He brought each volume to the Princess as it was finished, but her manner of receiving it was to shake her head over it with a kind, sad smile. "It's beautiful, I'm sure, but I've lost my sense for such things. Besides, you must always remember what you once told me, that a woman, even the most cultivated, is incapable of feeling the difference between a bad binding and a good. I remember your once saying that fine ladies had brought cobbled leather to your shop and wished it imitated. Certainly those are 233 not the differences I most feel. My dear fellow, such things have ceased to speak to me; they're doubtless charming, but they leave me cold. What will you have? One can't serve God and Mammon." Her thoughts were fixed on far other things than the delight of dainty covers, and she evidently considered that in caring so much for them Hyacinth resembled the mad emperor who fiddled in the flames of Rome. European society, to her mind, was in flames, and no frivolous occupation could give the measure of the emotion with which she watched them. It produced occasionally demonstrations of hilarity, of joy and hope, but these always took some form connected with the life of the people. It was the people she had gone to see when she accompanied Hyacinth to a music hall in the Edgeware Road, and all her excursions and pastimes this winter were prompted by her interest in the classes on whose behalf the fundamental change was to be wrought.

To ask himself if she were in earnest was now an old story to him, and indeed the conviction he might arrive at on this head had ceased to have any high importance. It was just as she was, superficial or profound, that she held him, and she was at any rate sufficiently animated by a purpose for her doings to have consequences actual and possible. Some of these might be serious even if she herself were shallow, and there were times when he was much visited by the apprehension of them. On the Sundays when she had gone with him into the darkest places, the most fetid holes in London, she had always taken money with her in considerable quantities and had always left it behind. She said very naturally that one couldn't go and stare at people for an impression without paying them, and she gave alms right and left, indiscriminately, without inquiry or judgement, as simply as the abbess of 234 some beggar-haunted convent or a lady-bountiful of the superstitious unscientific ages who should have hoped to be assisted to heaven by her doles. Hyacinth never said to her, though he sometimes thought it, that since she was so full of the modern spirit her charity should be administered according to the modern lights, the principles of economic science: partly because she wasn't a woman to be directed and regulated— she could take other people's meanings but could never take their forms. Besides, what did it matter? To himself what did it matter to-day whether he were drawn into right methods or into wrong ones, his time being too short for regret or for cheer? The Princess was an embodied passion—she was not a system: and her behaviour, after all, was more addressed to relieving herself than to relieving others. And then misery was sown so thick in her path that wherever her money was dropped it fell into some clutching palm. He wondered she should still have so much cash to dispose of till she explained that she came by it through putting her personal expenditure on a rigid footing. What she gave away was her savings, the margin she had succeeded in creating; and now that she had tasted of the satisfaction of making little hoards for such a purpose she regarded her other years, with their idleness and waste, their merely personal motives, as a long, stupid sleep of the conscience. To do something for others was not only so much more human—it was so much more amusing!

She made strange acquaintances under Hyacinth's conduct; she listened to extraordinary stories and formed theories about them, and about the persons who narrated them to her, which were often still more extraordinary. She took romantic fancies to vagabonds of either sex, attempted to establish social relations with them and was the cause of infinite 235 agitation to the gentleman who lived near her in the Crescent, who was always smoking at the window and who reminded our hero of Mr. Micawber. She received visits that were a scandal to the Crescent, and Hyacinth neglected his affairs, whatever they were, to see what tatterdemalion would next turn up at her door. This intercourse, it is true, took a more fruitful form as her intimacy with Lady Aurora deepened; her ladyship practised discriminations which she brought the Princess to recognise, and before the winter was over Mr. Robinson's services in the slums were found unnecessary. He gave way with relief, with delight, to Lady Aurora, for he had himself not in the least grasped the principle of his behaviour for the previous four months nor taken himself seriously as a *cicerone*. He had plunged into a sea of barbarism without having any civilising energy to put forth. He was aware the people were direfully wretched—more aware, it often seemed to him, than they themselves were; so frequently was he struck with their brutal insensibility, a grossness proof against the taste of better things and against any desire for them. He knew it so well that the repetition of contact could add no vividness to the conviction; it rather smothered and befogged his impression, peopled it with contradictions and difficulties, a violence of reaction, a sense of the inevitable and insurmountable. In these hours the poverty and ignorance of the multitude seemed so vast and preponderant, and so much the law of life, that those who had managed to escape from the black gulf were only the happy few, spirits of resource as well as children of luck: they inspired in some degree the interest and sympathy that one should feel for survivors and victors, those who have come safely out of a shipwreck or a battle. What was most in Hyacinth's mind was the idea, of which every <u>236</u> pulsation of the general life of his time was a syllable, that the flood of democracy was rising over the world; that it would sweep all the traditions of the past before it; that, whatever it might fail to bring, it would at least carry in its bosom a magnificent energy; and that it might be trusted to look after its own. When this high, healing, uplifting tide should cover the world and float in the new era, it would be its own fault (whose else?) if want and suffering and crime should continue to be ingredients of the human lot. With his mixed, divided nature, his conflicting sympathies, his eternal habit of swinging from one view to another, he regarded the prospect in different moods with different intensities. In spite of the example Eustache Poupin gave him of the reconcilement of disparities, he was afraid the democracy wouldn't care for perfect bindings or for the finer sorts of conversation. The Princess gave up these things in proportion as she advanced in the direction she had so audaciously chosen; and if the Princess could give them up it would take very transcendent natures to stick to them. At the same time there was joy and exultation in the thought of surrendering one's self to the wash of the wave, of being carried higher on the sun-touched crests of wild billows than one could ever be by a dry, lonely effort of one's own. That vision could deepen to ecstasy; make it indifferent if one's ultimate fate, in such a heaving sea, were not almost certainly to be submerged in bottomless depths or dashed to pieces on immovable rocks. Hyacinth felt that, whether his personal sympathy should rest finally with the victors or the vanquished, the victorious force was potentially infinite and would require no testimony from the irresolute.

The reader will doubtless smile at his mental debates and oscillations, and not understand why a <u>237</u> little bastard bookbinder should attach importance to his conclusions. They were not important for either cause, but they were important for himself—if only because they would rescue him from the torment of his present life, the perpetual, sore shock of the rebound. There was no peace for him between the two currents that flowed in his nature, the blood of his passionate, plebeian mother and that of his long-descended, supercivilised sire. They continued to toss him from one side to the other; they arrayed him in intolerable defiances and revenges against himself. He had a high ambition: he wanted neither more nor less than to get hold of the truth and wear it in his heart. He believed with the candour of youth that it is brilliant and clear-cut, like a royal diamond; but to whatever quarter he turned in the effort to find it he seemed to know that behind him, bent on him in reproach, was a tragic, wounded face. The thought of his mother had filled him with the vague, clumsy fermentation of his first impulses toward social criticism; but since the problem had become more complex by the fact that many things in the world as it was constituted were to grow intensely dear to him he had tried more and more to construct some conceivable and human countenance for his father— some expression of honour, of tenderness and recognition, of unmerited suffering, or at least of adequate expiation. To desert one of these presences for the other—that idea was the source of shame, as an act of treachery would have been; for he could almost hear the voice of his father ask him if it were the conduct of a gentleman to take up the opinions and emulate the crudities of fanatics and cads. He had quite got over holding that it would not have become his father to talk of what was proper to gentlemen, got over making the mental reflexion that from such a worthy's son at least the biggest 238 cad in London could not have deserved less consideration. He had worked himself round to allowances, to interpretations, to such hypotheses as the evidence in the *Times*, read in the British Museum on that never-to-be-forgotten afternoon, did not exclude. Though they had been frequent enough, and too frequent, his hours of hot resentment against the man who had attached to him the stigma he was to carry for ever, he threw himself, in other conditions and with a certain success, into the effort to find filial condonations and excuses. It was comparatively easy for him to accept himself as the son of a terribly light Frenchwoman; there seemed a deeper obloquy even than that in his having for his other parent a nobleman altogether wanting in nobleness. He was absolutely too poor to afford it. Sometimes, in imagination, he sacrificed one of the authors of his being to the other, throwing over Lord Frederick much the oftener; sometimes, when the theory failed that his father would have done great things for him if he had lived, or the assumption broke down that he had been Florentine Vivier's only lover, he cursed and disowned them alike; sometimes he arrived at conceptions which presented them side by side, looking at him with eyes infinitely sad but quite unashamed—eyes that seemed to tell him they had been surpassingly unfortunate but had not been base. Of course his worst moments now, as they had always been the worst, were those in which his grounds for holding that Lord Frederick had really been his father viciously fell away from him. It must be added that they always passed off, since the mixture in his tormenting, his incorrigible pulses could be accounted for by no other dream.

I mention these dim broodings not because they belong in an especial degree to the history of our young man during the winter of the Princess's residence 239 in Madeira Crescent, but because they were a constant element in his moral life and need to be remembered in any view of him at a given time. There were nights of November and December, as he trod the greasy pavements that lay between Westminster and Paddington, groping his way through the baffled lamplight and tasting the smoke-seasoned fog, when there was more happiness in his heart than he had ever known. The influence of his permeating London had closed over him again; Paris and Milan and Venice had shimmered away into reminiscence and picture; and as the great city which was most his own lay round him under her pall like an immeasurable breathing monster he felt with a vague excitement, as he had felt before, only now with more knowledge, that it was the richest expression of the life of man. His horizon had been immensely widened, but it was filled again by the expanse that sent dim night-gleams and strange, blurred reflexions and emanations into a sky without stars. He suspended, so to say, his small sensibility in the midst of it, to quiver there with joy and hope and ambition as well as with the effort of renunciation. The Princess's quiet fireside glowed with deeper assurances, with associations of intimacy, through the dusk and the immensity; the thought of it was with him always, and his relations with its mistress were more organised than they had been in his first vision of her. Whether or no it was better for the cause she cherished that she should have been reduced to her present simplicity, it was better at least for poor Mr. Robinson. It made her more near and him more free; and if there had been a danger of her nature's seeming really to take the tone of the vulgar things about her he would only have had to remember her as she was at Medley to restore the perspective. Her beauty 240 always appeared in truth to have the setting that best became it; her fairness made the element in which she lived and, among the meanest accessories, constituted a kind of splendour. Nature had emphasised the difficult, the deterrent, for her establishing properties in common with the horrible populace of London. Hyacinth used to smile at this pretension in his night-walks to Paddington or homeward; the populace of London were scattered upon his path, and he asked himself by what wizardry they could ever be raised to high participations. There were nights when every one he met appeared to reek with gin and filth and he found himself elbowed by figures as foul as lepers. Some of the women and girls in particular were appalling—saturated with alcohol and vice, brutal, bedraggled, obscene. "What remedy but another deluge, what alchemy but annihilation?" he asked himself as he went his way; and he wondered what fate there could be in the great scheme of things for a planet overgrown with such vermin, what redemption but to be hurled against a ball of consuming fire. If it was the fault of the rich, as Paul Muniment held, the selfish, congested rich who allowed such abominations to flourish, that made no difference and only shifted the shame; since the terrestrial globe, a visible failure, produced the cause as well as the effect.

It didn't occur to our young man that the Princess had withdrawn her confidence from him because, for the work of investigating still further the condition of the poor, she had placed herself in the hands of Lady Aurora. He could have no jealousy of the noble spinster; he had too much respect for her philanthropy, the thoroughness of her knowledge and her capacity to answer any question it could come into the Princess's extemporising head to ask, and too acute a consciousness of his own desultory 241 and superficial view of the great question. It was enough for him that the little parlour in Madeira Crescent was a spot round which his thoughts could revolve and toward which his steps could direct themselves with an unalloyed sense of security and privilege. The picture of it hung before him half the time in colours to which the feeling of the place gave a rarity that doubtless didn't literally characterise the scene. His relations with the Princess had long since ceased to appear to him to belong to the world of fable; they were as natural as anything else—everything in life was queer enough; he had by this time assimilated them, as it were, and they were an indispensable part of the happiness of each. "Of each"—Hyacinth risked that, for there was no particular vanity now involved in his perceiving that the most remarkable woman in Europe was simply quite fond of him. The quiet, familiar, fraternal welcome he found on the nasty winter nights was proof enough of that. They sat together like very old friends whom long pauses, during which they merely looked at each other with kind, acquainted eyes, couldn't make uncomfortable. Not that the element of silence was the principal part of their conversation, for it interposed only when they had talked a great deal. Hyacinth, on the opposite side of the fire, felt at times almost as if he were married to his hostess, so many things were taken for granted between them. For intercourse of that sort, intimate, easy, humorous, circumscribed by drawn curtains and shaded lamplight, interfused with domestic embarrassments and confidences that all turned to the jocular, the Princess was incomparable. It was her theory of her present existence that she was picnicking, but all the accidents of the business were happy accidents. There was a household quietude in her steps and gestures, in the way she sat, in the 242 way she listened, in the way she played with the cat or looked after the fire or folded Madame Grandoni's ubiquitous shawl; above all in the inveteracy with which she spent her evenings at home, never dining out nor going to parties, ignorant of the dissipations of the town. There was something in the isolation of the room when the kettle was on the hob and he had given his wet umbrella to the maid and his friend had made him sit in a certain place near the fire, the better to dry his shoes—there was something that evoked the idea of the *vie de province* he had read about in French fiction. The French term came to him because it represented more the especial note of the Princess's company, the cultivation, the facility, of talk. She expressed herself often in the French tongue itself; she could borrow that convenience for certain shades of meaning, though she had told Hyacinth she had her own intenser Latin view of the people to whom it was native. Certainly the strain of her discourse was not provincial; her talk was singularly free and unabashed; there was nothing one mightn't say to her or that she was not liable to say herself. She had cast off prejudices and gave no heed to conventional danger-posts. Hyacinth admired the movement—his eyes seemed to see it—with which in any direction, intellectually, she could fling open her windows. There was an extraordinary charm in this mixture of liberty and humility—in seeing a creature capable socially of immeasurable flights sit dove-like and with folded wings.

The young man met Lady Aurora several times in Madeira Crescent—her days, like his own, were filled with work, so that she came in the evening—and he knew that her friendship with the Princess had arrived at a rich maturity. The two ladies were a source of almost rapturous interest to each other, each rejoicing that the other was not a bit different. 243 The Princess prophesied freely that her visitor would give her up—all nice people did very soon; but to the acuteness of our hero's observation the end of her ladyship's almost breathless enthusiasm was not yet in view. She was bewildered but was fascinated; she thought her foreign friend not only the most distinguished, the most startling, the most edifying and the most original person in the world, but the most amusing and the most delightful to have tea with. As for that personage herself her sentiment about Lady Aurora was the same Hyacinth's had been: she held her a saint, the first she had ever seen, and the purest specimen conceivable; as good in her way as Saint Francis of Assisi, as tender and quaint and transparent, of a spirit of charity as sublime. She felt that when one met a human flower as fresh as that in the dusty ways of the world one should pluck it and wear it; and she was always inhaling Lady Aurora's fragrance, always kissing her and holding her hand. The spinster was frightened at her generosity, at the way her imagination embroidered; she wanted to convince her—as the Princess did on her own side—that such exaggerations destroyed their unfortunate subject. The Princess delighted in her clothes, in the way she put them on and wore them, in the economies she practised in order to have money for charity and the ingenuity with which these slender resources were made to go far—in the very manner in which she spoke, a kind of startled simplicity. She wished to emulate her in all these particulars; to learn how to economise still more cunningly, to get her bonnets at the same shop, to care as little for the fit of her gloves, to ask in the same tone, "Isn't it a bore Susan Crotty's husband has got a ticket-of-leave?" She said Lady Aurora made her feel like a French milliner and that if there was anything 244 in the world she loathed it was a French milliner. Each of these persons was powerfully affected by the other's idiosyncrasies, and each wanted the other to remain as she was while she herself should be transformed into the image of her friend.

One night, going to Madeira Crescent a little later than usual, Hyacinth met the pilgrim from Belgrave Square just leaving the house. She had a different air from any he had seen in her before; appeared flushed and even a little agitated, as if she had been learning a piece of bad news. She said, "Oh how do you do?" with her customary quick, vague laugh, but she went her way without stopping to talk. Three minutes later he mentioned to the Princess that he had encountered her, and this lady replied: "It's a pity you didn't come a little sooner. You'd have assisted at a scene."

"At a scene?" he repeated, not understanding what violence could have taken place between mutual adorers.

"She made me a scene of tears, of earnest remonstrance—perfectly well meant, I needn't tell you. She thinks I'm going too far."

"I imagine you tell her things you don't tell me," Hyacinth said.

"Oh you, my dear fellow!" his hostess murmured. She spoke absent-mindedly, as if she were thinking of what had passed with Lady Aurora and as if the futility of telling things to Mr. Robinson had become a commonplace.

There was no annoyance for him in this, his pretension to keep pace with her "views" being quite extinct. The tone they now for the most part took with each other was one of mutual derision, of shrugging commiseration for lunacy on the one hand and pusillanimity on the other. In discussing with her he exaggerated deliberately, went fantastic 245 lengths in the way of reaction, a point where it was their habit and their amusement to hurl all manner of denunciation at each other's head. They had given up serious discussion altogether and when not engaged in bandying, in the spirit of burlesque, the amenities I have mentioned, talked for a compromise of matters as to which it couldn't occur to them to differ. There were evenings when she did nothing but relate her life and all she had seen of humanity, from her earliest years, in a variety of countries. If evil appearances seemed mainly to have been presented to her view this didn't diminish the interest and vividness of her reminiscences, nor her power, the greatest Hyacinth had ever encountered, of light mimetic, dramatic evocation. She was irreverent and invidious, but she made him hang on her lips; and when she regaled him with anecdotes of foreign courts—he delighted to know how monarchs lived and conversed—there was often for hours together nothing to indicate that she would have liked to get into a conspiracy and he would have liked to get out of one. Nevertheless his mind was by no means exempt from wonder as to what she was really doing in such holes and in what queer penalties she might find herself landed. When he questioned her she wished to know by what title, with his sentiments, he pretended to inquire. He did so but little, not being himself altogether convinced of the validity of his warrant; but on an occasion when she had challenged him he replied, smiling and hesitating: "Well, I must say it seems to me that from what I've told you it ought to strike you I've rather a title."

"You mean your famous pledge to 'act' on demand? Oh that will never come to anything."

"Why won't it come to anything?"

"It's too absurd, it's too vague. It's like some silly humbug in a novel."
246

"*Vous me rendez la vie!*" Hyacinth said theatrically.

"You won't have to do it," she went on.

"I think you mean I won't do it. I've offered at least. Isn't that a title?"

"Well then you won't do it," said the Princess; after which they looked at each other a couple of minutes in silence.

"You will, I think, at the pace you're going," the young man resumed.

"What do you know about the pace? You're not worthy to know!"

He did know, however; that is he knew her to be in communication with strange birds of passage, to have, or to believe she had, irons on the fire, to hold in her hand some of the strings that are pulled in great movements. She received letters that made Madame Grandoni watch her askance, of which, though she knew nothing of their contents and had only her general suspicions and her scent for disaster, now dismally acute, the old woman had spoken more than once to Hyacinth. Madame Grandoni had begun to have sombre visions of the interference of the police: she was haunted with the idea of a search for compromising papers; of being dragged herself, as an accomplice in direful plots, into a court of justice, possibly into a prison. "If she would only burn—if she would only burn! But she keeps—I know she keeps!" she groaned to Hyacinth in her helpless gloom. He could only guess what it might be she kept; asking himself if she were seriously entangled, were being really exploited by plausible outlaws, predatory adventurers who counted on her getting frightened at a given moment and offering hush-money to be allowed to slip out—out of a complicity which they themselves of course would never have taken seriously; or were merely coquetting 247 with paper schemes, giving herself cheap sensations, discussing preliminaries that could have no second stage.

It would have been easy for him to smile at her impression that she was "in it," and to conclude that even the cleverest women fail to know when they are futile, had not the vibration remained which had been imparted to his nerves two years before and of which he had spoken to his hostess at Medley—the sense, vividly kindled and never quenched, that the forces secretly arrayed against the present social order were pervasive and universal, in the air one breathed, in the ground one trod, in the hand of an acquaintance that one might touch or the eye of a stranger that might rest a moment on one's own. They were above, below, within, without, in every contact and combination of life; and it was no disproof of them to say it was too odd they should lurk in a particular, improbable form. To lurk in improbable forms was precisely their strength, and they would doubtless have still queerer features to show than this of the Princess's being a genuine participant even when she most flattered herself she was.

"You do go too far," he none the less said to her the evening Lady Aurora had passed him at the door.

To which she answered: "Of course I do—that's exactly what I mean. How else does one know one has gone far enough? That poor, dear woman's an angel, yet isn't in the least in it," she added in a moment. She would give him no further satisfaction on the subject; when he pressed her she asked if he had brought the copy of Browning he had promised the last time. If he had he was to sit down and read it to her. In such a case as this Hyacinth had no disposition to insist; he was glad enough not to talk about the everlasting nightmare. He took *Men and Women* from his pocket and read aloud for twenty 248 minutes; but on his making some remark on one of the poems at the end of this time he noted that his companion had paid no attention. When he charged her with this levity she only replied, looking at him musingly: "How *can* one, after all, go too far? That's the word of cowards."

"Do you mean her ladyship's a coward?"

"Yes, in not having the courage of her opinions, of her conclusions. The way the English can go half-way to a thing and then stick in the middle!" the Princess exclaimed impatiently.

"That's not your fault, certainly!" said Hyacinth. "But it seems to me Lady Aurora, for herself, goes pretty far."

"We're all afraid of some things and brave about others," his friend pursued.

"The thing Lady Aurora's most afraid of is the Princess Casamassima," Hyacinth returned.

His companion looked at him but wouldn't take this up. "There's one particular in which she would be very brave. She'd marry her friend—your friend—Mr. Muniment."

"Marry him, do you think?"

"What else pray?" the Princess asked. "She adores the ground he walks on."

"And what would Belgrave Square and Inglefield and all the rest of it say?"

"What do they say already and how much does it make her swerve? She'd do it in a moment, and it would be fine to see it, it would be magnificent," said the Princess, kindling, as she was apt to kindle at the idea of any great, free stroke.

"That certainly wouldn't be a case of what you call sticking in the middle," Hyacinth declared.

"Ah it wouldn't be a matter of logic; it would be a matter of passion. When it's a question of that the English, to do them justice, don't stick!" 249

This speculation of the Princess's was by no means new to Hyacinth, and he had not thought it heroic, after all, that their high-strung associate should feel herself capable of sacrificing her family, her name, and the few habits of gentility that survived in her life, of making herself a scandal, a fable and a nine days' wonder, for Muniment's sake: the young chemical expert being, to his mind, as we know, exactly the type of man who produced convulsions, made ruptures and renunciations easy. But it was less clear to him what opinions Muniment himself might hold on the subject of a union with a young woman who should have come out of her class for him. He would marry some day, evidently, because he would do all the natural, human, productive things; but for the present he had business on hand which would be likely to pass first. Besides—Hyacinth had seen him give evidence of this—he didn't think people could really come out of their class; he believed the stamp of one's origin ineffaceable and that the best thing one can do is to wear it and fight for it. Hyacinth could easily imagine how it would put him out to be mixed up closely with a person who, like Lady Aurora, was fighting on the wrong side. "She can't marry him unless he asks her, I suppose—and perhaps he won't," he reflected.

"Yes, perhaps he won't," said the Princess thoughtfully. 250

XXXIX

On Saturday afternoons Paul Muniment was able to leave his work at four o'clock, and on one of these occasions, some time after his visit to Madeira Crescent, he came into Rosy's room at about five, carefully dressed and brushed and ruddy with the freshness of an abundant washing. He stood at the foot of her sofa with a conscious smile, knowing how she chaffed him when his necktie was new; and after a moment, during which she ceased singing to herself as she twisted the strands of her long black hair together and let her eyes travel over his whole person, inspecting every detail, she said to him: "My dear Mr. Muniment, you're going to see the Princess."

"Well, have you anything to say against it?" Mr. Muniment asked.

"Not a word; you know I like princesses. But *you* have."

"Well, my girl, I'll not speak it to you," the young man returned. "There's something to be said against everything if you give yourself trouble enough."

"I should be very sorry if ever anything was said against my big brother."

"The man's a sneak who's only and always praised," Paul lucidly remarked. "If you didn't hope to be finely abused where would be the encouragement?" 251

"Ay, but not with reason," said Rosy, who always brightened to an argument.

"The better the reason the greater the incentive to expose one's self. However, you won't hear of it—if people do heave bricks at me."

"I won't hear of it? Pray don't I hear of everything? I should like any one to keep anything from *me!*" And Miss Muniment gave a toss of her recumbent head.

"There's a good deal I keep from you, my dear," said Paul rather dryly.

"You mean there are things I don't want, I don't take any trouble, to know. Indeed and indeed there are: things I wouldn't hear of for the world—that no amount of persuasion would induce me, not if you were to go down on your knees. But if I did, if I did, I promise you that just as I lie here I should have them all in my pocket. Now there are others," the young woman went on, "there are special points on which you'll just be so good

- 163 -

as to enlighten me. When the Princess asked you to come and see her you refused and wanted to know what good it would do. I hoped you'd go then; I should have liked you to go, because I wanted to know how she lived and whether she really had things handsome or only in the poor way she said. But I didn't push you, because I couldn't have told you what good it would do you: that was only the good it would have done me. At present I've heard everything from Lady Aurora and that it's all quite decent and tidy— though not really like a princess a bit—and that she knows how to turn everything about and put it best end foremost, just as I do, like, though I oughtn't to say it, no doubt. Well, you've been, and more than once, and I've had nothing to do with it; of which I'm very glad now, for reasons you perfectly know—you're too honest a man to pretend you don't. 252 Therefore when I see you going again I just inquire of you, as you inquired of her, what good *does* it do you?"

"I like it—I like it, my dear," said Paul with his fresh, unembarrassed smile.

"I daresay you do. So should I in your place. But it's the first time I have heard you express the idea that we ought to do everything we like."

"Why not, when it doesn't hurt any one else?"

"Oh Mr. Muniment, Mr. Muniment!" Rosy exclaimed with exaggerated solemnity, holding up at him a straight, attenuated forefinger. Then she added: "No, she doesn't do you good, that beautiful, brilliant woman."

"Give her time, my dear—give her time," said Paul, looking at his watch.

"Of course you're impatient, but you *must* hear me. I've no doubt she'll wait for you—you won't lose your turn. But what would you do, please, if any one was to break down altogether?"

"My bonnie lassie," the young man returned, "if *you* only keep going I don't care who fails."

"Oh I shall keep going, if it's only to look after my friends and get justice for them," said Miss Muniment—"the delicate, sensitive creatures who require support and protection. Have you really forgotten that we've such a one as that?"

The young man walked to the window with his hands in his pockets and looked out at the fading light. "Why does she go herself then, if she doesn't like her?"

Rose Muniment hesitated a moment. "Well, I'm glad I'm not a man!" she broke out. "I think a woman on her back's sharper than a man on his two legs. And you such a wonderful one too!"

"You're all too sharp for me, my dear. If she goes—and twenty times a week too—why shouldn't I 253 go once in ever so long? Especially as I like her and Lady Aurora doesn't."

"Lady Aurora doesn't? Do you think she'd be guilty of hypocrisy? Lady Aurora delights in her; she won't let me say that she's fit to dust the Princess's shoes. I needn't tell *you* how she goes down before them she likes. And I don't believe you care a button; you've something in your head, some wicked game or other, that you think she can hatch for you."

At this he turned round and looked at her a moment, smiling still and whistling just audibly. "Why shouldn't I care? Ain't I soft, ain't I susceptible?"

"I never thought I should hear you ask that—after what I've seen these four years. For four years she has come, and it's all for you—as well it might be; yet with your never showing any more sense of what she'd be willing to do for you than if you had been that woollen cat on the hearthrug!"

"What would you like me to do? Would you like me to hang round her neck and hold her hand the same as you do?" Muniment asked.

"Yes, it would do me good, I can tell you. It's better than what I see— the poor lady getting spotted and dim like a mirror that wants rubbing."

"How the devil am I to rub her?" Muniment quaintly asked. "You know a good deal, Rosy, but you don't know everything," he pursued with a face that gave no sign of seeing a reason in what she said. "Your mind's too poetical—as full of sounding strings and silver chords as some old, elegant harp. There's nothing in the world I should care for that her ladyship would be willing to do for me."

"She'd marry you at a day's notice—she'd do that for you."

"I shouldn't care a hang for that. Besides, if I 254 was to lay it before her she'd never come into the place again. And I shouldn't care for that— for you."

"Never mind me; I'll take the risk!" cried Rosy with high cheer.

"But what's to be gained if I can have her for you without any risk?"

"You won't have her for me or for any one when she's dead of a broken heart."

"Dead of a broken tea-cup!" said the young man; "And pray what should we live on when you had got us set up?—the three of us without counting the kids."

He evidently was arguing from pure good nature and not in the least from curiosity; but his sister replied as eagerly as if he would be floored by her answer: "Hasn't she got a hundred a year of her own? Don't I know every penny of her affairs?"

Paul gave no sign of any inward judgement passed on Rosy's conception of the delicate course or of a superior policy; perhaps indeed, for it is perfectly possible, her question didn't strike him as having a mixture of motives. He only said with a small, pleasant, patient sigh: "I don't want the dear old girl's money."

His sister, in spite of her eagerness, waited twenty seconds; then she flashed at him: "Pray do you like the Princess's better?"

"If I did there'd be much more of it," he quietly returned.

"How can she marry you? Hasn't she got a husband?" Rosy cried.

"Lord, how you give me away!" laughed her brother. "Daughters of earls, wives of princes—I've only to pick."

"I don't speak of the Princess so long as there's a Prince. But if you haven't seen that Lady Aurora's a beautiful, wonderful exception and quite unlike any <u>255</u> one else in all the wide world—well, all I can say is that *I* have."

"I thought it was your opinion," Paul objected, "that the swells should remain swells and the high ones keep their place."

"And pray would she lose hers if she were to marry you?"

"Her place at Inglefield certainly," he answered as lucidly as if his sister could never tire him with any insistence or any minuteness.

"Hasn't she lost that already? Does she ever go there?"

"Surely you appear to think so from the way you always question her about it."

"Well, they think her so mad already that they can't think her any madder," Rosy continued. "They've given her up, and if she were to marry you———"

"If she were to marry me they wouldn't touch her with a ten-foot pole," Paul broke in.

She flinched a moment, then said serenely: "Oh I don't care for that!"

"You ought to, to be consistent, though possibly she shouldn't, admitting that she wouldn't. You've more imagination than logic—which of course for a woman is quite right. That's what makes you say that her ladyship's in affliction because I go to a place she herself goes to without the least compulsion."

"She goes to keep you off," said Rosy with decision.

"To keep me off?"

"To interpose with the Princess—and in a sense to interfere against her. To be nice to her and conciliate her, so she mayn't take you."

"Has she told you any such rigmarole as that?" Paul inquired, this time staring a little. 256

"Do I need to be told things to know them? I'm not a fine, strong, superior male; therefore I can discover them for myself," Rosy answered with a dauntless little laugh and a light in her eyes which might indeed have made it appear she was capable of wizardry.

"You make her out at once too passionate and too calculating," the young man returned. "She has no personal feelings, she wants nothing for herself. She only wants one thing in the world—to make the poor a little less poor."

"Precisely; and she regards you, a helpless, blundering bachelor, as one of them."

"She knows I'm not helpless so long as you're about the place, and that my blunders don't matter so long as you correct them."

"She wants to assist me to assist you then!" the girl exclaimed with the levity with which her earnestness was always interfused: it was a spirit that seemed of a sudden, in argument, to mock at her own contention. "Besides, isn't that the very thing you want to bring about?" she went on. "Isn't that what you're plotting and working and waiting for? She wants to throw herself into it—to work with you."

"My dear girl, she doesn't understand a pennyworth of what I think. She couldn't if she would."

"And no more do I, I suppose you mean."

"No more do you; but with you it's different. If you would you could. However, it matters little who understands and who doesn't, for all there happens to be of it. I'm not doing much, you know."

Rosy lay there looking up at him. "It must be pretty thick when you talk that way. However, I don't care what you bring on, for I know I shall be looked after."

"Nothing's going to happen—nothing's going to happen," Paul remarked simply. 257

Her rejoinder to this was to say in a moment: "You've a different tone since you've taken up the Princess."

She spoke with a certain severity, but he broke out as if he hadn't heard her: "I like your idea of the female aristocracy quarrelling over a dirty brute like me."

"I don't know how dirty you are, but I know you smell of soap," said his sister inexorably. "They won't quarrel; that's not the way they do it. Yes, you're taking a different tone for some purpose I can't discover just yet."

"What do you mean by that? When did I ever take a tone?" Paul demanded.

"Why then do you speak as if you weren't remarkable, immensely remarkable—more remarkable than anything any one, male or female, good or bad, of the aristocracy or of the vulgar sort, can ever do for you?"

"What on earth have I ever done to show it?" he asked as with amusement.

"Oh I don't know your secrets, and that's one of them. But we're out of the common beyond any one, you and I, and between ourselves, with the door fastened, we might as well admit it."

"I admit it for you with all my heart!" the young man promptly laughed.

"Well then if I admit it for you that's all that's required."

The pair considered themselves a while in silence, as if each were tasting agreeably the distinction the other conferred; then Muniment said: "If I'm such an awfully superior chap why shouldn't I behave in keeping?"

"Oh you do, you do!"

"For all that you don't like it."

"It isn't so much what you do. It's what *she* does." 258

"How do you mean, what she does?"

"She makes Lady Aurora suffer."

"Oh I can't go into that," said Paul. "A man feels such a muff, talking about the women who 'suffer' for him."

"Well, if they do it I think a man might bear it!" Rosy retorted. "That's what a man *is*. When it comes to being sorry, oh that's too ridiculous!"

"There are plenty of things in the world I'm sorry for," he patiently conceded. "One of them is that you should keep me gossiping here when I want to go out."

"Oh I don't care if I worry her a little. Does she do it on purpose?" Rosy continued.

"You ladies must settle all that together"—and he rubbed his hat with the cuff of his coat. It was a new one, the bravest he had ever possessed, and in a moment he put it on his head as if to re-enforce his reminder to his sister that it was time she should release him.

"Well, you do look genteel," she said with high complacency. "No wonder she has lost her head! I mean the Princess," she explained. "You never went to any such expense for her ladyship."

"My dear, the Princess is worth it, she's worth it." Which appeared at last on his part all seriously spoken.

"Will she help you very much?" Rosy demanded, as at the touch of it, with a strange, sudden transition to eagerness.

"Well," said Paul, "that's rather what I look for."

She threw herself forward on her sofa with a movement that was rare with her and, shaking her clasped hands, exclaimed: "Then go off, go off quickly!"

He came round and kissed her as if he were not more struck than usual with her freakish inconsistency. 259 "It's not bad to have a little person at home who wants a fellow to succeed."

"Oh I know they'll look after me." And she sank back on her pillow with an air of agreeable security.

He was aware that whenever she said "they," without further elucidation, she meant the populace surging up in his rear, and he met it with his usual ease. "I don't think we'll leave it much to 'them.'"

"No it's not much you'll leave to them, I'll be bound."

He gave a louder laugh at this and said: "You're the deepest of the lot, Miss Muniment."

Her eyes kindled at his praise and as she rested them on his own she brought out: "Ah I pity the poor Princess too, you know!"

"Well now, I'm not conceited, but I don't," Paul returned, passing in front of the little mirror on the mantel-shelf.

"Yes, you'll succeed, and so shall I—but *she* won't," Rosy went on.

He stopped a moment with his hand on the latch of the door and said gravely, almost sententiously: "She's not only handsome, handsome as a picture, but she's uncommon sharp and has taking ways beyond anything ever known."

"I know her ways," his sister replied. Then as he left the room she called after him: "But I don't care for anything so long as you become prime minister of England!"

Three-quarters of an hour after this he knocked at the door in Madeira Crescent, and was immediately ushered into the parlour, where the Princess, in her bonnet and mantle, sat alone. She made no movement as he came in; she only looked up at him with a smile.

"You're braver than I gave you credit for," she said in her rich voice.
260

"I shall learn to be brave if I associate a while longer with you. But I shall never cease to be shy," Muniment added, standing there and looking tall in the middle of the small room. He cast his eyes about him for a place to sit down, but she gave him no help to choose; she only watched him in silence from her own place, her hands quietly folded in her lap. At last, when without remonstrance from her he had selected the most uncomfortable chair in the room, she replied:

"That's only another name for desperate courage. I put on my things on the chance, but I didn't expect you."

"Well, here I am—that's the great thing," he said good-humouredly.

"Yes, no doubt it's a very great thing. But it will be a still greater thing when you're there."

"I'm afraid you hope too much," the young man observed. "Where is it? I don't think you told me."

The Princess drew a small folded letter from her pocket and, without saying anything, held it out to him. He got up to take it from her, opened it and as he read it remained standing in front of her. Then he went straight to the fire and thrust the paper into it. At this act she rose quickly, as to save the document, but the expression of his face while he turned round to her made her stop. The smile that came into her own was a little forced. "What are you afraid of?" she asked. "I take it the house is known. If we go I suppose we may admit that we go."

Paul's face showed he had been annoyed, but he answered quietly enough: "No writing—no writing."

"You're terribly careful," said the Princess.

"Careful of you—yes."

She sank upon her sofa again, asking her companion 261 to ring for tea; they would do much better to have it before going out. When the order had been given she went on: "I see I shall have much less keen emotion than when I acted by myself."

"Is that what you go in for—keen emotion?"

"Surely, Mr. Muniment. Don't you?"

"God forbid! I hope to have as little of any sort as possible."

"Of course one doesn't want any vague rodomontade, one wants to do something. But it would be hard if one couldn't have a little pleasure by the way."

"My pleasure's in keeping very cool," Muniment said.

"So is mine. But it depends on how you understand it. I like quietness in the midst of a tumult."

"You've rare ideas about tumults. They're not good in themselves."

The Princess considered this a moment. "I wonder if you're too prudent. I shouldn't like that. If it's made an accusation against you that you've been—where we're going—shall you deny it?"

"With that prospect it would be simpler not to go at all, wouldn't it?" he lucidly asked.

"Which prospect do you mean? That of being found out or that of having to lie?"

"I suppose that if you lie well enough you're not found out." And he spoke again as for amusement.

"You won't take me seriously," said the Princess—and without irritation, without resentment, with accepted, intelligent sadness. Yet there was a fineness of reproach in the tone in which she added: "I don't believe you want to go at all."

"Why else should I have come—especially if I don't take you seriously?"

"That has never been a reason for a man's not going to see a woman," said the Princess. "It's usually a reason in favour of it." 262

Paul turned his steady eyes over the room, looking from one article of furniture to another: this was a way he had when engaged in a discussion, and it suggested not so much his reflecting on what his interlocutor said as that his thoughts were pursuing a bravely independent course. Presently he took up her remark. "I don't know that I quite understand what you mean by that question of taking a woman seriously."

"Ah you're very perfect!" she lightly wailed. "Don't you consider that the changes you look for will be also for our benefit?"

"I don't think they'll alter your position."

"If I didn't hope for that I wouldn't do anything," said the Princess.

"Oh I've no doubt you'll do a great deal."

The young man's companion was silent for some minutes, during which he also was content to say nothing. "I wonder you can find it in your conscience to work with me," she observed at last.

"It isn't in my conscience I find it," he laughed.

The maid-servant brought in the tea, and while his hostess made a place for it on a table beside her she returned: "Well, I don't care, for I think I have you in my power."

"You've every one in your power," Paul declared.

"Every one's no one," she answered rather dryly; and a moment later she said to him: "That extraordinary little sister of yours—surely you take *her* seriously?"

"I'm particularly fond of her, if that's what you mean. But I don't think her position will ever be altered."

"Are you alluding to her position in bed? If you consider that she'll never recover her health," the Princess said, "I'm very sorry to hear it."

"Oh her health will do. I mean that she'll continue 263 to be, like all the most amiable women, just a kind of ornament to life."

She had already noted that he pronounced amiable "emiable"; but she had accepted this peculiarity of her visitor in the spirit of imaginative transfiguration in which she had accepted several others. "To *your* life of course. She can hardly be said to be an ornament to her own."

"Her life and mine are all one."

"She's a prodigious person"—the Princess dismissed her. But while he drank his tea she remarked that for a revolutionist he was certainly prodigious as well; and he wanted to know in answer if it weren't rather in keeping for revolutionists to be revolutionary. He drank three cups, declaring his hostess's decoction rare; it was better even than Lady Aurora's. This led him to observe as he put down his third cup, looking round the room again lovingly, almost covetously: "You've got everything so handy I don't see what interest you can have."

"How do you mean, what interest?"

"In getting in so uncommon deep."

The light in her face flashed on the instant into pure passion. "Do you consider that I'm in—really far?"

"Up to your neck, ma'am."

"And do you think that *il y va* of my neck—I mean that it's in danger?" she translated eagerly.

"Oh I understand your French. Well, I'll look after you," Muniment said.

"Remember then definitely that I expect not to lie."

"Not even for me?" Then he added in the same familiar tone, which was not rough nor wanting in respect, but only homely and direct, suggestive of growing acquaintance: "If I was your husband I'd come and take you away." 264

"Please don't speak of my husband," she returned gravely. "You've no qualification for doing so. You know nothing whatever about him."

"I know what Hyacinth has told me."

"Oh Hyacinth!" she sighed impatiently. There was another silence of some minutes, not disconnected apparently from this reference to the little bookbinder; but when Muniment spoke after the interval it was not to carry on the allusion.

"Of course you think me very plain and coarse."

"Certainly you've not such a nice address as Hyacinth"—the Princess had no wish, on her side, to evade the topic. "But that's given to very few," she added; "and I don't know that pretty manners are exactly what we're working for."

"Ay, it won't be very endearing when we cut down a few allowances," her visitor concurred. "But I want to please you; I want to be as much as possible like Hyacinth," he went on.

"That's not the way to please me. I don't forgive him—he's very foolish."

"Ah don't say that; he's a fine little flute!" Paul protested.

"He's a delightful nature, with extraordinary qualities. But he's deplorably conventional."

"Yes, if you talk about taking things seriously—*he* takes them so," Muniment again agreed.

"Has he ever told you his life?" the Princess asked.

"He hasn't required to tell me. I've seen a good bit of it."

"Yes, but I mean before you knew him."

Paul thought. "His birth and his poor mother? I think it was Rosy told me all that."

"And pray how did *she* know?"

"Ah when you come to the way Rosy knows——!" He gave that up. "She doesn't like people in such <u>265</u> a box at all. She thinks we ought all to be grandly born."

"Then they agree, for so does poor Hyacinth." The Princess had a pause, after which, as with a deep effort: "I want to ask you something. Have you had a visit from Mr. Vetch?"

"The old gentleman who fiddles? No, he has never done me that honour."

"It was because I prevented him then. I told him to leave it to me."

"To leave what now?" And Paul looked out in placid perplexity.

"He's in great distress about Hyacinth—about the danger he runs. You know what I mean."

"Yes, I know what you mean," Muniment answered slowly. "But where does *he* come in? I thought it was supposed to be a grand secret."

"So it is. He doesn't know anything; he only suspects."

"How do *you* know then?"

She had another wait. "Oh I'm like Rosy—I find out. Mr. Vetch, as I suppose you're aware, has been near Hyacinth all his life; he takes a most affectionate interest in him. He believes there's something hanging over him and wants it to be made impossible." She paused afresh, but her visitor made no response and she continued: "He was going to see you, to beg you to do something, to interfere; he seemed to suppose your power in such a matter would be very great. But as I tell you, I requested him—a particular favour to me—to let you alone."

"What favour would it be to you?" Muniment asked.

"It would give me the satisfaction of feeling you not worried."

He appeared struck with the curious inadequacy of this explanation, considering what was at stake; 266 so that he confessed to almost rude amusement. "That was considerate of you beyond everything."

"It was not meant as consideration for you; it was a piece of calculation." Having made this statement the Princess gathered up her gloves and turned away, walking to the chimney-piece, where she stood arranging her bonnet-ribbons in the mirror with which it was decorated. Paul watched her with clear curiosity; in spite both of his inaccessibility to nervous agitation and of the general scepticism he had cultivated about her he was not proof against her faculty of creating a feeling of suspense, a tension of interest, on the part of those involved with her. He followed her movements, but plainly didn't follow her calculations, so that he could only listen more attentively when she brought out suddenly: "Do you know why I asked you to come and see me? Do you know why I went to see your sister? It was all a plan," said the Princess.

"We hoped it was just an ordinary, humane, social impulse," the young man returned.

"It was humane, it was even social, but it was not ordinary. I wanted to save Hyacinth."

"To save him?"

"I wanted to be able to talk with you just as I'm talking now."

"That was a fine idea!" Paul candidly cried.

"I've an exceeding, a quite inexpressible regard for him. I've no patience with some of his opinions, and that's why I permitted myself to say just now that he's silly. But after all the opinions of our friends are not what we love them for—so I don't see why they should be a ground of aversion. Robinson's nature is singularly generous and his intelligence very fine, though there *are* things he muddles up. You just now expressed strongly your own interest in him; therefore we ought to be perfectly 267 agreed. Agreed I mean about getting him out of his scrape."

Muniment had the air of a man feeling he must consider a little before assenting to these successive propositions; it being a limitation of his intellect that he couldn't respond without understanding. After a moment he answered, referring to his hostess's last remark, in which the others appeared to culminate, and at the same time shaking his head with a rise of his strong eyebrows: "His scrape isn't important."

"You thought it was when you got him into it."

"I thought it would give him pleasure."

"That's not a reason for letting people do what isn't good for them."

"I wasn't thinking so much about what would be good for him as about what would be bad for some others. He can do as he likes."

"That's easy to say. They must be persuaded not to call him."

"Persuade them then, dear madam."

"How can I persuade them?" she cried. "If I could do that I wouldn't have approached you. I've no influence, and even if I had it my motives would be suspected. You're the one to come in."

"Shall I tell them he funks it?" Muniment asked.

"He doesn't—he doesn't!" she declared.

"On what ground then shall I put it?"

"Tell them he has changed his opinions."

"Wouldn't that be rather like denouncing him as a traitor—and doing it hypocritically?"

"Tell them then it's simply my wish."

"That won't do *you* much good," Paul said with his natural laugh.

"Will it put me in danger? That's exactly what I want."

"Yes; but as I understand you, you want to suffer *for* the people, not by them. You're very fond 268 of Robinson; it couldn't be otherwise," the young man argued. "But you ought to remember that in the line you've chosen our affections, our natural ties, our timidities, our shrinkings——" His voice had become low and grave, and he paused a little while the Princess's deep and lovely eyes, attaching themselves to his face, showed how quickly she had been affected by this unwonted adjuration. He spoke now as if he were taking her seriously. "All those things are as nothing, they must never weigh a feather, beside our service."

She began to draw on her gloves. "You're a most extraordinary man."

"That's what Rosy tells me."

"Why don't you do it yourself?"

"Do Hyacinth's job? Because it's better to do my own."

"And pray what *is* your own?"

"I don't know," said Paul Muniment with perfect equanimity. "I expect to be instructed."

"Have you taken an oath like Hyacinth?"

"Ah madam, the oaths *I* take I don't tell," he gravely returned.

"Oh *you*——!" she breathed with a deep ambiguous cadence. She appeared to dismiss the question, but to suggest at the same time that he was very abnormal. This imputation was further conveyed by the next words she uttered. "And can you see a dear friend whirled away like that?"

At this, for the first time, her visitor showed impatience. "You had better leave my dear friend to me."

The Princess, her eyes still fixed on him, gave a long, soft sigh. "Well then, shall we go?"

He took up his hat again, but made no movement toward the door. "If you did me the honour to seek my acquaintance, to ask me to come and 269 see you, only in order to say what you've just said about Hyacinth, perhaps we needn't carry out the form of going to the place you proposed. Wasn't this only your pretext?"

"I believe you *are* afraid!" she frankly returned; but in spite of her exclamation the pair presently went out of the house. They quitted the door together, after having stood on the step a little to look up and down, apparently for a cab. So far as the darkness, which was now complete, permitted the prospect to be scanned, there was no such vehicle within hail. They turned to the left and after a walk of several minutes, during which they were engaged in small dull by-streets, emerged on a more populous way, where they found lighted shops and omnibuses and the evident chance of a hansom. Here they stayed afresh and very soon an empty hansom passed and, at a sign, pulled up near them. Meanwhile, it should be recorded, they had been followed, at an interval, by a cautious figure, a person who, in Madeira Crescent, when they came out of the house, was stationed on the other side of the street, at a considerable distance. On their appearing he had retreated a little, still, however, keeping them in sight. When they moved away he had moved in the same direction, watching them but maintaining his distance. He had drawn nearer, seemingly because he couldn't control his eagerness, as they passed into Westbourne Grove, and during the minute they stood there had been exposed to recognition by the Princess should she have happened to turn her head. In the event of her having felt such an impulse she would have discovered, in the lamplight, that her noble husband was hovering in her rear. But she was otherwise occupied; she failed to see that at one moment he came so close as to suggest an intention of breaking out on her from behind. The reader 270 scarce need be informed, nevertheless, that his design was but to satisfy himself as to the kind of person his wife was walking with. The time allowed him for this research was brief, especially as he had perceived, more rapidly than he sometimes perceived things, that they were looking for a vehicle and that with its assistance they would pass out of his range— a reflexion which caused him to give half his attention to the business of hailing any second cab that should come that way. There are parts of London in which you may never see a cab at all, but there are none in which you may see only one; in accordance with which fortunate truth Prince Casamassima was able to wave his stick to good purpose as soon as the two objects of his pursuit had rattled away. Behind them now, in the gloom, he had no fear of being seen. In little more than an instant he had jumped into another hansom, the driver of which accompanied the usual exclamation of "All right, sir!" with a small, amused grunt, regarded by the Prince as eminently British, after he had hissed at him, over the hood, expressively and in a manner by no means indicative of that nationality, the injunction, "Follow, follow, follow!" 271

XL

An hour after her companion had left the house with Paul Muniment Madame Grandoni came down to supper, a meal for which she made use, in gloomy solitude, of the little back parlour. She had pushed away her plate and sat motionless, staring at the crumpled cloth with her hands folded on the edge of the table, when she became aware that a gentleman had been ushered into the drawing-room and was standing before the fire in discreet suspense. At the same moment the maid-servant approached the old lady, remarking with bated breath: "The Prince, the Prince, mum! It's you he 'ave asked for, mum!" Upon this Madame Grandoni called out to the visitor from her place, addressed him as her poor, dear, distinguished friend and bade him come and give her his arm. He obeyed with solemn alacrity, conducting her to the front room and the fire. He helped her to arrange herself in her chair and gather her shawl about her; then he seated himself at hand and remained with his dismal eyes bent on her. After a moment she said: "Tell me something about Rome. The grass in Villa Borghese must already be thick with flowers."

"I would have brought you some if I had thought," he answered. Then he turned his gaze about the room. "Yes, you may well ask in such a black little hole as this. My wife shouldn't live here," he added. 272

"Ah my dear friend, for all she's your wife——!" the old woman exclaimed.

The Prince sprang up in sudden, sharp agitation, and then she saw that the stiff propriety with which he had come into the room and greeted her was only an effort of his good manners. He was really trembling with excitement. "It's true—it's true! She *has* lovers—she *has* lovers!" he broke out. "I've seen it with my eyes and I've come here to know!"

"I don't know what you've seen, but your coming here to know won't have helped you much. Besides, if you've seen you know for yourself. At any rate I've ceased to be able to tell you."

"You're afraid—you're afraid!" cried the visitor with a wild, accusatory gesture.

The old woman looked up at him with slow speculation. "Sit down and be quiet, very quiet. I've ceased to pay attention—I take no heed."

"Well, I do then," said the Prince, subsiding a little. "Don't you know she has gone out to a house in a horrible quarter with a man?"

"I think it highly probable, dear Prince."

"And who is he? That's what I want to discover."

"How can I tell you? I haven't seen him."

He looked at her with eyes of anguish. "Dear lady, is that kind to me when I've counted on you?"

"Oh I'm not kind any more; it's not a question of that. I'm angry—as angry almost as you."

"Then why don't you watch her, eh?"

"It's not with her I'm angry. It's with myself," said Madame Grandoni, all in thought.

"For becoming so indifferent, do you mean?"

"On the contrary, for staying in the house."

"Thank God you're still here, or I couldn't have come. But what a lodging for the Princess!" the 273 visitor exclaimed. "She might at least live in a manner befitting."

"Eh, the last time you were in London you thought it too expensive!" she cried.

He cast about him. "Whatever she does is wrong. Is it because it's so bad that you must go?" he went on.

"It's foolish—foolish—foolish," said his friend, slowly and impressively.

"Foolish, *che, che*! He was in the house nearly an hour, this one."

"In the house? In what house?"

"Here where you sit. I saw him go in, and when he came out it was after a long time, and she with him."

"And where were you meanwhile?"

Again the Prince faltered. "I was on the other side of the street. When they came out I followed them. It was more than an hour ago."

"Was it for that you came to London?"

"Ah what I came for——! To put myself in hell!"

"You had better go back to Rome," said Madame Grandoni.

"Of course I'll go back, but only if you'll tell me who this one is! How can you be ignorant, dear friend, when he comes freely in and out of the place?—where I have to watch at the door for a moment I can snatch. He wasn't the same as the other."

"As the other?"

"Doubtless there are fifty! I mean the little one I met in the house that Sunday afternoon."

"I sit in my room almost always now," said the old woman. "I only come down to eat."

"Dear lady, it would be better if you would sit here," the Prince returned.

"Better for whom?"

"I mean that if you didn't withdraw yourself you could at least answer my questions." 274

"Ah but I haven't the slightest desire to answer them," Madame Grandoni replied. "You must remember that I'm not here as your spy."

"No," said the Prince in a tone of extreme and simple melancholy. "If you had given me more information I shouldn't have been obliged to come here myself. I arrived in London only this morning, and this evening I spent two hours walking up and down opposite there, like a groom waiting for his master to come back from a ride. I wanted a personal impression. It was so I saw him come in. He's not a gentleman—not even one of the strange ones of this country."

"I think he's Scotch or Welsh," Madame Grandoni explained.

"Ah then you *have* seen him?"

"No, but I've heard him. He speaks straight out (the floors of this house are not built as we build in Italy) and his voice is the same I've noticed in the people of the wild parts, where they 'shoot.' Besides, she has told me—some few things. He's a chemist's assistant."

"A chemist's assistant? *Santo Dio!* And the other one, a year ago—more than a year ago—was a bookbinder."

"Oh the bookbinder——!" the old woman wailed.

"And does she associate with no people of good? Has she no other society?"

"For me to tell you more, Prince, you must wait till I'm free," she pleaded.

"How do you mean, free?"

"I must choose. I must either go away—and then I can tell you what I've seen—or if I stay here I must hold my tongue."

"But if you go away you'll have seen nothing," the Prince objected.

"Ah plenty as it is—more than I ever expected to!" <u>275</u>

He clasped his hands as in strenuous suppliance but at the same time smiled as to conciliate, to corrupt. "Dearest friend, you torment my curiosity. If you'll tell me this I'll never ask you anything more. Where did they go? For the love of God, what is that house?"

"I know nothing of their houses," she returned with an impatient shrug.

"Then there are others? there are many?" She made no answer but to sit intent, her chin in her bulging kerchief. Her visitor presently continued with his pressure of pain and his beautiful Italian distinctness, as if his lips cut and carved the sound, while his fine fingers quivered into quick, emphasising gestures: "The street's small and black, but it's like all the dreadful streets. It has no importance; it's at the end of a long imbroglio. They drove for twenty minutes, then stopped their cab and got out. They went together on foot some minutes more. There were many turns; they seemed to know them well. For me it was very difficult—of course I also got out; I had to stay so far behind—close against the houses. Chiffinch Street, N.E.—that was the name," the Prince continued, pronouncing the word with difficulty; "and the house is number 32—I looked at that after they went in. It's a very bad house—worse than this; but it has no sign of a chemist and there are no shops in the street. They rang the bell—only once, though they waited a long time; it seemed to me at least that they didn't touch it again. It was several minutes before the door was opened, and that was a bad time for me, because as they stood there they looked up and down. Fortunately you know the air of this place! I saw no light in the house—not even after they went in. Who opened to them I couldn't tell. I waited nearly half an hour, to see how long they might <u>276</u> stay and what they would do on coming out; then at last my impatience brought me here, for to know she was absent made me hope I might see you. While I was there two persons went in: two men together, both smoking, who looked like *artisti*—I saw them badly—but no one came out. I could see they took their cigars—and you can fancy what tobacco!—into the presence of the Princess. Formerly," pursued Madame Grandoni's visitor with a touching attempt at pleasantry on this point, "she never tolerated smoking—never mine at least. The street's very quiet—very few people pass. Now what's the house? Is it where that man lives?" he almost panted.

He had been encouraged by her consenting, in spite of her first protests, to listen to him—he could see she *was* listening; and he was still more encouraged when after a moment she answered his question by a question of her own. "Did you cross the river to go there? I know he lives over the water!"

"Ah no, it was not in that part. I tried to ask the cabman who brought me back to explain to me what it's called; but I couldn't make him understand. They've heavy minds," the Prince declared. Then he pursued, drawing a little closer to his hostess: "But what were they doing there? Why did she go with him?"

"They think they're conspiring. Ecco!" said Madame Grandoni.

"You mean they've joined a secret society, a band of revolutionists and murderers? *Capisco bene*—that's not new to me. But perhaps they only pretend it's for that," added the Prince.

"Only pretend? Why should they pretend? That's not Christina's way."

"There are other possibilities," he portentously observed. <u>277</u>

"Oh of course when your wife goes off with strange, low men in the dark, goes off to *des maisons louches*, you can think anything you like and I've nothing to say to your thoughts. I've my own, but they're my affair, and I shall not undertake to defend Christina, who's indefensible. When she commits these follies she provokes, she invites, the worst construction; there let it rest save for this one remark which I will content myself with making. That is that if she were a real wretch, capable of *all*, she wouldn't behave as she does now, she wouldn't expose herself to *the* supposition; the appearance of everything would be good and proper. I simply tell you what I believe. If I believed that what she's doing concerned you alone I should say nothing about it—at least sitting here. But it concerns others, it concerns every one, so I open my mouth at last. She has gone to that house to break up society."

"To break it up, yes, as she has wanted before?"

"Oh more than ever before! She's very much entangled. She has relations with people who are watched by the police. She hasn't told me, but I've grown sure of it by simply living with her."

The poor Prince stared. "And is *she* watched by the police?"

"I can't tell you; it's very possible—except that the police here isn't like that of other countries."

"It's more stupid." He gazed at his cold comforter with a flush of shame on his face. "Will she bring us to *that* scandal? It would be the worst of all."

"There's one chance—the chance she'll get tired of it," the old lady remarked. "Only the scandal may come before that."

"Dear friend, she's the Devil in person," said the Prince woefully. 278

"No, she's not the Devil, because she wishes to do good."

"What good did she ever wish to do to me?" he asked with glowing eyes.

She shook her head with a gloom that matched his own. "You can do no good of any kind to each other. Each on your own side you must be quiet."

"How can I be quiet when I hear of such infamies?" He got up in his violence and, after a fashion that caused his companion to burst into a short, incongruous laugh as soon as she heard the words, pronounced: "She shall *not* break up society!"

"No, she'll bore herself to death before the *coup* is ripe. Make up your mind to that."

"That's what I expected to find—that the caprice was over. She has passed through so many madnesses."

"Give her time—give her time," replied Madame Grandoni.

"Time to drag my name into an assize-court? Those people are robbers, incendiaries, murderers!"

"You can say nothing to me about them that I haven't said to her."

"And how does she defend herself?"

"Defend herself? Did you ever hear Christina do that?" the old woman asked. "The only thing she says to me is: 'Don't be afraid; I promise you by all that's sacred you personally shan't suffer.' She speaks as if she had it all in her hands. That's very well. No doubt I'm a selfish old pig, but after all one has a heart for others."

"And so have I, I think I may pretend," said the Prince. "You tell me to give her time, and it's certain she'll take it whether I give it or no. But I can at least stop giving her money. By heaven it's my duty as an honest man." 279

"She tells me that as it is you don't give her much."

"Much, dear lady? It depends on what you call so. It's enough to make all these scoundrels flock round her."

"They're not all scoundrels any more than she's all one. That's the tiresome part of it!" she wearily sighed.

"But this fellow, the chemist—to-night—what do you call *him*?"

"She has spoken to me of him as a fine young man."

"But she thinks it fine to blow us all up," the Prince returned. "Doesn't *he* take her money?"

"I don't know what he takes. But there are some things—heaven forbid one should forget them! The misery of London's fearful."

"*Che vuole?* There's misery everywhere," our personage opined. "It's the will of God. *Ci vuol pazienza!* And in this country does no one give alms?"

"Every one, I believe. But it appears that that's not enough."

He said nothing for a moment; this statement of Madame Grandoni's seemed to present difficulties. The solution, however, soon suggested itself; it was expressed in the inquiry: "What will you have in a country that hasn't the true faith?"

"Ah the true faith's a great thing, but there's suffering even in countries that have it."

"*Evidentemente.* But it helps suffering to be borne and, later, makes it up; whereas here——!" said the visitor with a sad if inconclusive smile. "If I may speak of myself it's to me, in my circumstances, a support."

"That's good," she returned a little curtly.

He stood before her, resting his eyes for a moment 280 on the floor. "And the famous Cholto—Godfrey Gerald—does he come no more?"

"I haven't seen him for months. I know nothing about him."

"He doesn't like the chemists and the bookbinders, eh?" asked the Prince.

"Ah it was he who first brought them—to gratify your wife."

"If they've turned him out then that's very well. Now if only some one could turn *them* out!"

"*Aspetta, aspetta!*" said the old woman.

"That's very good advice, but to follow it isn't amusing." Then the Prince added: "You alluded, just now, as to something particular, to *quel giovane*, the young artisan whom I met in the other house. Is he also still proposed to our admiration, or has he paid the penalty of his crimes?"

"He has paid the penalty, but I don't know of what. I've nothing bad to tell you of him except that I think his star's on the wane."

"*Poverino!*" the Prince exclaimed.

"That's exactly the manner in which I addressed him the first time I saw him. I didn't know how it would happen, but I felt it would happen somehow. It has happened through his changing his opinions. He has now the same idea as you—*ci vuol pazienza*."

Her friend listened with the same expression of wounded eagerness, the same parted lips and excited eyes, to every added fact that dropped from Madame Grandoni's lips. "That at least is more honest. Then *he* doesn't go to Chiffinch Street?"

"I don't know about Chiffinch Street, though it would be my impression that he doesn't go to any place visited by Christina and the other one, by the Scotchman, together. But these are delicate matters," the old woman pursued.

They seemed much to impress her interlocutor. <u>281</u> "Do you mean that the Scotchman is—what shall I call it?—his successor?"

For a time she made no reply. "I imagine this case different. But I don't understand; it was the other, the little one, who helped her to know the Scotchman."

"And now they've quarrelled—about my wife? It's all tremendously edifying!" the Prince wailed.

"I can't tell you, and shouldn't have attempted it, only that Assunta talks to me."

"I wish she would talk to me," he said wistfully.

"Ah my friend, if Christina were to find you getting at her servants——!"

"How could it be worse for me than it is now? However, I don't know why I speak as if I cared, for I don't care any more. I've given her up. It's finished."

"I'm glad to hear it," said Madame Grandoni gravely.

"You yourself made the distinction perfectly. So long as she endeavoured only to injure *me*, and in my private capacity, I could condone, I could wait, I could hope. But since she has so shamelessly thrown herself into criminal undertakings, since she lifts her hand with a determined purpose, as you tell me, against the most sacred institutions—it's too much; ah yes, it's too much! She may go her way; she's no wife of mine. Not another penny of mine shall go into her pocket and into that of the wretches who prey upon her, who have corrupted her."

"Dear Prince, I think you're right. And yet I'm sorry!" sighed his hostess, extending her hand for assistance to rise from her chair. "If she becomes really poor it will be much more difficult for me to leave her. *This* is not poverty, and not even a good imitation of it, as she would like it to be. But what will be said of me if, having remained with her through 282 so much of her splendour, I turn away from her the moment she begins to want?"

"Dear lady, do you ask that to make me relent?" the Prince uneasily quavered.

"Not in the least; for whatever's said and whatever you do there's nothing for me in decency at present but to pack my trunk. Judge by the way I've tattled."

"If you'll stay on she shall have everything." He spoke in a very low tone, with a manner that betrayed the shame he felt for his attempt at bribery.

Madame Grandoni gave him an astonished glance and moved away from him. "What does that mean? I thought you didn't care."

I know not what explanation of his inconsequence her guest would have given her if at that moment the door of the room hadn't been pushed open to permit the entrance of Hyacinth Robinson. He stopped short on finding a stranger in the field, but before he had time to say anything the old lady addressed him rather shortly. "Ah you don't fall well; the Princess isn't at home."

"That was mentioned to me, but I ventured to come in to see you as I've done before," our young man replied. Then he added as to accommodate: "I beg many pardons. I was not told you were not alone."

"My visitor's going, but I'm going too," said Madame Grandoni. "I must take myself to my room—I'm all falling to pieces. Therefore kindly excuse me."

Hyacinth had had time to recognise the Prince, and this nobleman paid him the same compliment, as was proved by his asking of their companion in a rapid Italian aside: "Isn't it the bookbinder?"

"*Sicuro*," said the old lady; while Hyacinth, murmuring a regret that he should find her indisposed, turned back to the door. 283

"One moment—one moment, I pray!" the Prince interposed, raising his hand persuasively and looking at Mr. Robinson with an unexpected, exaggerated smile. "Please introduce me to the gentleman," he added in English to Madame Grandoni.

She manifested no surprise at the request—she had none left for anything—but pronounced the name of Prince Casamassima and then added for Hyacinth's benefit: "He knows who you are."

"Will you permit me to keep you a very little minute?" The Prince appealed to his fellow-visitor, after which he remarked to Madame Grandoni: "I'll talk with him a little. It's perhaps not necessary we should incommode you if you don't wish to stay."

She had for an instant, as she tossed off a small satirical laugh, a return of her ancient drollery. "Remember that if you talk long she may come back! Yes, yes, I'll go upstairs. *Felicissima notte, signori!*" She took her way to the door, which Hyacinth, considerably bewildered, held open for her.

The reasons for which Prince Casamassima wished to converse with him were mysterious; nevertheless he was about to close the door behind their friend as a sign that he was at the service of the greater personage. At this moment the latter raised again a courteous, remonstrant hand. "After all, as my visit is finished and as yours comes to nothing, might we not go out?"

"Certainly I'll go with you," said Hyacinth. He spoke with an instinctive stiffness in spite of the Prince's queer affability, and in spite also of the fact that he felt sorry for the nobleman to whose countenance Madame Grandoni's last injunction, uttered in English, could bring a deep and painful blush. It is forbidden us to try the question of what Hyacinth, face to face with an aggrieved husband, may have had on his conscience, but he assumed, naturally 284 enough, that the situation might be grave, though indeed the Prince's manner was for the moment incongruously bland. He invited his new, his grand acquaintance to pass, and in a minute they were in the street together.

"Do you go here—do you go there?" the Prince inquired as they stood a moment before the house. "If you permit I'll take the same direction." On Hyacinth's answering that it was indifferent to him he said, turning to the right: "Well then here, but *adagio*, if that pleases you, and only a little way." His English was far from perfect, but his errors were like artificial flowers of accent: Hyacinth was struck with his effort to express himself very distinctly, so that in intercourse with a small untutored Briton his foreignness should not put him at a disadvantage. Quick to perceive and appreciate, our hero noted how the quality of breeding in him just enabled him to compass that coolness, and he mentally applauded the success of a difficult feat. Difficult he judged it because it seemed to him that the purpose for which the Prince wished to speak to him was one requiring an immensity of explanation, and it was a sign of training to explain adequately, in a strange tongue, especially if one were agitated, to a person in a social position very different from one's own. Hyacinth knew what the Prince's estimate of *his* importance must be—he could have no illusions as to the character of the people his wife received; but while he heard him carefully put one word after the other he was able to smile to himself at his needless precautions. Our young man reflected that at a pinch he could have encountered him in his own tongue: during his stay at Venice he had picked up an Italian vocabulary. "With Madame Grandoni I spoke of you," the Prince announced dispassionately as they walked along. "She told me a thing that <u>285</u> interested me," he added; "that's why I walk with you." Hyacinth said nothing, deeming that better by silence than in any other fashion he held himself at the disposal of his interlocutor. "She told me you've changed—you've no more the same opinions."

"The same opinions?"

"About the arrangement of society. You desire no more the assassination of the rich."

"I never desired any such thing!" said Hyacinth indignantly.

"Oh if you've changed you can confess," his friend declared in an encouraging tone. "It's very good for some people to be rich. It wouldn't be right for all to be poor."

"It would be pleasant if all could be rich," Hyacinth more mildly suggested.

"Yes, but not by stealing and shooting."

"No, not by stealing and shooting. I never desired that."

"Ah no doubt she was mistaken. But to-day you think we must have patience?" the Prince went on as if greatly hoping Hyacinth would allow this valuable conviction to be attributed to him. "That's also my view."

"Oh yes, we must have patience," said his companion, who was now smiling to himself in the dark.

They had by this time reached the end of the little Crescent, where the Prince paused under the street-lamp. He considered the small bookbinder's countenance for a moment by its help and then pronounced: "If I'm not mistaken you know very well the Princess."

Hyacinth hung back: "She has been very kind to me."

"She's my wife—perhaps you know."

Again Mr. Robinson faltered, but after a moment he replied: "She has told me that she's married." 286 As soon as he had spoken these words he thought them idiotic.

"You mean you wouldn't know if she hadn't told you, I suppose. Evidently there's nothing to show it. You can think if that's agreeable to me."

"Oh I can't think, I can't judge."

"You're right—that's impossible." The Prince stood before his companion, and in the pale gaslight the latter saw more of his face. It had an unnatural expression, a look of wasted anxiety; the eyes seemed to glitter, and our fond observer conceived the unfortunate nobleman to be feverish and ill. He pursued in a moment: "Of course you think it strange—my conversation. I want you to tell me something."

"I'm afraid you're very unwell," said Hyacinth.

"Yes, I'm very unwell; but I shall be better if you'll tell me. It's because you've come back to good ideas—that's why I ask you."

A sense that the situation of the Princess's husband was really pitiful, that at any rate he suffered and was helpless, that he was a gentleman and even a person who would never have done any great harm—a perception of these appealing truths came into Hyacinth's heart and stirred there a desire to be kind to him, to render him any service that in reason he might ask. It struck him he must be pretty sick to ask any at all, but that was his own affair. "If you'd like me to see you safely home I'll do that," our young friend brought out; and even while he spoke he was struck with the oddity of his being already on such friendly terms with a person whom he had hitherto supposed to be the worst enemy of the rarest of women. He found himself unable to consider the Prince with resentment.

This personage acknowledged the civility of the offer with a slight inclination of his high slimness. 287

"I'm very much obliged to you, but I don't go home. I don't go home till I know this—to what house she has gone. Will you tell me that?"

"To what house?" Hyacinth repeated.

"She has gone with a person whom you know. Madame Grandoni told me that. He's a Scotch chemist."

"A Scotch chemist?" Hyacinth stared.

"I saw them myself—an hour, two hours, ago. Listen, listen; I'll be very clear," said the Prince, laying his forefinger on the other hand with a pleading emphasis. "He came to that house—this one, where we've been, I mean—and stayed there a long time. I was here in the street—I've passed my day in the street! They came out together and I watched them—I followed them."

Hyacinth had listened with wonder and even with suspense; the Prince's manner gave an air of such importance and such mystery to what he had to relate. But at this he broke out: "This's not my business—I can't hear it! *I* don't watch, *I* don't follow."

His friend stared in surprise, but then rejoined, more quickly than he had spoken yet: "Do you understand that they went to a house where they conspire, where they prepare horrible acts? How can you like that?"

"How do you know it, sir?" Hyacinth gravely asked.

"It's Madame Grandoni who has told me."

"Why then do you question me?"

"Because I'm not sure, I don't think she knows. I want to know more, to be sure of what's the truth. Does she go to such a place only for the revolution, or does she go to be alone with him?"

"With *him*?" The Prince's tone and his excited eyes had somehow made the suggestion live.

"With the tall man—the chemist. They got into 288 a hansom together; the house is far away, in the lost quarters."

Hyacinth drew himself together. "I know nothing about the matter and I don't care. If that's all you wish to ask me we had better separate."

The Prince's high face grew long; it seemed to grow paler. "Then it's not true that you hate those abominations!"

Hyacinth frankly wondered. "How can you know about my opinions? How can they interest you?"

The Prince looked at him with sick eyes; he raised his arms a certain distance and then let them drop at his sides. "I hoped you'd help me."

"When we're in trouble we can't help each other much!" our young man exclaimed. But this austere reflexion was lost on the Prince, who at the moment it was uttered had already turned to look in the direction from which they had moved, the other end of the Crescent, his attention suddenly jerked round by the sound of a rapid hansom. The place was still and empty and the wheels of this vehicle reverberated. He glowered at it through the darkness and in an instant cried, under his breath, excitedly: "They've come back—they've come back! Now you can see—yes, the two!" The hansom had slackened pace and pulled up; the house before which it stopped was clearly the house the two men had lately quitted. Hyacinth felt his arm seized by his strange confidant, who hastily, with a strong effort, drew him forward several yards. At this moment a part of the agitation that possessed the Princess's unhappy husband seemed to pass into his own blood; a wave of anxiety rushed through him—anxiety as to the relations of the two persons who had descended from the cab: he had in short for several instants a very exact revelation of the state of feeling of those who love in the rage of jealousy. If he had been told half an hour before 289 that he was capable of surreptitious peepings in the interest of that passion he would have resented the insult; yet he allowed himself to be checked by his companion just at the nearest point at which they might safely consider the proceedings of the couple who alighted. It was in fact the Princess accompanied by Paul Muniment. Hyacinth noticed that the latter paid the cabman, who immediately drove away, from his own pocket. He stood with the Princess for some minutes at the door of the house— minutes during which Mr. Robinson felt his heart beat insanely, ignobly. He couldn't tell why.

"What does he say? what does *she* say?" hissed the Prince; and when he went on the next moment, "Will he go in again or will he go away?" our stricken youth felt a voice given to his own sharpest thought. The pair were talking together with rapid sequences, and as the door had not yet been opened it was clear that, to prolong the conversation on the steps, the Princess delayed to ring. "It will make three, four hours he has been with her," moaned the Prince.

"He may be with her fifty hours!" Hyacinth laughed as he turned away ashamed of himself.

"He has gone in—*sangue di Dio!*" cried the Prince, catching his companion again by the arm and making him look. All our friend saw was the door just closing; Paul and the Princess were on the other side of it. "Is *that* for the revolution?" the trembling nobleman panted. But Mr. Robinson made no answer; he only gazed at the closed door an instant and then, disengaging himself, walked straight away, leaving the victim of the wrong he could even then feel as deeper than his own to shake, in the dark, a helpless, foolish, gold-headed stick at the indifferent house where Madame Grandoni's bedroom light glimmered aloft. 290

XLI

Hyacinth waited a long time, but when at last Millicent came to the door the splendour of her appearance did much to justify her delay. He heard an immense rustling on the staircase, accompanied by a creaking of that inexpensive structure, and then she brushed forward into the narrow, dusky passage where he had been standing a quarter of an hour. Highly flushed, she exhaled a strong, cheap perfume, and she instantly thrust her muff, a tight, fat, beribboned receptacle, at him to be held while she adjusted her gloves to her large, vulgar hands. He opened the door—it was so natural an assumption that they shouldn't be able to talk properly in the passage—and they came out to the low steps, lingering there in the yellow Sunday sunshine. A loud ejaculation on the beauty of the day broke from Millicent, though, as we know, she was not addicted to facile admirations. Winter was not over but spring had begun, and the smoky London air allowed the baffled vision, by way of a change, to pierce it almost through. The town could refresh its recollections of the sky, and the sky could ascertain the geographical position of the town. The essential dimness of the low perspectives had by no means disappeared, but it had loosened its folds; it lingered as a blur of mist interwoven with pretty sun-tints and faint transparencies. There was warmth and 291 iridescence and a view of the shutters of shops, and the church-bells were ringing. Miss Henning remarked that it was a "shime" she couldn't have a place to ask a gentleman to sit down; but what were you to do when you had such a grind for your living and a room, to keep yourself tidy, no bigger than a pill-box? She couldn't herself abide waiting outside; she knew something about it when she took things home to ladies to choose—the time they spent was long enough to choose a husband!—and it always made her feel quite wicked. It was something "croo'l." If she could have what she liked she knew what she'd have; and she hinted at a mystic bower where a visitor could sit and enjoy himself—with the morning paper or a nice view out of the window or even a glass of sherry—so that, close at hand but perfectly private, she could dress without getting in a fidget, which always made her red in the face.

"I don't know how I 'ave pitched on my things," she remarked as she offered her magnificence to Hyacinth, who became aware she had put a small plump book into her muff. He explained that, the day being so fine, he had come to propose to her a walk in the manner of ancient times. They might spend an hour or two in the Park and stroll beside the Serpentine, or even paddle about on it if she liked; they might watch the lambkins or feed the ducks if she would put a crust in her pocket. The privilege of paddling Millicent entirely declined; she had no idea of wetting her flounces and she left those rough pleasures, especially of a Sunday, to a lower class of young woman. But she didn't mind if she did go a turn, though he didn't deserve any such favour after the way he hadn't been near her, not if she had died in her garret. She wasn't one that was to be dropped and taken up at any man's convenience—she didn't 292 keep one of those offices for servants out of place. Her conviction was strong that if the day hadn't been so grand she would have sent her friend about his business; it was lucky for him she was always forgiving—such was her sensitive, generous nature—when the sun was out. Only there was one thing—she couldn't abide making no difference for Sunday; it was her personal habit to go to church and she should have it on her conscience if she gave that up for a lark. Hyacinth had already been impressed, more than once, by the manner in which his old playmate stickled for the religious observance: of all the queer disparities of her nature her devotional turn struck him as perhaps the queerest. She held her head erect through the longest and dullest sermon and quitted the sacred edifice with her fine face embellished by the publicity of her virtue. She was exasperated by the general secularity of Hyacinth's behaviour, especially taken in conjunction with his general straightness, and was only consoled a little by the fact that if he didn't drink or fight or steal he at least dabbled in unlimited wickedness of opinion— theories as bad as anything people often got ten years for. He had not yet revealed to her that his theories had somehow lately come to be held with less of a clutch; an instinct of kindness had forbidden him to deprive her of a grievance doing so much for sociability. He had not reflected that she would have been more aggrieved, and consequently more delightful, if her condemnation of his godlessness had missed corroborative signs.

On the present occasion she let him know he might have his pleasure if he would first accompany her to church; and it was in vain he represented to her that this proceeding would deprive them of their morning, inasmuch as after church she would have to dine and in the interval there would be no time 293 left. She replied with a toss of her head that she dined when she liked; besides, on Sundays she had cold fare—it was left out for her: an argument to which Hyacinth had to assent, his ignorance of her domestic economy being complete, thanks to the maidenly mystery, the vagueness of reference and explanation in which, despite great freedom of complaint, perpetual announcements of intended change, of impending promotion and of high bids for her services in other quarters, she had always enshrouded her private affairs. He walked by her side to the place of worship she preferred—her choice was made apparently from a large experience; and as they went he observed that it was a good job he wasn't married to her. Lord, how she would bully him, how she would "squeeze" him, in such a case! The worst of it would be that—such was his amiable, peace-loving nature—he should obey like a showman's poodle. And pray who *was* a man to obey, asked Millicent, if he wasn't to obey his own wife? She sat up in her pew with a majesty that carried out this idea; she seemed to answer in her proper person for creeds and communions and sacraments; she was more than devotional, she was individually almost pontifical. Hyacinth had never felt himself under such distinguished protection; the Princess Casamassima came back to him in comparison as a loose Bohemian, a shabby adventuress. He had sought her out to-day not for the sake of her austerity—he had had too gloomy a week for that—but for that of her genial side; yet now that she treated him to the severer spectacle it struck him for the moment as really grand sport, a kind of magnification of her rich vitality. She had her phases and caprices like the Princess herself, and if they were not the same as those of the lady of Madeira Crescent they proved at least that she was as brave a woman. No one but <u>294</u> a really big creature could give herself such airs; she would have a consciousness of the large reserve of pliancy required to make up for them. The Princess wanted to destroy society and Millicent to uphold it; and as Hyacinth, by the side of his childhood's friend, listened to practised intonings and felt the brush of a rich unction, he was obliged to recognise the liberality of a fate that had sometimes appeared invidious. He had been provided with the best opportunities for choosing between the beauty of the original and the beauty of the conventional.

On this particular Sunday there was by luck no sermon—by the luck, I mean, of his heretical impatience—so that after the congregation dispersed there was still plenty of time for a walk in the Park. Our friends traversed that barely-interrupted expanse of irrepressible herbage which stretches from the Birdcage Walk to Hyde Park Corner and took their way to Kensington Gardens beside the Serpentine. Once her religious exercises were over for the day—she as rigidly forbore to repeat them in the afternoon as she made a point of the first service—once she had lifted her voice in prayer and praise Millicent changed her carriage; moving to a different measure, uttering her sentiments in a high, free manner and not minding if it was noticed she had on her very best gown and was out if need be for the day. She was mainly engaged at first in overhauling Hyacinth for his long absence and demanding as usual some account of what he had been up to. He listened at his ease, liking and enjoying her chaff, which seemed to him, oddly enough, wholesome and refreshing, and amusedly and absolutely declining to satisfy her. He alleged, as he had had occasion to do before, that if he asked no explanations of her the least he had a right to expect in return was that she should let him off as easily; and even the indignation with <u>295</u> which she received this plea didn't make him feel that a clearing-up between them could be a serious thing. There was nothing to clear up and nothing to forgive; they were a pair of very fallible creatures, united much more by their weaknesses than by any consistency or fidelity they might pretend to practise toward each other. It was an old acquaintance—the oldest thing to-day, except Mr. Vetch's friendship, in Hyacinth's life; and, oddly enough, it inspired our young man with a positive indulgent piety. The probability that the girl "kept company" with other men had quite ceased to torment his imagination; it was no longer necessary to his happiness to be so certain about it that he might dismiss her from his mind. He could be as happy without it as with it, and he felt a new modesty over prying into her affairs. He was so little in a position to be stern with her that her assumption of his recognising a right in her to pull him to pieces seemed but a part of her perpetual clumsiness—a clumsiness that was not soothing, yet was nevertheless, in its rich spontaneity, one of the things he liked her for.

"If you've come to see me only to make low jokes at my expense you had better have stayed away altogether," she said with dignity as they came out of the Green Park. "In the first place it's rude, in the second place it's silly, and in the third place I see through you."

"My dear Milly, the motions you go through, the resentment you profess, are all a kicking up of dust which I blow away with a breath," her companion replied. "But it doesn't matter; go on—say anything you like. I came to see you for recreation, to enjoy myself without effort of my own. I scarcely ventured to hope, however, that you'd make me laugh—I've been so dismal for a long time. In fact I'm dismal still. I wish I 296 had your disposition. My mirth, as you see, is a bit feverish."

"The first thing I require of any friend is that he should respect me," Miss Henning announced. "You lead a bad life. I know what to think about that," she continued irrelevantly.

"And is it through respect for *you* that you wish me to lead a better one? To-day then is so much saved out of my wickedness. Let us get on the grass," Hyacinth pursued; "it's innocent and pastoral to feel it under one's feet. It's jolly to be with you. You understand everything."

"I don't understand everything you say, but I understand everything you hide," the young woman returned as the great central expanse of the Park, looking intensely green and browsable, stretched away before them.

"Then I shall soon become a mystery to you, for I mean from this time forth to cease to seek safety in concealment. You'll know nothing about me then—for it will be all under your nose."

"Well, there's nothing so pretty as nature," Millicent observed at a venture, surveying the smutty sheep who find pasturage in the fields that extend from Knightsbridge to the Bayswater Road. "What will you do when you're so bad you can't go to the shop?" she added with a sudden transition. And when he asked why he should ever be so bad as that she said she could see he *was* in a fever: she hadn't noticed it at first because he never had had any more complexion than a cheese. Was it something he had caught in some of those back slums where he went prying about with his mad ideas? It served him right for taking as little good into such places as ever came out of them. Would his fine friends—a precious lot *they* were, that put it off on him to do all the nasty part—would they find the doctor and the port 297 wine and the money and all the rest when he was laid up, perhaps for months, through their putting such rot into his head and his putting it into others that could carry it even less? She stopped on the grass in the watery sunshine and bent on her companion a pair of eyes in which he noted afresh a stirred curiosity, a friendly, reckless ray, a possibility of ardour, a pledge of really closer comradeship. Suddenly she brought out, quitting the tone of exaggerated derision she had employed a moment before: "You precious little rascal, you've got something on your heart! Has your Princess given you the sack?"

"My poor girl, your talk's a queer mixture," he resignedly sighed. "But it may well be. It's not queerer than my life."

"Well, I'm glad you admit that!" Milly cried as she walked on with a flutter of ribbons.

"Your ideas about my ideas!" Hyacinth wailed. "Yes, you should see me in the back slums. I'm a bigger Philistine than you, Miss Henning."

"You've got more ridiculous names, if that's what you mean. I don't believe you half the time know what you do mean yourself. I don't believe you even know with all your thinking what you do think. That's your disease."

"It's astonishing how you sometimes put your finger on the place," he now returned with interest. "I mean to think no more—I mean to give it up. Avoid it yourself, dear friend—avoid it as you would a baleful vice. It confers no true happiness. Let us live in the world of irreflective contemplation—let us live in the present hour."

"I don't care how I live nor where I live," she cried, "so long as I can do as I like. It's them that are over you—it's them that cut it fine! But you never were really satisfactory to me—not as one 298 friend should be to another," she pursued, reverting irresistibly to the concrete and turning still upon her companion that fine fairness which had no cause to shrink from a daylight exhibition. "Do you remember that day I came back to the Plice, ever so long ago, and called on poor dear Miss Pynsent—she couldn't abide me, she never understood my form—and waited till you came in, and then went a walk with you and had tea at a coffee-shop? Well, I don't mind telling you that you weren't satisfactory to me even that night, and that I consider myself remarkably good-natured, ever since, to have kept you so little up to the mark. You always tried to carry it off as if you were telling one everything, and you never told one nothing at all."

"What is it you want me to tell, my dear child?" Hyacinth freely fluted, putting his hand into her arm. "I'll tell you anything in life you like."

"I daresay you'll tell me no end of rot. Certainly I tried kindness on you," Miss Henning declared.

"Try it again; don't give it up," said her friend while he moved with her in close association.

She stopped short, detaching herself, though not with intention. "Well then, *has* she clean chucked you?"

Hyacinth's eyes turned away; he looked at the green expanse, misty and sunny, dotted with Sunday-keeping figures which made it seem larger; at the wooded boundary of the Park, beyond the grassy moat of the Gardens; at a shining reach of the Serpentine on the one side and the far façades of Bayswater, brightened by the fine weather and the privilege of their view, on the other. "Well, you know, I rather fancy it," he replied in a moment.

"Ah the vile brute!" she rang out as they resumed their walk.

Upwards of an hour later they were sitting under 299 the great trees of Kensington, those scattered, in the Gardens, over the slope which rises gently from the side of the water most distant from the old red palace. They had taken possession of a couple of the chairs placed there to the convenience of that superior part of the public for which a penny is not prohibitive, and Millicent, of whom such speculations were highly characteristic, had devoted considerable conjecture to the question of whether the functionary charged with collecting the penny would omit to come and demand his fee. Miss Henning liked to enjoy her pleasures *gratis* as well as to see others do so, and even that of sitting in a penny chair could touch her more deeply in proportion as she might feel she was "doing" some vested interest by it. The man came round, however, and after that her pleasure could only take the form of sitting as long as possible, to recover her money. This issue had been met, and two or three others of a much weightier kind had come up. At the moment we again participate in them she was leaning forward, earnest and attentive, her hands clasped in her lap and her multitudinous silver bracelets tumbled forward on her thick wrists. Her face, with its parted lips and eyes clouded to gentleness, wore an expression Hyacinth had never seen there before and which caused him to say to her: "After all, dear Milly, you're a sweet old boy!"

"Why did you never tell me before—years ago?" she asked.

"It's always soon enough to make a fool of one's self! I don't know why I've slobbered over to-day—sitting here in a charming place, in balmy air, amid pleasing suggestions and without any reason or practical end. The story's hideous and I've kept it down so long! It would have been an effort to me, an impossible effort at any time, to do otherwise. 300 Somehow, just now it hasn't been an effort; and indeed I've spoken just *because* the air's sweet and the place ornamental and the day a holiday and your person so lovely and your presence so moving. All this has had the effect an object has if you plunge it into a cup of water—the water overflows. Only in my case it's not water, but a very foul liquid indeed. Pardon the bad odour!"

There had been a flush of excitement in Millicent's face while she listened to what had gone before; it lingered, and as a fine colour still further refined by an access of sensibility is never unbecoming to a handsome woman it enriched her unwonted expression. "I wouldn't have been so rough with you," she presently remarked.

"My dear lass, *this* isn't rough!" Hyacinth protested.

"You're all of a tremble." She put out her hand and laid it on his own as if she had been a nurse feeling his pulse.

"Very likely. I'm a nervous little beast," he said.

"Any one would be nervous to think of anything so awful. And when it's yourself!" The girl's manner represented the dreadfulness of such a contingency. "You require sympathy," she added in a tone that made him perversely grin; the words sounded like a medical prescription.

"A tablespoonful every half-hour." And he kept her hand, which she was about to draw away.

"You'd have been nicer too," Millicent went on.

"How do you mean, I'd have been nicer?"

"Well, I like you now," said Miss Henning. And this time she drew away her hand as if, after such a speech, to recover her dignity.

"It's a pity I've always been so terribly under the influence of women," Hyacinth sighed again as he folded his arms. 301

He was surprised at the delicacy with which she replied. "You must remember they've a great deal to make up to you."

"Do you mean for my mother? Ah *she*'d have made it up if they had let her! But the sex in general have been very nice to me," he declared. "It's wonderful the kindness they've shown me and the amount of pleasure I've derived from their society."

It would perhaps be inquiring too closely to consider whether this reference to sources of consolation other than those that sprang from her own bosom had an irritating effect on Milly; she at all events answered it by presently saying: "Does *she* know—your trumpery Princess?"

"Yes, but she doesn't mind it."

"That's most uncommonly kind of her!" cried the girl with a scornful laugh.

"It annoys me very much," he interposed—though still with detachment—"to hear you apply invidious epithets to her. You know nothing about her."

"How do you know what I know, please?" She asked this question with the habit of her natural pugnacity, but the next instant she dropped her voice as in remembrance of the appeal made by a great misfortune. "Hasn't she treated you most shamefully, and you such a regular dear?"

"Not in the least. It is I who, as you may say, have rounded on her. She made my acquaintance because I was interested in the same things as herself. Her interest has continued, has increased, but mine, for some reason or other, has declined. She has been consistent and I've been beastly fickle."

"Your interest in the Princess has declined?" Millicent questioned, following imperfectly this somewhat complicated statement. 302

"Oh dear, no. I mean only in some opinions I used to hold." And he might have been speaking of "shaky" shares, to a considerable amount, of which he had at a given moment shrewdly directed his broker to relieve him.

"Ay, when you thought everything should go to the lowest! That's a good job!"—and Miss Henning's laugh suggested that, after all, Hyacinth's views and the changes in his views were not what was most important. "And your grand lady still goes in for the costermongers?"

"She wants to take hold of the great question of material misery; she wants to do something to make that misery less. I don't care for her means, I don't like her processes. But when I think of what there is to be done, and of the courage and devotion of those who set themselves to do it, it seems to me sometimes that with my reserves and scruples I'm a very poor creature."

"You *are* a poor creature—to sit there and put such accusations on yourself!" the girl flashed out. "If you haven't a spirit for yourself I promise I've got one for you! If she hasn't kicked you out why in the name of common sense did you say just now she has? And why is your dear old face as white as my stocking?"

Hyacinth looked at her a while without answering and as if he took a placid pleasure in her violence. "I don't know—I don't understand."

She put out her own hand now and took possession of his; for a minute she held it as wishing to check herself, as finding some influence in his touch that would help her. They sat in silence, looking at the ornamental water and the landscape-gardening reflected in it, till Milly turned her eyes again and brought out: "Well, that's the way I'd have served him too!" 303

It took him a moment to perceive she was alluding to the vengeance wrought on Lord Frederick. "Don't speak of that; you'll never again hear a word about it on my lips. It's all darkness."

"I always knew you were a gentleman," the girl went on with assurance.

"A queer variety, *cara mia*," her companion rejoined—not very candidly, as we know the theories he himself had cultivated on this point. "Of course you had heard poor Pinnie's wild maunderings. They used to exasperate me when she was alive, but I forgive her now. It's time I should, when I begin to talk myself. I think I'm breaking up."

"Oh it wasn't Miss Pynsent; it was just yourself."

"Pray what did I ever say—in those days?"

"It wasn't what you said," she answered with refinement. "I guessed the whole business—except of course what she got her time for and you being taken to that death-bed—the very day I came back to the Plice. Couldn't you see I was turning it over? And did I ever throw it up at you, whatever high words we might have had? Therefore what I say now is no more than I thought then. It only makes you nicer."

She was crude, she was common, she even had the vice of pointless exaggeration, for he himself honestly couldn't understand how the situation he had described could make him nicer. But when the faculty of affection that was in her rose to the surface it diffused a glow of rest, almost of protection, deepening at any rate the luxury of their small cheap pastoral, the interlude in the grind of the week's work; so that though neither of them had dined he would have been delighted to sit with her there the whole afternoon. It seemed a pause in something harsh that was happening to him, making it all easier, pushing it off to a distance. His thoughts 304 hovered about that with a pertinacity of which they themselves wearied, but they hung there now with an ache of indifference. It would be too much, no doubt, to say that Millicent's society appeared a compensation, yet he felt it at least a resource. For her too, evidently, the time had a taste; she made no proposal to retrace their steps. She questioned him about his father's family and as to their letting him go on like that without ever holding out so much as a little finger; and she declared in a manner that was meant to gratify him by the indignation it conveyed, though the awkwardness of the turn made him smile, that if she had been one of such a bloated crew she should never have been able to "abear" the thought of a relation in such a poor way. Hyacinth already knew what Miss Henning thought of his business at old Crook's and of the feeble show of a young man of his parts contented with a career that was after all a mere getting of one's living by one's 'ands. He had to do with books, but so had any shop-boy who should carry such articles to the residence of purchasers; and plainly Millicent had never discovered wherein the art he practised differed from that of a plumber or a saddler. He had not forgotten the shock once administered to her by his letting her know he wore an apron; she looked down on such conditions from her own so much higher range, since *she* wore mantles and jackets and shawls and the long trains of robes exhibited behind plate glass on dummies of wire and drawn forth to be transferred to her own undulating person, and had moreover never a scrap to do with making them up, but just with talking about them and showing them off and persuading people—people too quite gaping with the impression—of their beauty and cheapness. It had been a source of endless comfort to her, in her arduous evolution, that she 305 herself never worked with her 'ands. Hyacinth answered her inquiries, as she had answered his own of old, by asking her what "his family" owed to the son of a person who had brought murder and mourning into their bright sublimities, and whether she thought he was very highly recommended to them. His question pulled her up a moment; after which she returned with the finest spirit: "Well, if your position was so low ain't that all the more reason they should give you a lift? Oh it's something cruel!" she cried; and she added that in his place she would have found a way to bring herself under their notice. *She* wouldn't have drudged out her life in Soho if she had had the blood of half the Peerage in her veins! "If they had noticed you they'd have liked you," she was so good as to observe; but she immediately remembered also that in that case he would have been carried away quite over her head. She wasn't prepared to say that she would have given him up, little good as she had ever got of him. In that case he would have been thick with real swells, and she emphasised the "real" by way of a thrust at the fine lady of Madeira Crescent—an artifice wasted, however, inasmuch as Hyacinth was sure she had extracted from Sholto a tolerably detailed history of the Princess. Millicent was tender and tenderly sportive, and he was struck with the fact that his base birth really made little impression on her: she accounted it an accident much less grave than he had been in the habit of doing. She was touched and moved, but what moved her was his story of his mother's dreadful revenge, her long imprisonment and his childish visit to the jail, with his later discovery of his peculiar footing in the world. These things produced in her a generous agitation—something the same in kind as the emotion she had occasionally owed to the perusal of the 306 *Family Herald*. What affected her most and what she came back to was the whole element of Lord Frederick and the mystery of Hyacinth's having got so little good out of his affiliation to that nobleman. She couldn't get over his friends' not having done something, though her imagination was still vague as to what they might have done. It was the queerest thing in the world to find her apparently assuming that if he hadn't been so inefficient he might have "worked" the whole dark episode as a source of distinction, of glory, of profit. *She* wouldn't have been a nobleman's daughter for nothing! Oh the left hand was as good as the right; her respectability, for the moment, made nothing of that! His long silence was what most astonished her; it put her out of patience, and there was a strange candour in her wonderment at his not having bragged about his ancestry. The generations representing it were vivid and concrete to her now in comparison with the timid shadows Pinnie had set into spasmodic circulation. Millicent bumped about in his hushed past with the oddest mixture of enthusiasm and criticism, and with good intentions which had the effect of profane voices bawling for sacred echoes.

"Me only—me and her? Certainly I ought to be obliged, even though it's late in the day. The first time you saw her I suppose you told her—that night you went into her box at the theatre, eh? She'd have worse to tell you, I'm sure, if she could ever bring herself to speak the proper truth. And do you mean to say you never broke it to your big friend in the chemical line?"

"No, we've never talked about it."

"Men are rare creatures!" Millicent cried. "You never so much as mentioned it?"

"It wasn't necessary. He knew it otherwise—he knew it through his sister." 307

"How do you know that if he never spoke?"

"Oh because he was jolly good to me," said Hyacinth.

"Well, I don't suppose that ruined him," Miss Henning rejoined. "And how did his sister know it?"

"Oh I don't know. She guessed it."

The girl stared, then fairly snorted. "It was none of her business." Then she added: "He *was* jolly good to you? Ain't he good to you now?" She asked this question in her loud free voice, which rang through the bright stillness of the place.

Hyacinth delayed for a minute to meet it, and when at last he did so it was without looking at her. "I don't know. I can't make it out."

"Well, I can then!" And she jerked him round toward her and inspected him with her big bright eyes. "You silly baby, has *he* been serving you?" She pressed her curiosity upon him; she asked if that was what disagreed with him. His lips gave her no answer, but apparently after an instant she found one in his face. "Has he been making up to her Serene Highness—is that his game?" she broke out. "Do you mean to say she'd look at the likes of him?"

"The likes of him? He's as fine a man as stands!" said Hyacinth. "They've the same views, they're doing the same work."

"Oh he hasn't changed *his* opinions then—not like you?"

"No, he knows what he wants; he knows what he thinks."

"Very much the 'same work,' I'll be bound!" cried Millicent in large derision. "He knows what he wants, and I daresay he'll get it."

He was now on his feet, turning away from her; but she also rose and passed her hand into his arm. 308 "It's their own business; they can do as they please."

"Oh don't try to be a blamed saint; you put me out of patience!" the girl responded with characteristic energy. "They're a precious pair, and it would do me good to hear you say so."

"A man shouldn't turn against his friends," he went on with desperate sententiousness.

"That's for them to remember; there's no danger of *your* forgetting it." They had begun to walk but she stopped him; she was suddenly smiling at him and her face was radiant. She went on with caressing inconsequence: "All you've terribly told me—it *has* made you nicer."

"I don't see that, but it has certainly made *you* so. My dear girl, you're a comfort," Hyacinth added as they moved further. Soon after which, the protection offered by the bole of a great tree being sufficiently convenient, he had, on a large look about them, passed his arm round her and drawn her closer and closer—so close that as they again paused together he felt her yield with a fine firmness, as it were, and with the full mass of her interest. 309

XLII

He had no intention of going later on to Madeira Crescent, and that is why he asked her before they separated if he mightn't see her again after tea. The evenings were bitter to him now and he feared them in advance. The darkness had become a haunted element; it had visions for him that passed even before his closed eyes—sharp doubts and fears and suspicions, suggestions of evil, revelations of pain. He wanted company to light up his gloom, and this had driven him back to Millicent in a manner not altogether consistent with the respect which it was still his theory that he owed to his nobler part. He felt no longer free to drop in at the Crescent and tried to persuade himself, in case his mistrust should be overdone, that his reasons were reasons of magnanimity. If Paul were seriously occupied with the Princess, if they had work in hand for which their most earnest attention was required (and Sunday was all likely to be the day they would take: they had spent so much of the previous Sunday together) his absence would have the superior, the marked motive of his leaving his friend a clear field. There was something inexpressibly representative to him in the way that friend had abruptly decided to re-enter the house, after pausing outside with its mistress, at the moment he himself stood glaring through the fog with the Prince. The movement <u>310</u> repeated itself innumerable times to his inward sense, suggesting to him things he couldn't bear to learn. Hyacinth was afraid of being jealous even after he had become so, and to prove to himself he was not he had gone to see the Princess one evening in the middle of the week. Hadn't he wanted Paul to know her months and months before, and was he now to entertain a vile feeling at the first manifestation of an intimacy which rested, in each party to it, on aspirations that he respected? The Princess had not been at home, and he had turned away from the door without asking for Madame Grandoni: he had not forgotten that on the occasion of his previous visit she had excused herself from staying below. After the little maid in the Crescent had told him her mistress was out he walked away with a quick curiosity—a curiosity which, if he had listened to it, would have led him to mount the first omnibus that travelled in the direction of Camberwell. Was Paul Muniment, he such a rare one in general for stopping at home of an evening, was he also out, and would Rosy in this case be in the humour to mention—for of course she would know—where he had gone? Hyacinth let the omnibus pass, for he suddenly became aware with a rueful pang that he was in danger of playing the spy. He had not been near Muniment since, on purpose to leave his curiosity unsatisfied. He allowed himself, however, to notice that the Princess had now not written him a word of consolation, as she had been kind enough to do in the old days when he had knocked at her door without finding her. At present he had missed her twice in succession, and yet she had given no sign of regret—regret even on his own behalf. This determined him to stay away a bit longer; it was such a proof that she was absorbingly occupied. Hyacinth's glimpse of her in earnest talk with her friend—or 311 rather with his—as they returned from the excursion described by the Prince, his memory of Paul's beguiled figure crossing the threshold once more, could leave him no doubt as to the degree of that absorption.

Milly meanwhile hung back a little when he proposed to her that they should finish the day together. She smiled indeed and her splendid eyes rested on his with an air of indulgent wonder; they seemed to ask if it were worth her pains, in face of his probable incredulity, to mention the *real* reason why she couldn't have the pleasure of acceding to his delightful pressure. Since he would be sure to deride her explanation wouldn't some trumped-up excuse do as well, something he could knock about without hurting her? We are not to know exactly in what sense Miss Henning decided; but she confessed at last that there *was* an odious obstacle to their meeting again later—a promise she had made to go and see a young lady, the forewoman of her department, who was kept indoors with a bad face and nothing in life to help her pass the time. She was under a pledge to spend the evening with her, and it was not in her nature to fail of such a charity. Hyacinth made no comment on this speech; he received it in silence, looking at the girl gloomily.

"I know what's passing in your mind!" Millicent suddenly broke out. "Why don't you say it at once and give me a chance to contradict it? I oughtn't to care, but I do care!"

"Stop, stop—don't let us fight!" He spoke in a tone of pleading weariness; she had never heard just that accent before.

Millicent just considered: "I've a mind to play her false. She's a real lady, highly connected, and the best friend I have—I don't count men," she sarcastically sniffed—"and there isn't one in the world I'd do such a thing for but you." 312

"No, keep your promise; don't play any one false," said Hyacinth.

"Well, you *are* a gentleman!" she returned with a sweetness her voice occasionally took.

"Especially——" Hyacinth began; but he suddenly stopped.

"Especially what? Something impudent, I'll engage! Especially as you don't believe me?"

"Oh no! Don't let's fight!" he repeated.

"Fight, my darling? I'd fight *for* you!" Miss Henning declared.

He offered himself after tea the choice between a visit to Lady Aurora and a pilgrimage to Lisson Grove. He was a little in doubt about the former experiment, having an idea her ladyship's family might be reinstalled in Belgrave Square. He reflected, however, that he couldn't recognise this as a reason for not going to see her; his relations with her had nothing of the underhand, and she had given him the kindest general invitation. If her haughty parents were at home she was probably at dinner with them: he would take that risk. He had taken it before without disastrous results. He was determined not to spend the evening alone, and he would keep the Poupins as a more substantial alternative in case Lady Aurora shouldn't be able to receive him.

As soon as the great portal in Belgrave Square was drawn open before him he saw the house was occupied and animated—if animation might be talked about in a place which had hitherto mainly answered to his idea of a magnificent mausoleum. It was pervaded by subdued light and tall domestics; he found himself looking down a kind of colonnade of colossal footmen, an array more imposing even than the retinue of the Princess at Medley. His inquiry died away on his lips and he stood there struggling with dumbness. It was manifest to him that some 313 high festival was taking place, a scene on which his presence could only be a blot; and when a large official, out of livery, bending over him for a voice that didn't issue, suggested, not unencouragingly, that it might be Lady Aurora he wished to see, he replied with detachment and despair: "Yes, yes, but it can't be possible!" The butler took no pains to controvert this proposition verbally; he merely turned round with a majestic air of leading the way, and as at the same moment two of the footmen closed the wings of the door behind the visitor Hyacinth judged it his cue to follow. In this manner, after crossing a passage where, in the perfect silence of the servants, he heard the shorter click of his plebeian shoes upon a marble floor, he found himself ushered into a small room, lighted by a veiled lamp, which, when he had been left there alone, without further remark on the part of his conductor, he recognised as the place—only now more amply decorated—of one of his former interviews. Lady Aurora kept him waiting a little, but finally fluttered in with an anxious, incoherent apology. The same transformation had taken place in her own aspect as in that of her parental halls: she had on a light-coloured, crumpled-looking, faintly-rustling dress; her head was adorned with a languid plume that flushed into little pink tips, and in her hand she carried a pair of white gloves. All her repressed eagerness was in her face, and she smiled as if wishing to anticipate any scruples or embarrassments on the part of her visitor; frankly admitting herself disguised and bedizened and the shock the fact might convey. Hyacinth said to her that, no doubt, on inferring the return of her family to town, he ought to have backed out; he knew this must make a difference in her life. But he had been marched in, for all his protest, and now it was clear he had <u>314</u> interrupted her at dinner. She answered that no one who asked for her at any hour was ever turned away; she had managed to arrange that and was very happy in her success. She didn't usually dine—there were so many of them and it took so long. Most of her friends couldn't come at visiting-hours and it wouldn't be right she shouldn't ever receive them. On that occasion she *had* been dining, but it was all over; she was only sitting there because she was going to a party. Her parents were dining out and she was just in the drawing-room with some of her sisters. When they were alone it wasn't so long, though it was rather long afterwards, when they went up again. It wasn't time yet: the carriage wouldn't come for nearly half an hour. She hadn't been to an evening thing for months and months, but—didn't he know?—one sometimes had to do it. Lady Aurora expressed the idea that one ought to be fair all round and that one's duties were not all of the same species; some of them would come up from time to time that were quite different from the others. Of course it wasn't just unless one did all, and that was why she was in for something to-night. It was nothing of consequence; only the family meeting the family, as they might do of a Sunday, at one of their houses. It was there that papa and mamma were dining. Since they had given her that room for any hour she wanted—it was really tremendously convenient—she had resolved to do a party now and then, like a respectable young woman, because it pleased them: though why it should create even that thrill to see *her* at a place was more than she could imagine. She supposed it was because it would perhaps keep some people, a little, from thinking she was mad and not safe to be at large—which was of course a sort of thing that people didn't like to have thought of their <u>315</u> belongings. Lady Aurora explained and expatiated with a kind of yearning superabundance; she talked more continuously than Hyacinth had ever heard her do before, and the young man made out that she was not, so to speak, in equilibrium. He thought it scarcely probable she was excited by the simple prospect of again dipping into the great world she had forsworn, and he soon became aware of his having himself in a manner upset her. His senses were fine enough to hint to him that there were associations and wounds he revived and quickened. She suddenly stopped talking and the two sat there looking at each other in an odd, an occult community of suffering. He made mechanical remarks, explaining insufficiently why he had come, and in the course of a very few moments, quite independently of these observations, it seemed to him there was a deeper, a measurelessly deep, confidence between them. A tacit confession passed and repassed, and each understood the situation of the other. They wouldn't speak of it—

it was very definite they would never do that; for there was something in their common consciousness that was inconsistent with the grossness of accusation. Besides, the grievance of each was an apprehension, an instinct of the soul—not a sharp, definite wrong supported by proof. It was in the air and in their restless pulses, and not in anything they could exhibit or complain of for comfort. Strange enough it seemed to him that the history of each should be the counterpart of that of the other. What had each done but lose that which he or she had never so much as had? Things had gone ill with them; but even if they had gone well, even if the Princess had not combined with his friend in that manner which made his heart sink and produced an effect exactly corresponding on Lady Aurora's—even in this case what would felicity, what 316 would success, have amounted to? They would have been very barren. He was sure the singular creature before him would never have had a chance to take the unprecedented social step for the sake of which she was ready to go forth from Belgrave Square for ever; Hyacinth had judged the smallness of Paul Muniment's appetite for that complication sufficiently to have begun really to pity her ladyship long ago. And now, even when he most felt the sweetness of her sympathy, he might wonder what she could have imagined for him in the event of his not having been supplanted—what security, what completer promotion, what honourable, satisfying sequel. They were unhappy because they were unhappy, and they were right not to rail about that.

"Oh I like to see you—I like to talk with you," she said simply. They talked for a quarter of an hour, and he made her such a visit as any clever gentleman might have made any gentle lady. They exchanged remarks about the lateness of the spring, about the loan-exhibition at Burlington House—which Hyacinth had paid his shilling to see—about the question of opening the museums on Sunday, about the danger of too much coddling legislation on behalf of the working classes. He declared that it gave him great pleasure to catch any sign of her amusing herself; it was unnatural never to do that, and he hoped that now she had taken a turn she would keep it up. At this she looked down, smiling, at her frugal finery and then she said: "I daresay I shall begin to go to balls—who knows?"

"That's what our friends in Audley Court think, you know—that it's the worst mistake you can make not to drink deep of the cup while you have it."

"Oh I'll do it then—I'll do it for *them*!" Lady Aurora exclaimed. "I daresay that, as regards all 317 that, I haven't listened to them enough." This was the only allusion that passed on the subject of the Muniments.

Hyacinth got up, he had stayed long enough, since she was going out; and as he put forth his hand to her she seemed to him a heroine. She would try to cultivate the pleasures of her class if the brother and sister in Camberwell thought it right—try even to be a woman of fashion in order to console herself. Paul Muniment didn't care for her, but she was capable of considering that it might be her duty to regulate her life by the very advice that made an abyss between them. Hyacinth didn't believe in the success of this attempt; there passed before his imagination a picture of the poor lady coming home and pulling off her feathers for evermore after an evening spent watching the agitation of a ball-room from the outer edge of the circle and with a white, irresponsive face. "Let us eat and drink, for to-morrow we die," he said, laughing.

"Oh I don't mind dying."

"I think I do," Hyacinth declared as he turned away. There had been no mention whatever of the Princess.

It was early enough in the evening for him to risk a visit to Lisson Grove; he calculated that the Poupins would still be sitting up. When he reached their house he found this calculation justified; the brilliancy of the light in the window appeared to announce that Madame was holding a salon. He ascended to this apartment without delay—it was free to a visitor to open the house-door himself—and, having knocked, he obeyed the hostess's invitation to enter. Poupin and his wife were seated, with a third person, at a table in the middle of the room, round a staring kerosene lamp adorned with a globe of clear glass, of which the transparency was mitigated <u>318</u> only by a circular pattern of bunches of grapes. The third person was his friend Schinkel, who had been a member of the little party that had waited that wet, black night upon Hoffendahl. No one said anything as he came in; but in their silence the three others got up, looking at him, he thought, as he had on occasion imagined his being looked at before, only never quite so unmistakably. <u>319</u>

BOOK SIXTH

XLIII

"My child, you're always welcome," said Eustache Poupin, taking Hyacinth's hand in both his own and holding it for some moments. An impression had come to our young man, immediately, that they were talking about him before he appeared and that they would rather have been left to talk at their ease. He even thought he saw in Poupin's face the kind of consciousness that comes from detection, or at least interruption, in a nefarious act. With Poupin, however, it was difficult to tell; he always looked so heated and exalted, so like a conspirator defying the approach of justice. Hyacinth took in the others: they were standing as if they had shuffled something on the table out of sight, as if they had been engaged in the manufacture of counterfeit coin. Poupin kept hold of his hand; the Frenchman's ardent eyes, fixed, unwinking, always expressive of the greatness of the occasion, whatever the occasion was, had never seemed to him to protrude so far from the head. "Ah my dear friend, *nous causions justement de vous,*" Eustache remarked as if this were a very extraordinary fact.

"Oh *nous causions, nous causions*——!" his wife exclaimed as if to deprecate a loose overstatement. "One may mention a friend, I suppose, in the way of conversation, without taking such a liberty."

"A cat may look at a king, as your English proverb says," added Schinkel jocosely. He smiled so hard 322 at his own pleasantry that his eyes closed up and vanished—an effect which Hyacinth, who had observed it before, thought particularly unbecoming to him, appearing as it did to administer the last perfection to his ugliness. He would have consulted his facial interests by cultivating blankness.

"Oh a king, a king——!" Poupin demurred, shaking his head up and down. "That's what it's not good to be, *au point où nous en sommes.*"

"I just came in to wish you good-night," said Hyacinth. "I'm afraid it's rather late for a call, though Schinkel doesn't seem to think so."

"It's always too late, *mon très-cher,* when you come," the Frenchman returned. "You know if you've a place at our fireside."

"I esteem it too much to disturb it," said Hyacinth, smiling and looking round at the three.

"We can easily sit down again; we're a comfortable party. Put yourself beside me." And the Frenchman drew a chair close to the one, at the table, that he had just quitted.

"He has had a long walk, he's tired—he'll certainly accept a little glass," Madame Poupin pronounced with decision as she moved toward the tray containing the small gilded service of liqueurs.

"We'll each accept one, *ma bonne*; it's a very good occasion for a drop of *fine*," her husband interposed while Hyacinth seated himself in the chair marked by his host. Schinkel resumed his place, which was opposite; he looked across at the new visitor without speaking, but his long face continued to flatten itself into a representation of mirth. He had on a green coat which Hyacinth had seen before; this was a garment of ceremony, such as our young man judged it would have been impossible to procure in London or in any modern time. It was eminently German and of high antiquity, and had a 323 tall, stiff, clumsy collar which came up to the wearer's ears and almost concealed his perpetual bandage. When Hyacinth had sat down Eustache Poupin remained out of his own chair and stood beside him resting a hand on his head. At this touch something came over Hyacinth that brought his heart into his throat. The possibility that occurred to him, conveyed in Poupin's whole manner as well as in the reassuring intention of his caress and in his wife's instant, uneasy offer of refreshment, explained the confusion of the circle and reminded our hero of the engagement he had taken with himself to live up to a grand conception of the quiet when a certain crisis in his fate should have arrived. It struck him this crisis was in the air, very near—that he should touch it if he made another movement: the pressure of the Frenchman's hand, which was meant as an attenuation, only worked as a warning. As he looked across at Schinkel he felt dizzy and a little sick; for a moment, to his senses, the room whirled round. His resolution to be quiet appeared only too easy to keep; he couldn't break it even to the extent of speaking. He knew his voice would tremble, and this was why he made no answer to Schinkel's rather honeyed words, uttered after an hesitation. "*Also*, my dear Robinson, have you passed your Sunday well—have you had an 'appy day?" Why was every one so treacherously mild? His eyes questioned the table, but encountered only its well-wiped surface, polished for so many years by the gustatory elbows of the Frenchman and his wife, and the lady's dirty pack of cards for "patience"—she had apparently been engaged in this exercise when Schinkel came in—which indeed gave a little the impression of startled gamblers who might have shuffled away the stakes. Madam Poupin, diving into a cupboard, came back with a bottle of green chartreuse, an 324 apparition which led the German to exclaim: "*Lieber Gott*, you Vrench, you

Vrench, how well you always arrange! What on earth would you have more?"

The hostess distributed the liquor, but our youth could take none of it down, leaving it to the high appreciation of his friends. His indifference to this luxury excited discussion and conjecture, the others bandying theories and contradictions and even ineffectual jokes about him over his head—all with a volubility that seemed to him unnatural. For Poupin and Schinkel there was something all wrong with a man who couldn't smack his lips over a drop of that tap; he must either be in love or have some still more insidious complaint. It was true Hyacinth *was* always in love—that was no secret to his friends; but it had never been observed to stop his thirst. The Frenchwoman poured scorn on this view of the case, declaring that the effect of the tender passion was to make one enjoy one's victual—when everything went straight, *bien entendu*; and how could an ear be deaf to the wily words of a person so taking?—in proof of which she deposed that she had never eaten and drunk with such relish as at the time (oh far away now) when she had a soft spot in her heart for her rascal of a husband. For Madame Poupin to allude to the companion of her trials as a rascal indicated a high degree of conviviality. Hyacinth sat staring at the empty table with the feeling that he was somehow a detached, irresponsible witness of the evolution of his doom. Finally he looked up and said to his mates collectively: "What's up and what the deuce is the matter with you all?" He followed this inquiry by a request they would tell him what it was they had been saying about him, since they admitted he had been the subject of their talk. Madame Poupin answered for them that they had simply been saying how much they loved him, but that they 325 wouldn't love him any more if he became suspicious and *grincheux*. She had been telling Mr. Schinkel's fortune on the cards and she would tell Hyacinth's if he liked. There was nothing much for Mr. Schinkel, only that he would find something some day that he had lost, but would probably lose it again, and serve him right if he did! He had objected that he had never had anything to lose and never expected to have; but that was a vain remark, inasmuch as the time was fast coming when every one would have something—though indeed it was to be hoped Schinkel would keep it when he had got it. Eustache rebuked his wife for her levity, reminded her that their young friend cared nothing for old women's tricks, and said he was sure Hyacinth had come to talk over a very different matter: the question—he was so good as to take an interest in it, as he had done in everything that related to them—of the terms which M. Poupin might owe it to himself, to his dignity, to a just though not exaggerated sentiment of his value, to make in accepting Mr. "Crook's" offer of the foremanship of the establishment in Soho; an offer not yet formally enunciated but visibly in the air and destined—it would seem at least—to arrive within a day or two. The actual old titulary was going, late in the day, to set up for himself. The Frenchman intimated that before accepting any such proposal he must have the most substantial guarantees. "*Il me faudrait des conditions très-particulières.*" It was strange to Hyacinth to hear M. Poupin talk so comfortably about these high contingencies, the chasm by which he himself was divided from the future having suddenly doubled its width. His host and hostess sat down on either side of him, and Poupin gave a sketch, in somewhat sombre tints, of the situation in Soho, enumerating certain elements of decomposition which he perceived 326 to be at work there and which he would not undertake to deal with unless he should be given a completely free hand. Did Schinkel understand—and if so what was he grinning at? Did Schinkel understand that poor Eustache was the victim of an absurd hallucination and that there was not the smallest chance of his being invited to assume a lieutenancy? He had less capacity for tackling the British workman to-day than on originally beginning to rub shoulders with him, and old Crook had never in his life made a mistake, at least in the use of his tools. Hyacinth's responses were few and mechanical, and he presently ceased to try and look as if he were entering into his host's ideas.

"You've some news—you've some news about me," he brought out abruptly to Schinkel. "You don't like it, you don't like to have to give it to me, and you came to ask our friends here if they wouldn't help you out with it. But I don't think they'll assist you particularly, poor dears! Why do you mind? You oughtn't to mind more than I do. That isn't the way."

"*Qu'est-ce qu'il dit—qu'est-ce qu'il dit, le pauvre chéri?*" Madame Poupin demanded eagerly; while Schinkel looked very hard at her husband and as to ask for wise direction.

"My dear child, *vous vous faites des idées!*" the latter exclaimed, again laying his hand on his young friend all soothingly.

But Hyacinth pushed away his chair and got up. "If you've anything to tell me it's cruel of you to let me see it as you've done and yet not satisfy me."

"Why should I have anything to tell you?" Schinkel almost whined.

"I don't know that—yet I believe you have. I make out things, I guess things quickly. That's my nature at all times, and I do it much more now." 327

"You do it indeed; it's very wonderful," Schinkel feebly conceded.

"Mr. Schinkel, will you do me the pleasure to go away—I don't care where: out of this house?" Madame Poupin broke out in French.

"Yes, that will be the best thing, and I'll go with you," said Hyacinth.

"If you'd retire, my child, I think it would be a service that you'd render us," Poupin returned, appealing to him as with indulgence for his temper. "Won't you do us the justice to believe you may leave your interests in our hands?"

Hyacinth earnestly debated; it was now perfectly clear to him that Schinkel had some sort of message for him, and his curiosity as to what it might be had become nearly intolerable. "I'm surprised at your weakness," he observed as sternly as he could manage it to Poupin.

The Frenchman stared at him and then fell on his neck. "You're sublime, my young friend—you're truly sublime!"

"Will you be so good as to tell me what you're going to do with that young man?" demanded Madame Poupin with a glare at Schinkel.

"It's none of your business, my poor lady," Hyacinth replied, disengaging himself from her husband. "Schinkel, I wish you'd just walk away with me."

"*Calmons-nous, entendons-nous, expliquons-nous!* The situation's very simple," Poupin went on.

"I'll go with you if it will give you pleasure," said Schinkel very obligingly to Hyacinth.

"Then you'll give me that letter, the sealed one, first!" Madame Poupin, erecting herself, declared to the German.

"My wife, you're *bien sotte!*" Poupin groaned, lifting his hands and shoulders and turning away. 328

"I may be anything you like, but I won't be a party—no, God help me, not to that!" the good woman protested, planted before Schinkel as to prevent his moving.

"If you've a letter for me you ought to give it to me, hang you!" said Hyacinth to Schinkel. "You've no right to give it to any one else."

"I'll bring it to you in your house, my good friend," Schinkel replied with a vain, public wink which seemed to urge how Madame Poupin must be considered.

"Oh in his house—I'll go to his house!" this lady cried. "I regard you, I've always regarded you, as my child," she continued to Hyacinth, "and if this isn't an occasion for a mother——!"

"It's you who are making it an occasion. I don't know what you're talking about," said Hyacinth. He had been questioning Schinkel's face and believed he found in it a queer, convulsed but honest appeal to depend on him. "I've disturbed you and I think I had better go away."

Poupin had turned round again; he seized the young man's arm eagerly, as to prevent his retiring without taking in his false position. "How can you care when you know everything's changed?"

"What do you mean—everything's changed?"

"Your opinions, your sympathies, your whole attitude. I don't approve of it—*je le constate*. You've withdrawn your confidence from the people; you've said things on this spot, where you stand now, that have given pain to my wife and me."

"If we didn't love you we should say you had madly betrayed us!"— she quickly took her husband's idea.

"Oh I shall never madly betray you," Hyacinth rather languidly smiled.

"You'll never hand us over—of course you think <u>329</u> so. But you've no right to act for the people when you've ceased to believe in the people. *Il faut être conséquent, nom de Dieu!*" Poupin went on.

"You'll give up all thoughts of acting for me—*je ne permets pas ça!*" grandly added his wife.

"The thing's probably not of importance—only a little word of consideration," Schinkel suggested soothingly.

"We repudiate you, we deny you, we denounce you!" shouted Poupin with magnificent heat.

"My poor friends, it's you who have broken down, not I," said Hyacinth. "I'm much obliged to you for your solicitude, but the inconsequence is yours. At all events good-night."

He turned away from them and was leaving the room when Madame Poupin threw herself upon him as her husband had done a moment before, but in silence and with an extraordinary force of passion and distress. Being stout and powerful she quickly got the better of him and pressed him to her ample bosom in a long, dumb embrace.

"I don't know what you want me to do," he said as soon as he could speak. "It's for me to judge of my convictions."

"We want you to do nothing, because we *know* you've changed," Poupin insisted. "Doesn't it stick out of you, in every glance of your eye and every breath of your lips? It's only for that, because that alters everything."

"Does it alter my sacred vow? There are some things in which one can't change. I didn't promise to believe; I promised to obey."

"We want you to be sincere—that's the great thing," Poupin all edifyingly urged. "I'll go to see them—I'll make them understand."

"Ah you should have done that before!" his poor wife flashed. 330

"I don't know who you're talking about, but I'll allow no one to meddle in my affairs." Hyacinth spoke now with vehemence; the scene was cruel to his nerves, which were not in a condition to bear it.

"When it's a case of Hoffendahl it's no good to meddle," Schinkel gravely contributed.

"And pray who's Hoffendahl and what authority has *he* got?" demanded Madame Poupin, who had caught his meaning. "Who has put him over us all, and is there nothing to do but to lie down in the dust before him? Let him attend to his little affairs himself and not put them off on innocent children, no matter whether the poor dears are with us or against us."

This protest went so far that Poupin clearly felt bound to recover a dignity. "He has no authority but what we give him; but you know how we respect him and that he's one of the pure, *ma bonne*. Hyacinth can do exactly as he likes; he knows that as well as we do. He knows there's not a feather's weight of compulsion; he knows that for my part I long ago ceased to expect anything of him."

"Certainly there's no compulsion," said Schinkel. "It's to take or to leave. Only *they* keep the books."

Hyacinth stood there before the three with his eyes on the floor. "Of course I can do as I like, and what I like is what I *shall* do. Besides, what are we talking about with such sudden passion?" he asked, looking up. "I've no summons, I've no sign, I've no order. When the call reaches me it will be time to discuss it. Let it come or not come: it's not my affair."

"*Ganz gewiss*, it's not your affair," said Schinkel.

"I can't think why M. Paul has never done anything, all this time, knowing that everything's different now!" Madame Poupin threw in.

"Yes, my dear boy, I don't understand our friend," 331 her husband remarked, watching Hyacinth with suspicious, contentious eyes.

"It's none of his business any more than ours; it's none of any one's business!" Schinkel earnestly opined.

"Muniment walks straight; the best thing you can do is to imitate him," said Hyacinth, trying to pass Poupin, who had placed himself before the door.

"Promise me only this—not to do anything till I've seen you first," the Frenchman almost piteously begged.

"My poor old friend, you're very weak." And Hyacinth opened the door in spite of him and passed out.

"Ah well, if you *are* with us that's all I want to know!" the young man heard him call from the top of the stairs in a different voice, a tone of sudden, extravagant fortitude. 332

XLIV

Hyacinth had hurried down and got out of the house, but without the least intention of losing sight of Schinkel. The odd behaviour of the Poupins was a surprise and annoyance, and he had wished to shake himself free from it. He was candidly astonished at the alarm they were so good as to feel for him, since he had never taken in their having really gone round to the faith that the note he had signed to Hoffendahl would fail to be presented. What had he said, what had he done, after all, to give them the right to fasten on him the charge of apostasy? He had always been a free critic of everything, and it was natural that on certain occasions in the little parlour at Lisson Grove he should have spoken in accordance with that freedom; but it was with the Princess alone that he had permitted himself really to rail at their grimy "inferiors" and give the full measure of his scepticism. He would have thought it indelicate to express contempt for the opinions of his old foreign friends, to whom associations that made them venerable were attached; and, moreover, for Hyacinth a change of heart was in the nature of things much more an occasion for a hush of publicity and a kind of retrospective reserve: it couldn't prompt one to aggression or jubilation. When one had but lately discovered what could be said on the opposite side one didn't want to boast of one's 333 sharpness—not even when one's new convictions cast shadows that looked like the ghosts of the old.

He lingered in the street a certain distance from the house, watching for Schinkel's exit and prepared to remain there if necessary till the dawn of another day. He had said to the agitated trio just before that the manner in which the communication they looked so askance at should reach him was none of his business—it might reach him as it either smoothly or clumsily could. This was true enough in theory, but in fact his desire was overwhelming to know what Madame Poupin had meant by her allusion to a sealed letter, destined for him, in Schinkel's possession—an allusion confirmed by Schinkel's own virtual acknowledgment. It was indeed this eagerness that had driven him out of the house, for he had reason to believe the German wouldn't fail him, and it galled his suspense to see the foolish Poupins try to interpose, to divert the missive from its course. He waited and waited in the faith that Schinkel was dealing with them in his slow, categorical, Germanic way, and only reprehended him for having in the first place paltered with his sacred trust. Why hadn't he come straight to him—whatever the mysterious document was—instead of talking it over with French featherheads? Passers were rare at this hour in Lisson Grove and lights mainly extinguished; there was nothing to look at but the vista of the low black houses, the dim interspaced street-lamps, the prowling cats who darted occasionally across the road and the terrible mysterious far-off stars, which appeared to him more than ever to see everything of our helplessness and tell nothing of help. A policeman creaked along on the opposite side of the way, looking across at him as he passed, and stood for some minutes on the corner as to keep an eye on him. Hyacinth had leisure to reflect that the day was <u>334</u> perhaps not far off when a policeman might have an eye on him for a very good reason—might walk up and down, pass and repass as he mounted guard on him.

It seemed horribly long before Schinkel came out of the house, but it was probably only half an hour. In the stillness of the street he heard Poupin let his visitor out, and at the sound he stepped back into the recess of a doorway on the same side, so that in looking out the Frenchman shouldn't see him waiting. There was another delay, for the two stood talking together interminably and without seizable sounds on the doorstep. At last, however, Poupin went in again, and then Schinkel came down the street toward Hyacinth, who had felt sure he would proceed to that quarter, it being, as our young friend happened to know, that of his habitation. After he had heard Poupin go in he stopped and looked up and down; it was evidently his idea that Hyacinth would be awaiting him. Our hero stepped out of the shallow recess in which he had flattened himself, and came straight to him, and the two men stood there face to face in the dusky, empty, sordid street.

"You didn't let them have the letter?"

"Oh no, I retained it," said Schinkel with his eyes more than ever like invisible points.

"Then hadn't you better give it to me?"

"We'll talk of that—we'll talk." Schinkel made no motion to satisfy him; having his hands in the pockets of his trousers and an appearance marked by the exasperating assumption that they had the whole night before them. As one of the "dangerous" he was too intolerably for order.

"Why should we talk? Haven't you talked enough with those people all the evening? What have they to say about it? What right have you to detain a letter that belongs to me?" <u>335</u>

"*Erlauben Sie.* I'll light my pipe," the German simply returned. And he proceeded to this business methodically, while Hyacinth's pale, excited face showed in the glow of the match that ignited on the rusty railing beside them. "It isn't yours unless I've given it you," Schinkel went on as they walked along. "Be patient and I'll tell you," he added, passing his hand into his comrade's arm. "Your way, not so? We'll go down toward the Park." Hyacinth tried to be patient and listened with interest when Schinkel added: "She tried to take it; she attacked me with her hands. But that wasn't what I went for, to give it up."

"Is she mad? I don't recognise them"—and Hyacinth spoke as one scandalised.

"No, but they lofe you."

"Why then do they try to disgrace me?"

"They think it no disgrace if you've changed."

"That's very well for her; but it's pitiful for him, and I declare it surprises me."

"Oh *he* came round—he helped me to resist. He pulled his wife off. It was the first shock," said Schinkel.

"You oughtn't to have shocked them, my dear fellow," Hyacinth pronounced.

"I was shocked myself—I couldn't help it."

"Lord, how shaky you all are!" He was more and more aware now of all the superiority still left him to cling to.

"You take it well. I'm very sorry. But it is a fine chance," Schinkel went on, smoking away.

His pipe seemed for the moment to absorb him, so that after a silence Hyacinth resumed:

"Be so good as to remember that all this while I don't in the least understand what you're talking about."

"Well, it was this morning, early," said the 336 German. "You know in my country we don't lie in bett late, and what they do in my country I try to do everywhere. I think it's good enough. In winter I get up of course long before the sun, and in summer I get up almost at the same time. I should see the fine picture of the sunrise if in London you *could* see. The first thing I do of a Sunday is to smoke a pipe at my window, which is at the front, you remember, and looks into a little dirty street. At that hour there's nothing to see there—you English are so slow to leave the bett. Not much, however, at any time; it's not important, my bad little street. But my first pipe's the one I enjoy most. I want nothing else when I have that pleasure. I look out at the new fresh light—though in London it's not very fresh— and I think it's the beginning of another day. I wonder what such a day will bring—if it will bring anything good to us poor devils. But I've seen a great many pass and nothing has come. This morning, *doch*, brought something—something at least to you. On the other side of the way I saw a young man who stood just opposite my house and looking up at my window. He looked at me straight, without any ceremony, and I smoked my pipe and looked at him. I wondered what he wanted, but he made no sign and spoke no word. He was a very neat young man; he had an umbrella and he wore spectacles. We remained that way, face to face, perhaps for a quarter of an hour, and at last he took out his watch—he had a watch too—and held it in his hand, just glancing at it every few minutes, as if to let me know that he would rather not give me the whole day. Then it came over me that he wanted to speak to me! You would have guessed that before, but we good Germans are slow. When we understand, however, we act; so I nodded at him to let him know I'd 337 come down. I put on my coat and my shoes, for I was only in my shirt and stockings—though of course I had on my trousers—and I went down into the street. When he saw me come he walked slowly away, but at the end of a little distance he waited for me. When I came near him I saw him to be a very neat young man indeed—very young and with a very nice friendly face. He was also very clean and he had gloves, and his umbrella was of silk. I liked him very much. He said I should come round the corner, so we went round the corner together. I thought there would be some one there waiting for us; but there was nothing—only the closed shops and the early light and a little spring mist that told that the day would be fine. I didn't know what he wanted; perhaps it was some of our business—that's what I first thought—and perhaps it was only a little game. So I was very careful; I didn't ask him to come into the house. Yet I told him that he must excuse me for not understanding more quickly that he wished to speak with me; and when I said this he said it was not of consequence—he would have waited there, for the chance to see me, all day. I told him I was glad I had spared him that at least, and we had some very polite conversation. He *was* a very pleasant young man. But what he wanted was simply to put a letter in my hand; as he said himself he was only a good private postman. He gave me the letter—it was not addressed; and when I had taken it I asked him how he knew and if he wouldn't be sorry if it should turn out that I was not the man for whom the letter was meant. But I didn't give him a start; he told me he knew all it was necessary for him to know—he knew exactly what to do and how to do it. I think he's a valuable member. I asked him if the letter required an answer, and he 338 told me he had nothing to do with that; he was only to put it in my hand. He recommended me to wait till I had gone into the house again to read it. We had a little more talk—always very polite; and he mentioned that he had come so early because he thought I might go out if he delayed, and because also he had a great deal to do and had to take his time when he could. It's true he looked as if he had plenty to do—as if he was in some very good occupation. I should tell you he spoke to me always in English, but he was not English; he sounded his words only as if he had learnt them very well. I could see he has learnt everything very well. I suppose he's not German—so he'd have spoken to me in German. But there are so many, of all countries! I said if he had so much to do I wouldn't keep him; I would go to my room and open my letter. He said it wasn't important; and then I asked him if he wouldn't come into my room also and rest. I told him it wasn't very handsome, my room—because he looked like a young man who would have for himself a very neat lodging. Then I found he meant it wasn't important that we should talk any more, and he went away without even offering to shake hands. I don't know if he had other letters to give, but he went away, as I have said, like a good postman on his rounds, without giving me any more information."

It took Schinkel a long time to tell this story—his calm and conscientious thoroughness made no allowance for any painful acuteness of curiosity his auditor might feel. He went from step to step, treating all his points with lucidity and as if each would have exactly the same interest for his companion. The latter made no attempt to hurry him, and indeed listened now with a rare intensity of patience; for he *was* interested and it was moreover 339 clear to him that he was safe with Schinkel, who would satisfy him in time—wouldn't worry him with attaching conditions to their business in spite of the mistake, creditable after all to his conscience, he had made in going for discussion to Lisson Grove. Hyacinth learned in due course that on returning to his apartment and opening the little packet of which he had been put into possession, Mr. Schinkel had found himself confronted with two separate articles: one a sealed letter superscribed with our young man's name, the other a sheet of paper containing in three lines a request that within two days of receiving it he would hand the letter to the "young Robinson." The three lines in question were signed D. H., and the letter was addressed in the same hand. Schinkel professed that he already knew the writing; it was the neat fist—neatest in its very flourishes—of Diedrich Hoffendahl. "Good, good," he said, bearing as to soothe on Hyacinth's arm. "I'll walk with you to your door and I'll give it to you there; unless you like better I should keep it till to-morrow morning, so that you may have a quiet sleep—I mean in case it might contain anything that will be unpleasant to you. But it's probably nothing; it's probably only a word to say you need think no more about your undertaking."

"Why should it be that?" Hyacinth asked.

"Probably he has heard that you've cooled off."

"That I've cooled off?" Our hero stopped him short; they had just reached the top of Park Lane. "To whom have I given a right to say that?"

"Ah well, if you haven't, so much the better. It may be then for some other reason."

"Don't be an idiot, Schinkel," Hyacinth returned as they walked along. And in a moment he went on: "What the devil did you go and tattle to the Poupins for?" 340

"Because I thought they'd like to know. Besides, I felt my responsibility; I thought I should carry it better if they knew it. And then I'm like them—I lofe you."

Hyacinth made no answer to this profession; he only said the next instant: "Why didn't your young man bring the letter directly to me?"

"Ah I didn't ask him that! The reason was probably not complicated, but simple—that those who wrote it knew my address and didn't know yours. And wasn't I one of your backers?"

"Yes, but not the principal one. The principal one was Paul Muniment. Why wasn't any communication made me through Paul Muniment?" And this now struck him as a question that would reverberate the more one thought of it.

"My dear Robinson, you want to know too many things. Depend on it there are always good reasons. I should have preferred—yes—it had been Muniment. But if they didn't send to him——!" With which Schinkel's lucidity dropped and lost itself in a thick cloud of smoke.

"Well, if they didn't send to him——?" Hyacinth persisted.

"You're a great friend of his—how can I tell you?"

At this Hyacinth looked up at him askance and caught an ambiguous, an evasive roll in his companion's small, mild eye. "If it's anything against him my being his friend makes me just the man to hear it. I can defend him."

"Well, it's a possibility they're not satisfied."

"How do you mean it—not satisfied?"

"How shall I say it?—that they don't trust him."

"Don't trust him? And yet they trust me!"

"Ah my boy, depend upon it there are reasons," Schinkel replied; and in a moment he added: "They 341 know everything—everything. They're like the great God of the believers: they're searchers of hearts; and not only of hearts, but of all a man's life—his days, his nights, his spoken, his unspoken words. Oh they go deep and they go straight!"

The pair pursued the rest of their course for the most part in silence, Hyacinth being considerably struck with something that dropped from his companion in answer to a question he asked as to what Eustache Poupin had said when Schinkel, this evening, first told him what he had come to see him about. "*Il vaut du galme—il vaut du galme*": that was the German's version of the Frenchman's words; and Hyacinth repeated them over to himself several times and almost with the same accent. They had a certain soothing effect. In fact the good Schinkel was somehow salutary altogether, as our hero felt when they stopped at last at the door of his lodging in Westminster and stood there face to face while Hyacinth waited—just waited. The sharpness of his impatience had passed away and he watched without irritation the loving manner in which his mate shook the ashes out of the big smoked-out—so vehemently smoked-out—pipe and laid it to rest in its coffin. It was only after he had gone through this business with his usual attention to every detail of it that he said "*Also*, now for the letter" and, putting his hand inside his old waistcoat, drew forth the portentous missive. It passed instantly into Hyacinth's grasp, and our young man transferred it to his own pocket without looking at it. He thought he saw disappointment in Schinkel's ugly, kindly face at this indication that he himself should have no knowledge—present and relieving at least—of its contents; but he liked that better than his pretending to attribute to it again some silly comfortable sense. Schinkel had now the shrewdness or the good taste not to repeat 342 that remark, and as the letter pressed against his heart Hyacinth felt it still more distinctly, not as a vain balm to apprehension, but as the very penetration of a fatal knife. What his friend did say in a moment was: "Now you've got it I'm very glad. It's easier for me." And he effected a poor strained grin.

"I should think so!" Hyacinth exclaimed. "If you hadn't done your job you'd have paid for it."

Schinkel mumbled as for accommodation while he lingered, and then as Hyacinth turned away, putting in his door-key, brought out: "And if you don't do yours so will you."

"Yes, as you say, they themselves go straight! Good-night." And our young man let himself in.

The passage and staircase were never lighted and the lodgers either groped their way bedward with the infallibility of practice or scraped the wall with a casual match the effect of which, in the milder gloom of day, was a rude immensity of laceration. Hyacinth's room was a second floor back, and as he approached it he was startled by seeing a light proceed from the crevice under the door, the imperfect fitting of which figured to him thus as quite squalid. He stopped and considered this new note of his crisis, his first impulse being to connect it with the case just presented by Schinkel—since what could anything that touched him now be but a part of the same business? It was doubtless all in order that some second portent should now await him there. Yet it occurred to him that when he went out to call on Lady Aurora after tea he must simply have left a tallow candle burning, and that it showed a cynical spirit on the part of his landlady, who could be so close-fisted for herself, not to have gone in and put it out. Lastly it came over him that he had had a visitor in his absence and that the visitor 343 had taken possession of his apartment till his return, seeking such poor sources of comfort as were perfectly just. When he opened the door this last prevision proved the correct one, though the figure in occupation was not one of the possible presences that had loomed. Mr. Vetch sat beside the little table at which Hyacinth did his writing; he showed a weary head on a supporting hand and eyes apparently closed. But he looked up when his young man appeared. "Oh I didn't hear you; you're very quiet."

"I come in softly when I'm late, for the sake of the house—though I'm bound to say I'm the only lodger who has that refinement. Besides, you've been asleep," Hyacinth said.

"No, I've not been asleep," the old man returned. "I don't sleep much nowadays."

"Then you've been plunged in meditation."

"Yes, I've been thinking." With which Mr. Vetch explained that the woman of the house had begun by refusing him admittance without proper assurances that his intentions were pure and that he was moreover the oldest friend Mr. Robinson had in the world. He had been there an hour; he had thought he might find him by coming late.

Mr. Robinson was very glad he had waited and was delighted to see him and expressed regret that he hadn't known in advance of his visit, so that he might have something to offer him. He sat down on the bed, vaguely expectant; he wondered what special purpose had brought the fiddler so far at that unnatural hour. Yet he spoke but the truth in saying he was glad to see him. Hyacinth had come upstairs in such a pain of desire to be alone with the revelation carried in his pocket that the sight of a guest had given him positive relief by postponing solitude. The place where he had put his letter seemed to throb 344 against his side, yet he was thankful to his old friend for forcing him still to leave it so. "I've been looking at your books," the fiddler said; "you've two or three exquisite specimens of your own. Oh yes, I recognise your work when I see it; there are always certain little finer touches. You've a manner, as who should say, like one of the masters. With such a hand and such feeling your future's assured. You'll make a fortune and become famous."

Mr. Vetch sat forward to sketch this vision; he rested his hands on his knees and looked very hard at his young host, as if to challenge him to dispute a statement so cheering and above all so authoritative. The effect of what Hyacinth saw in his face was to produce immediately the idea that the fiddler knew something, though there was no guessing how he could know it. The Poupins, for instance, had had no time to communicate with him, even granting them capable of that baseness—all inconceivable in spite of Hyacinth's having seen them, less than an hour before, fall so much below their own standard. With this suspicion there rushed into his mind an intense determination to dissemble before his visitor to the last: he might imagine what he liked, but he should have no grain of satisfaction—or rather should have only that of being led to believe if possible that his suspicions were "rot." Hyacinth glanced over the books he had taken down from the shelf and admitted that they were pleasing efforts and that so long as one didn't become blind or maimed the ability to produce that sort of thing was a legitimate source of confidence. Then suddenly, as they continued simply to look at each other, the pressure of the old man's curiosity, the expression of his probing, beseeching eyes, which had become strange and tragic in these latter times and completely changed their character, grew so intolerable that to defend himself our hero <u>345</u> took the aggressive and asked him boldly if it were simply to look at his work, of which he had half-a-dozen specimens in Lomax Place, that he had made a nocturnal pilgrimage. "My dear old friend, you've something on your mind—some fantastic fear, some extremely erroneous *idée fixe*. Why has it taken you to-night in particular? Whatever it is it has brought you here at an unnatural hour under some impulse you don't or can't name. I ought of course to be thankful to anything that brings you here; and so I am in so far as that it makes me happy. But I can't like it if it makes *you* miserable. You're like a nervous mother whose baby's in bed upstairs; she goes up every five minutes to see if he's all right—if he isn't uncovered or hasn't tumbled out of bed. Dear Mr. Vetch, don't, don't worry; the blanket's up to my chin and I haven't tumbled yet."

He heard himself say these things as if he were listening to another person; the impudence of them in the grim conditions seemed to him somehow so rare. But he believed himself to be on the edge of a form of action in which impudence evidently must play a considerable part, and he might as well try his hand at it without delay. The way the old man looked out might have indicated that he too was able to take the measure of his perversity—judged him false to sit there declaring there was nothing the matter while a brand-new revolutionary commission burned in his pocket.

But in a moment Mr. Vetch said very mildly and as if he had really been reassured: "It's wonderful how you read my thoughts. I don't trust you; I think there are beastly possibilities. It's not true at any rate that I come to look at you every five minutes. You don't know how often I've resisted my fears—how I've forced myself to let you alone."

"You had better let me come and live with you 346 as I proposed after Pinnie's death. Then you'll have me always under your eyes," Hyacinth smiled.

The old man got up eagerly and, as Hyacinth did the same, laid firm hands on his shoulders, holding him close. "Will you now really, my boy? Will you come to-night?"

"To-night, Mr. Vetch?"

"To-night has worried me more than any other, I don't know why. After my tea I had my pipe and a glass, but I couldn't keep quiet; I was very, very bad. I got to thinking of Pinnie—she seemed to be in the room. I felt as if I could put out my hand and touch her. If I believed in ghosts, in signs or messages from the dead, I should believe I had seen her. She wasn't there for nothing; she was there to add her fears to mine—to talk to me about you. I tried to hush her up, but it was no use—she drove me out of the house. About ten o'clock I took my hat and stick and came down here. You may judge if I thought it important—I took a cab."

"Ah why do you spend your money so foolishly?" Hyacinth asked in a tone of the most affectionate remonstrance.

"Will you come to-night?" said his companion for rejoinder, holding him still.

"Surely it would be simpler for you to stay here. I see perfectly you're ill and nervous. You can take the bed and I'll spend the night in the chair."

The fiddler thought a moment. "No, you'll hate me if I subject you to such discomfort as that; and that's just what I don't want."

"It won't be a bit different in your room. There as here I shall have to sleep in a chair."

"I'll get another room. We shall be close together," the fiddler went on.

"Do you mean you'll get another room at this hour of the night, with your little house stuffed full 347 and your people all in bed? My poor Anastasius, you're very bad; your reason totters on its throne," said Hyacinth with excellent gaiety.

"Very good, we'll get a room to-morrow. I'll move into another house where there are two side by side." His "boy's" tone was evidently soothing to him.

"*Comme vous y allez!*" the young man continued. "Excuse me if I remind you that in case of my leaving this place I've to give a fortnight's notice."

"Ah you're backing out!" Mr. Vetch lamented, dropping his hands.

"Pinnie wouldn't have said that," Hyacinth returned. "If you're acting, if you're speaking, at the behest of her pure spirit, you had better act and speak exactly as she'd have done. She'd have believed me."

"Believed you? Believed what? What's there to believe? If you'll make me a promise I'll believe that."

"I'll make you any promise you like," said Hyacinth.

"Oh any promise I like—that isn't what I want! I want just one very particular little proof—and that's really what I came here for to-night. It came over me that I've been an ass all this time never to have got it out of you before. Give it to me now and I'll go home quietly and leave you in peace." Hyacinth, assenting in advance, requested again that he would formulate his demand, and then Mr. Vetch said: "Well, make me a promise—on your honour and as from the man you are, God help you, to the man I am—that you'll never, under any circumstances whatever, 'do' anything."

"'Do' anything——?"

"Anything those people expect of you."

"Those people?" Hyacinth repeated.

"Ah don't torment me—worried as I already am—with pretending not to understand!" the old 348 man wailed. "You know the people I mean. I can't call them by their names, because I don't know their names. But you do, and they know *you*."

Hyacinth had no desire to torment him, but he was capable of reflecting that to enter into his thought too easily would be tantamount to betraying himself. "I suppose I know the people you've in mind," he said in a moment; "but I'm afraid I don't grasp the need of such solemnities."

"Don't they want to make use of you?"

"I see what you mean," said Hyacinth. "You think they want me to touch off some train for them. Well, if that's what troubles you, you may sleep sound. I shall never do any of their work."

A radiant light came into the fiddler's face; he stared as if this assurance were too fair for nature. "Do you take your oath to that? Never anything, anything, anything?"

"Never anything at all."

"Will you swear it to me by the memory of that good woman of whom we've been speaking and whom we both loved?"

"My dear old Pinnie's memory? Willingly."

Mr. Vetch sank down in his chair and buried his face in his hands; the next moment his companion heard him sobbing. Ten minutes later he was content to take his departure and Hyacinth went out with him to look for another cab. They found an ancient four-wheeler stationed languidly at a crossing of the ways, and before he got into it he asked his young friend to kiss him. The young friend did so with a fine accolade and in the frank foreign manner, on both cheeks, and then watched the vehicle get itself into motion and rattle away. He saw it turn a neighbouring corner and then approached the nearest gas-lamp to draw from his breast-pocket the sealed letter Schinkel had given him. <u>349</u>

XLV

"And Madame Grandoni then?" he asked, all loth to turn away. He felt pretty sure he should never knock at that door again, and the desire was strong in him to see once more, for the last time, the ancient, afflicted, titular "companion" of the Princess, whom he had always liked. She had struck him as ever in the slightly ridiculous position of a confidant of tragedy in whom the heroine, stricken with reserves unfavourable to the dramatic progression, should have ceased to confide.

"*È andata via, caro signorino*," said Assunta, smiling at him as she held the door open.

"She has gone away? Bless me! when did she go?"

"It's now five days, dear young sir. She has returned to *our* fine country."

"Is it possible?" He felt it somehow as a personal loss.

"*È possibilissimo!*" Then Assunta added: "There were many times when she almost went; but this time, *capisce*——!" And without finishing her sentence this most exiled of Romans and expertest of tire-women indulged in a subtle, suggestive, indefinable play of expression to which hands and shoulders contributed as well as lips and eyebrows.

Hyacinth looked at her long enough to catch any meaning she might have wished to convey, but 350 gave no sign of apprehending it. He only remarked gravely: "In short she's off!"

"Eh, and the worst is she'll probably never come back. She didn't move, as she kept threatening, for a long time; but when at last she decided——!" And Assunta's flattened hand, sweeping the air sidewise, figured the straightness of the old lady's course. "*Peccato!*" she ended with a sigh.

"I should have liked to see her again—I should have liked to bid her good-bye." He lingered, suddenly helpless, though, informed of the Princess's own more temporary absence, he had no reason for remaining save the possibility she might reappear before he turned away. This possibility, however, was small, since it was only nine o'clock, the middle of the evening—too early an hour for her return if, as Assunta said, she had gone out after tea. He looked up and down the Crescent, gently swinging his stick, and became aware in a moment of some tender interest on the part of his humbler friend.

"You should have come back sooner; then perhaps Madama wouldn't have gone, *povera vecchia*," she rejoined in a moment. "It's too many days since you've been here. She liked you—I know that."

"She liked me, but she didn't like me to come," said Hyacinth. "Wasn't that why she went—because we keep coming?"

"Ah that other one—with the long legs—yes. But you're better."

"The Princess doesn't think so, and she's the right judge," Hyacinth smiled.

"Eh, who knows what she thinks? It's not for me to say. But you had better come in and wait. I daresay she won't be long, and she'll be content to find you."

Hyacinth wondered. "I'm not sure of that." Then he asked: "Did she go out alone?" 351

"*Sola, sola.* Oh don't be afraid; you were the first!" And Assunta, delightfully, frankly insidious, flung open the door of the little drawing-room.

He sat there nearly an hour, in the chair the Princess habitually used, under her shaded lamp, with a dozen objects round him which seemed as much a part of herself as if they had been folds of her dress or even tones of her voice. His thoughts rattled like the broken ice of a drink he had once wistfully seen mixed at an "American Bar," but he was too tired for unrest; he had not been to work and had walked about all day to fill the time; so that he simply lay back there with his head on one of the Princess's cushions, his feet on one of her little stools—one of the ugly ones that belonged to the house—and his respiration coming as quick as that of a man in sharp suspense. He was agitated beneath his fatigue, yet not because he was waiting for the Princess; a deeper source of emotion had been opened to him and he had not on the present occasion more mere "nervous" intensity than he had known at other moments of the past twenty hours. He had not closed his eyes the night before, and the day had not made up for that torment. A fever of reflexion had descended on him and the range of his imagination been wide. It whirled him through circles of immeasurable compass; and this is the reason for which, thinking of many things while he sat in the Princess's place, he wondered why, after all, he had come to Madeira Crescent and what interest he could have in seeing the lady of the house. Wasn't everything over between them and the link snapped which had for its brief hour bound them so closely together? And this not simply because for a long time now he had received no sign nor communication from her, no invitation to come back, no inquiry as to why his visits had stopped; not even because he had seen her 352 go in and out with Paul Muniment and it had suited Prince Casamassima to point to him the moral of her doing so; nor still because, quite independently of the Prince, he believed her to be more deeply absorbed in her acquaintance with that superior young man than she had ever been in her relations with himself. The ground of his approach, so far as he became conscious of it in his fitful meditations, could only be a strange, detached curiosity—strange and detached because everything else of his past had been engulfed in the abyss that opened before him when, after his separation from Mr. Vetch, he stood under the lamp in the paltry Westminster street. That had swallowed up all familiar feelings, and yet out of the ruin had sprung the impulse of which this vigil was the result.

The solution of his difficulty—he flattered himself he had arrived at it—involved a winding-up of his affairs; and though, even had no solution been required, he would have felt clearly that he had been dropped, yet since even in that case it would have been sweet to him to bid her good-bye, so at present the desire for some last vision of her own hurrying fate could still appeal to him. If things had not gone well for him he was still capable of wondering if they looked better for her. There rose in his mind all perversely, yet all humanly, a yearning need to pity her. These were odd feelings enough, and by the time half an hour had elapsed they had throbbed themselves into the stupor of exhaustion. While it came to him in how different a frame he was waiting now from that of his first visit in South Street he closed his eyes and lost himself. His unconsciousness lasted, he afterwards supposed, nearly half an hour; it ended in his feeling the lady of the house stand there before him. Assunta was behind and as he opened his eyes took from her the bonnet and mantle of which she divested 353 herself. "It's charming of you to have waited," the Princess said, smiling down at him with all her old kindness. "You're very tired— don't get up; that's the best chair and you must keep it." She made him remain where he was; she placed herself near him on a smaller seat; she declared she wasn't tired herself, that she didn't know what was the matter with her—nothing tired her now; she exclaimed on the time that had elapsed since he had last called, as if she were reminded of it simply by seeing him again; and she insisted that he should have some tea—he looked so much as if he needed it. She considered him with deeper attention and wished to know where he ailed—what he had done to use himself up; adding that she must begin to look after him again, since while she had had the care of him that kind of thing didn't happen. In response to this Hyacinth made a great confession: he admitted he had stayed away from work and simply amused himself—amused himself by loafing about London all day. This didn't pay—he had arrived at that wisdom as he grew older; it was doubtless a sign of increasing years when one felt one's self finding wanton pleasures hollow and that to stick to one's tools was not only more profitable but more refreshing. However, he did stick to them as a general thing: that was no doubt partly why, from the absence of the habit of it, a day off turned out rather a sell. Meanwhile, when he hadn't seen her for some time he always on meeting the Princess again had a renewed, formidable sense of her beauty, and he had it to-night in an extraordinary degree. Splendid as that beauty had ever been it shone on this occasion, like a trimmed lamp, clearer and further, so that—if what was already supremely fine could be capable of greater refinement—it might have worked itself free of all earthly grossness and been purified and consecrated by her new 354 life. Her gentleness, when she turned it on, was quite divine—it had always the irresistible charm that it was the humility of a high spirit—and on this occasion she gave herself up to it. Whether it was because he had the consciousness of resting his eyes on her for the last time, or because she wished to be particularly pleasant to him in order to make up for having amid other preoccupations rather dropped him of late—it was probable the effect sprang from both causes—at all events the sight of each great, easy, natural, yet all so coercive, fact of her seemed no poorer a privilege than when, the other year, he had gone into her box at the play. She affected him as raising and upholding the weight that rested on him very much after the form of some high, bland caryatid crowned with a crushing cornice. He suffered himself to be coddled and absently, even if radiantly, smiled at, and his state of mind was such that it could produce no alteration of his pain to see that these were on the Princess's part inexpensive gifts. She had sent Assunta to bring them tea, and when the tray arrived she gave him cup after cup with every grace of hospitality; but he had not sat with her a quarter of an hour before he was sure she scarcely measured a word he said to her or a word she herself uttered. If she had the best intention of being "balmy" by way of making up, she was still rather vague about what she was to make up *for*. Two points became perfectly clear: first that she was thinking of something quite other than her present, her past, or her future relations with Hyacinth Robinson; second that he was superseded indeed. This was so completely the case that it didn't even occur to her, evidently, how cruel the sense of supersession might be to one who was sick and sore. If she was charming to such weakness wasn't it because she was good-natured and he had 355 been hanging off, and not because she had done him an injury? Perhaps after all she hadn't, for he got the impression it might be no great loss of comfort to any shuffler not to constitute part of her intimate life to-day. It was manifest from things in her face, from her every movement and tone, and indeed from all the irradiation of her beauty, that this life was involving intimacies and efforts arduous all round. If he had called from curiosity about her success it was sufficiently implied for him that her success was good: she was living more than ever on high hopes and bold plans and far-reaching combinations. These things, from his own point of view, were not now so quite the secret of joy, and to be mixed up with them was perhaps not so much greater a sign that one hadn't lived for nothing than the grim understanding he had in the interest of peace just arrived at with himself. She asked why he hadn't been to her for so long, much as if this failure were only a vulgar form of social neglect; and she scarce seemed to note it either as a good or as a poor excuse when he said he had stayed away because he knew her to be deep in business. But she didn't deny the impeachment; she admitted she had been busier than ever in her life before. She looked at him as if he would know what that meant, and he said he was very sorry for her.

"Because you think it's all a mistake? Yes, I know that. Perhaps it is, but if so it's a magnificent one. If you were scared about me three or four months ago I don't know what you'd think to-day—if you knew! I've risked," she yet all portentously simply stated, "everything."

"Fortunately I don't know anything," he said.

"No indeed. How should you?"

"And to tell the truth," he went on, "that's really the reason I haven't been back here till to-night. I 356 haven't wanted to know—I've feared and hated to know."

"Then why did you come at last?"

"Well, out of the most illogical of curiosities."

"I suppose then you'd like me to tell you where I've been to-night, eh?" she asked.

"No, my curiosity's satisfied. I've learnt something—what I mainly wanted to know—without your telling me."

She stared an instant. "Ah you mean whether Madame Grandoni had gone? I suppose Assunta told you."

"Yes, Assunta told me, and I was sorry to hear it."

The Princess looked grave, as if her old friend's departure had been indeed a very awkward affair. "You may imagine how I feel it! It leaves me completely alone; it makes, in the eyes of the world, an immense difference in my position. However, I don't consider the eyes of the world. At any rate she couldn't put up with me any more; it appears I'm more and more of a scandal—and it was written!" On Hyacinth's asking what the old lady would do she said: "I suppose she'll go and live with my husband. Funny, isn't it? that it should have always to be with one of us and that it should matter so little which." Five minutes later she inquired of him if the same reason he had mentioned just before was the explanation of his absence from Audley Court. Mr. Muniment had told her he hadn't been near him and the sister for more than a month.

"No, it isn't the fear of learning something that would make me uneasy: because somehow, in the first place, it isn't natural to feel uneasy about Paul, and because in the second, if it were, he never lets one see anything—of any effect or impression on 357 him. It's simply the general sense of real divergence of view. When that divergence becomes sharp there are forms and lame pretences——"

"It's best not to try to keep up? I see what you mean—when you're grimly sincere. But you might go and see the sister."

"I don't like the sister," Hyacinth frankly averred.

"Ah neither do I!" the Princess said; while her visitor remained conscious of the perfect composure, the absence of false shame, with which she had named their common friend. But she was silent after this, and he judged he had stayed long enough and sufficiently taxed a preoccupied attention. He got up and was bidding her good-night when she suddenly brought out: "By the way, your not going to see so good a friend as Mr. Muniment because you disapprove to-day of his work suggests to me that you'll be in an awkward fix, with your disapprovals, the hour you're called upon to serve the cause according to your vow."

"Oh of course I've thought of that," Hyacinth smiled.

"And would it be indiscreet to ask what you've thought?"

"Ah so many things, Princess! It would take me a long time to say."

"I've never talked to you of this, because it seemed to me indelicate and the whole thing too much a secret of your own breast for even so intimate a friend as I've been to have a right to meddle with it. But I've wondered much, seeing you take all the while less and less interest—in the real business, I mean, less and less—how you'd reconcile your change of heart with your meeting your engagement. I pity you, my poor friend," she went on with a noble benignity, "for I can imagine nothing more terrible than to find yourself face to face with your 358 obligation and to feel at the same time the spirit originally prompting it dead within you."

"Terrible, terrible, most terrible." And he looked at her gravely.

"But I pray God it may never be your fate!" The Princess had a pause, after which she added: "I see you feel it. Heaven help us all! Why shouldn't I tell you when I worry?" she went on. "A short time ago I had a visit from Mr. Vetch."

"It was kind of you to see him," Hyacinth said.

"He was delightful, I assure you. But do you know what he came for? To beg me on his knees to snatch you away."

"Away from what?"

"From the danger that hangs over you. He was most touching."

"Oh yes, he has talked to me about it," our young man said. "He has picked up the idea, but is utterly at sea. And how did he expect you'd be able to snatch me?"

"He left that to me; he had only a general—and such a flattering—belief in my possible effect on you."

"And he thought you'd set it in motion to make me back out? He does you injustice. You wouldn't!" Hyacinth finely laughed. "In that case, taking one false position with another, yours would be no better than mine."

"Oh, speaking seriously, I'm perfectly quiet about you and about myself. I know you won't be called," the Princess returned.

"May I be told how you know it?"

She waited but an instant. "Mr. Muniment keeps me informed."

"And how does *he* know?"

"We've information. My poor dear friend," the Princess went on, "you're so much out of it now that if I were to tell you I fear you wouldn't understand." 359

"Yes, no doubt I'm out of it; but I still have a right to say, all the same, in contradiction to your charge of a moment ago, that I take interest in the 'real business' exactly as much as I ever did."

"My poor Hyacinth, my dear, infatuated, little aristocrat, was that ever very much?" she asked.

"It was enough, and it's still enough, to make me willing to lay down my life for anything that will clearly help."

"Yes, and of course you must decide for yourself what that is—or rather what it's not."

"I didn't decide when I gave my promise. I agreed to abide by the decision of others," Hyacinth answered.

"Well, you said just now that in relation to this business of yours you had thought of many things," his friend pursued. "Have you ever by chance thought of anything that *will* do their work?"

"Their work?"

"The people's."

"Ah you call me fantastic names, but I'm one of them myself!" he cried.

"I know what you're going to say," the Princess broke in. "You're going to say it will help them to do what you do—to do their work themselves and earn their wages. That's beautiful so far as it goes. But what do you propose for the thousands and hundreds of thousands for whom no work—on the overcrowded earth, under the pitiless heaven—is to be found? There's less and less work in the world, and there are more and more people to do the little there is. The old ferocious selfishness *must* come down. They won't come down gracefully, so they must just be assisted."

The tone in which she spoke made his heart beat fast, and there was something so inspiring in the great union of her beauty, her sincerity and her energy that the image of a heroism not less great <u>360</u> flashed up again before him in all the splendour it had lost—the idea of a tremendous risk and an unregarded sacrifice. Such a woman as that, at such an hour, one who could shine like silver and ring like crystal, made every scruple a poor prudence and every compunction a cowardice. "I wish to God I could see it as you see it!" he wailed after he had looked at her some seconds in silent admiration.

"I see simply this: that what we're doing is at least worth trying, and that as none of those who have the power, the place, the means, will bethink themselves of anything else, on *their* head be the responsibility, on *their* head be the blood!"

"Princess," said Hyacinth, clasping his hands and feeling that he trembled, "dearest Princess, if anything should happen to *you*——!" But his voice fell; the horror of it, a dozen hideous images of her possible perversity and her possible punishment were again before him, as he had already seen them in sinister musings: they seemed to him worse than anything he had imagined for himself.

She threw back her head, looking at him almost in anger. "To me! And pray why not to me? What title have I to exemption, to security, more than any one else? Why am I so sacrosanct and so precious?"

"Simply because there's no one in the world and has never been any one in the world like you."

"Oh thank you!" said the Princess impatiently. And she turned from him as with a beat of great white wings that raised her straight out of the bad air of the personal. It took her up too high, it put an end to their talk; expressing an indifference to what it might interest him to think of her to-day, and even a contempt for it, which brought tears to his eyes. His tears, however, were concealed by the fact that he bent his head low over the hand he had taken to kiss; after which he left the room without looking at her. 361

XLVI

"I've received a letter from your husband," Paul Muniment said to her the next evening as soon as he came into the room. He announced this truth with an unadorned directness as well as with a freedom of manner that showed his visit to be one of a closely-connected series. The Princess was evidently not a little surprised and immediately asked how in the world the Prince could know his address. "Couldn't it have been by your old lady?" Muniment returned. "He must have met her in Paris. It's from Paris he writes."

"What an incorrigible cad!" she exclaimed.

"I don't see that—for writing to me. I've his letter in my pocket and I'll show it to you if you like."

"Thank you, nothing would induce me to touch anything he has touched."

"You touch his money, my dear lady," Muniment remarked with one of the easy sequences of a man who sees things as they are.

The Princess considered. "Yes, I make an exception for that, because it hurts him, it makes him suffer."

"I should think on the contrary it would gratify him by showing you in a state of weakness and dependence."

"Not when he knows I don't use it for myself. What exasperates him is that it's devoted to ends 362 which he hates almost as much as he hates me and yet which he can't call selfish."

"He doesn't hate you," said Muniment with the same pleasant reasonableness—that of a man who has mastered not two or three but all the possible aspects of a question. "His letter satisfies me of that." The Princess stared at this and asked what he was coming to—if he were leading up to the hint that she should go back and live with her husband. "I don't know that I'd go so far as to advise it," he replied; "when I've so much benefit from seeing you here on your present footing, that wouldn't sound well. But I'll just make bold to prophesy you'll go before very long."

"And on what does that extraordinary prediction rest?"

"On this plain fact—that you'll have nothing to live upon. You decline to read the Prince's letter, but if you were to look at it it would give you evidence of what I mean. He informs me that I need count on no more supplies from your hands, since you yourself will receive no more."

"He addresses you in those plain terms?"

"I can't call them very plain, because the letter's in French and I naturally have had a certain difficulty in making it out, in spite of my persevering study of the tongue and the fine example set me by poor Robinson. But that appears to be the gist of the matter."

"And you can repeat such an insult to me without the smallest apparent discomposure? You're indeed the most extraordinary of men!" the Princess broke out.

"Why is it an insult? It's the simple truth. I do take your money," Muniment said.

"You take it for a sacred cause. You don't take it for yourself." 363

"The Prince isn't obliged to look at that," he answered amusedly.

His companion had a pause. "I didn't know you were on his side."

"Oh you know on what side I am!"

"What does *he* know? What business has he to address you so?"

"I suppose, as I tell you, that he knows from Madame Grandoni. She has told him I've great influence with you."

"Ah she was welcome to tell him that!" the Princess tossed off.

"His reasoning, therefore, has been that when I find you've nothing more to give to the cause I'll let you go."

"Nothing more? And does he count *me* myself, and every pulse of my being, every capacity of my nature, as nothing?" the Princess cried with shining eyes.

"Apparently he thinks *I* do."

"Oh as for that, after all, I've known you care far more for my money than for me. But it has made no difference to me," she finely said.

"Then you see that by your own calculation the Prince is right."

"My dear sir," Muniment's hostess replied, "my interest in you never depended on your interest in me. It depended wholly on a sense of your great destinies. I suppose that what you began to tell me," she went on, "is that he stops my allowance."

"From the first of next month. He has taken legal advice. It's now clear—so he tells me—that you forfeit your settlements."

"Can't I take legal advice too?" she demanded. "I can fight that to the last inch of ground. I can forfeit my settlements only by an act of my own. The act that led to our separation was *his* act; he turned me out of his house by physical violence." 364

"Certainly," said her visitor, displaying even in this simple discussion his easy aptitude for argument; "but since then there *have* been acts of your own——!" He stopped a moment, smiling; then went on: "Your whole connexion with a league working for as great ends as you like, but for ends and by courses necessarily averse to the eye of day and the observation of the police—this constitutes an act; and so does your exercise of the pleasure, which you appreciate so highly, of feeding it with money extorted from an old Catholic and princely family. You know how little it's to be desired that these matters should come to light."

"Why in the world need they come to light? Allegations in plenty of course he'd have, but not a particle of proof. Even if Madame Grandoni were to testify against me, which is inconceivable, she wouldn't be able to produce a definite fact."

"She'd be able to produce the fact that you had a little bookbinder staying for a month in your house."

"What has that to do with it?" she promptly asked. "If you mean that that's a circumstance which would put me in the wrong as against the Prince, is there not on the other side this marked detail that while our young friend was staying with me Madame Grandoni herself, a person of the highest and most conspicuous respectability, never saw fit to withdraw from me her countenance and protection? Besides, why shouldn't I have my bookbinder just as I might have—and the Prince should surely appreciate my consideration in not having—my physician and my chaplain?"

"Am I not your chaplain?" Muniment again amusedly inquired. "And does the bookbinder usually dine at the Princess's table?"

"Why not—when he's an artist? In the old 365 times, I know, artists dined with the servants; but not to-day."

"That would be for the court to appreciate," he said. And in a moment he added: "Allow me to call your attention to the fact that Madame Grandoni *has* left you—*has* withdrawn her countenance and protection."

"Ah but not for Hyacinth!" the Princess returned in a tone which would have made the fortune of an actress if an actress could have caught it.

"For the bookbinder or for the chaplain, it doesn't matter. But that's only a detail. In any case," he noted, "I shouldn't in the least care for your going to law."

The Princess rested her eyes on him a while in silence and at last replied: "I was speaking just now of your great future, but every now and then you do something, you say something, that makes me really doubt you. It's when you seem afraid. That's terribly against your being a first-rate man."

"Ah I know you've thought me little better than a smooth sneak from the first of your knowing me. But what does it matter? I haven't the smallest pretension to being a first-rate man."

"Oh you're deep and you're provoking!" she said with sombre eyes.

"Don't you remember," he went on without heeding this rich comment, "don't you remember how the other day you accused me of being not only a coward but a traitor; of playing false, of wanting, as you said, to back out?"

"Most distinctly. How can I help its coming over me at times that you've incalculable ulterior views and are but consummately using me—but consummately using us all? Well, I don't care!"

"No, no; I'm genuine," said Muniment simply, yet in a tone which might have implied that their 366 discussion was idle. And he made a transition doubtless too abrupt for perfect civility. "The best reason in the world for your not going to law with your husband is this: that when you haven't a penny left you'll be obliged to go back and live with him."

"How do you mean, when I haven't a penny left? Haven't I my own property?" the Princess demanded.

"The Prince assures me you've drawn on your own property at such a rate that the income to be derived from it amounts, to his positive knowledge, to no more than a thousand francs—forty pounds—a year. Surely with your habits and tastes you can't live on forty pounds. I should add that your husband implies that your property originally was rather a small affair."

"You've the most extraordinary tone," she answered gravely. "What you appear to wish to express is simply this: that from the moment I've no more money to give you I'm of no more value than the washed-out tea-leaves in that pot."

Muniment looked down a while at his substantial boot. His companion's words had brought a flush to his cheek; he appeared to admit to himself and to her that at the point their conversation had reached there was a natural difficulty in his delivering himself. But presently he raised his head, showing a face still slightly embarrassed, but more for her than for himself. "I've no intention whatever of saying anything harsh or offensive to you, but since you challenge me perhaps it's well that I should let you know how inevitably I *do* consider that in giving your money—or rather your husband's—to our business you gave the most valuable thing you had to contribute."

"This is the day of plain truths!" she rang out with a high mildness. "You don't count then any 367 devotion, any intelligence that I may have placed at your service—even rating my faculties modestly?"

"I count your intelligence, but I don't count your devotion, and one's nothing without the other. You're not trusted—well, where it makes the difference."

"Not trusted!" the Princess repeated with her splendid stare. "Why I thought I could be hanged to-morrow!"

"They may let you hang, perfectly, without letting you act. You're liable to be weary of us," he went on; "and indeed I think you're weary even now."

"Ah you *must* be a first-rate man—you're such a brute!" she replied, noticing, as she had noticed before, that he pronounced "weary" *weery*.

"I didn't say you were weary of *me*," he said with a certain awkwardness. "But you can never live poor—you don't begin to know the meaning of it."

"Oh no, I'm not tired of you," she declared as if she wished she were. "In a moment you'll make me cry with rage, and no man has done that for years. I was very poor when I was a girl," she added in a different manner. "You yourself recognised it just now in speaking of the insignificant character of my fortune."

"It had to be a fortune to be insignificant," Muniment smiled. "You'll go back to your husband!"

To this she made no answer, only looking at him with a high, gradual clearance of her heat. "I don't see after all why they trust you more than they trust me," she said at last.

"I am not sure they do. I've heard something this evening that suggests that."

"And may one know what it is?"

"A communication which I should have expected to be made through me has been made through another person." 368

"A communication———?"

"To Hyacinth Robinson."

"To Hyacinth———?" The Princess sprang up; she had turned pale in a moment.

"He has got his billet, but they didn't send it through me."

"Do you mean his 'call'? He was here last night," the Princess said.

"A fellow, a worker, named Schinkel, a German—whom you don't know, I think, but who was originally a witness, with me and another, of his undertaking—came to see me this evening. It was through him the call came, and he put Hyacinth up to it on Sunday night."

"On Sunday night?" The Princess stared. "Why he was here yesterday, and he talked of it and told me nothing."

"That was quite right of him, bless his pluck!" Muniment returned.

She closed her eyes a moment and when she opened them again he had risen and was standing before her. "What do they want him to do?" she asked.

"I'm like Hyacinth; I think I had better not tell you—at least till it's over."

"And when will it be over?"

"They give him several days and, I believe, minute instructions—with, however," Paul went on, "considerable discretion in respect to seizing his chance. The thing's made remarkably easy for him. All this I know from Schinkel, who himself knew nothing on Sunday, being merely the fellow to see he got the thing, and who saw him in fact yesterday morning."

"Schinkel trusts you then?" the Princess remarked.

Muniment looked at her steadily. "Yes, but he 369 won't trust you. Hyacinth's to receive a card of invitation to a certain big house," he explained, "a card with the name left in blank, so that he may fill it out himself. It's to be good for each of two grand parties which are to be given at a few days' interval. That's why they give him the job—because at a grand party he'll look in his place."

"He'll like that," she said musingly—"repaying hospitality with a pistol-shot."

"If he doesn't like it he needn't do it."

She made no return to this, but in a moment said: "I can easily find out the place you mean—the big house where two parties are to be given at a few days' interval and where the master—or is it to be the principal guest?—is worth your powder."

"Easily, no doubt. And do you want to warn him?"

"No, I want to do the business myself first, so that it won't be left for another. If Hyacinth will look in his place at a grand party shall not I look still more in mine? And as I know the individual I should be able to approach him without exciting the smallest suspicion."

Muniment appeared for a little to consider her suggestion as if it were practical and interesting; but presently he answered quietly enough: "To fall by your hand would be too good for him."

"However he falls, will it be useful, valuable?" the Princess asked.

"It's worth trying. He's a very bad institution."

"And don't you mean to go near Hyacinth?"

"No, I wish to leave him free."

"Ah, Paul Muniment," she said, "you *are* a first-rate man!" She sank down on the sofa and sat looking up at him. "In God's name, why have you told me this?" 370

"So that you shall not be able to throw it up at me later that I haven't."

She flung herself over, burying her face in the cushions, and remained so for some minutes in silence. He watched her a while without speaking, then at last brought out: "I don't want to aggravate you, but you *will* go back!" The words failed to cause her even to raise her head, and after a moment he—as for the best attenuation of any rudeness—stepped out of the room. 371

XLVII

That she had done with him, done with him for ever, was to remain the most vivid impression Hyacinth had carried away from Madeira Crescent the night before. He went home and threw himself on his narrow bed, where the consolation of sleep again descended on him. But he woke up with the earliest dawn, and the beginning of a new day was a quick revival of pain. He was overpast, he had become vague, he was extinct. Things Sholto had said came back to him, and the compassion of foreknowledge Madame Grandoni had shown him from the first. Of Paul Muniment he only thought to wonder if this great fellow-worker knew. An insurmountable desire to do more than justice to him for the very reason that there might be a temptation to do less forbade him to challenge his friend even in imagination. He vaguely asked himself if *he* would ever be superseded; but this possibility faded away in a stronger light—a dazzling vision of some great tribuneship which swept before him now and again and in which the figure of the Princess herself seemed merged and blurred. When full morning came at last and he got up it brought with it in the restlessness making it impossible he should remain in his room a return of that beginning of an answerless question, "After all, after all——?" which the Princess had planted there the night before when she spoke so <u>372</u> bravely in the name of the Revolution. "After all, after all, since nothing else was tried or would apparently ever be tried——!" He had a sense that his mind, made up as he believed, would fall to pieces again; but that sense in turn lost itself in a shudder which was already familiar—the horror of the public reappearance, in his person, of the imbrued hands of his mother. This loathing of the idea of a *repetition* had not been sharp, strangely enough, till he felt the great, hard hand on his shoulder; in all his previous meditations the growth of his reluctance to act for the "party of action" had not been the fear of a personal stain, but the simple growth of yearning observation. Yet now the idea of the personal stain made him horribly sick; it seemed by itself to make service impossible. It passed before him, or rather it stayed, like a blow dealt back at his mother, already so hideously disfigured; to suffer it to start out in the life of her son was in a manner to place her own forgotten, redeemed pollution again in the eye of the world. The thought that was most of all with him was that he had time, he had time; he was grateful for that and saw a delicacy, a mercy, in their having given him a margin, not condemned him to be pressed by the hours. He had another day, he had two days, he might take three, he might take several. He knew he should be terribly weary of them before they were over; but for that matter they would be over whenever he liked.

Anyhow he went forth again into the streets, into the squares, into the parks, solicited by an aimless desire to steep himself yet once again in the great, indifferent city he so knew and so loved and which had had so many of his smiles and tears and confidences. The day was grey and damp, though no rain fell, and London had never appeared to him to wear more proudly and publicly the stamp of her 373 imperial history. He passed slowly to and fro over Westminster bridge and watched the black barges drift on the great brown river; looked up at the huge fretted palace that rose there as a fortress of the social order which he, like the young David, had been commissioned to attack with a sling and pebble. At last he made his way to Saint James's Park and wandered and pointlessly sat. He watched the swans as from fascination and followed the thoroughfare that communicates with Pimlico. He stopped here presently and came back again; then, over the same pavement, he retraced his steps westward. He looked in the windows of shops—looked especially into the long, glazed expanse of that establishment in which at that hour of the day Millicent Henning discharged superior functions. Her image had descended on him after he came out, and now it moved before him as he went, it clung to him, it refused to quit him. He made in truth no effort to drive it away; he held fast to it in return, and it murmured strange things in his ear. She had been so jolly to him on Sunday; she was such a strong, obvious simple nature, with such a generous breast and such a freedom from the sophistries of civilisation. All he had ever liked in her came back to him now with a finer air, and there was a moment, during which he again made time on the bridge that spans the lake in the Park, seemingly absorbed in the pranks of a young ass in a boat, when he asked himself if at bottom he hadn't liked her better almost than any one. He tried to think he had, he wanted to think he had, and he seemed to see the look her eyes would have if he should swear to her he had. Something of that sort had really passed between them on Sunday, only the business coming up since had brushed it away. Now the taste of the vague, primitive comfort his Sunday had given him revived, 374 and he asked himself if he mightn't have a second and even a deeper draught of it. After he had thought he couldn't again wish for anything he found himself wishing he might believe there was something Millicent could do for him. Mightn't she help him—mightn't she even extricate him? He was looking into a window—not that of her own shop— when a vision rose before him of a quick flight with her, for an undefined purpose, to an undefined spot; and he was glad at that moment to have his back turned to the people in the street, because his face suddenly grew red to the tips of his ears. Again and again, all the same, he indulged in the reflexion that spontaneous, uncultivated minds often have inventions, inspirations. Moreover, whether Millicent should have any or not, he might at least feel the firm roundness of her arms about him. He didn't exactly know what good this would do him or what door it would open, but he should like it. The sensation was not one he could afford to defer, but the nearest moment at which he should be able to enjoy it would be that evening. He had thrown over everything, but she herself would be busy all day; nevertheless it would be a gain, it would be a kind of foretaste, to see her earlier, to have three words with her. He wrestled with the temptation to go into her haberdasher's, because he knew she didn't like it—he had tried it once of old; as the visits of gentlemen even when ostensible purchasers (there were people watching about who could tell who was who) compromised her in the eyes of her employers. This was not an ordinary case, however; and though he hovered a long time, undecided, embarrassed, half-ashamed, at last he went in as by the force of the one, the last, sore personal need left him. He would just make an appointment with her, and a glance of the eye and a single word would suffice. 375

He remembered his way through the labyrinth of the shop; he knew her department was on the upper floor. He walked through the place, which was crowded, as if he had as good a right as any one else; and as he had entertained himself on rising with putting on his holiday garments, in which he made such a tidy figure, he was not suspected of any purpose more nefarious than that of looking for some nice thing to give a lady. He ascended the stairs and found himself in a large room where made-up articles were ranged and where, though there were twenty people in it, a glance told him he shouldn't find Millicent. She was perhaps in the next one, into which he passed by a wide opening. Here also were numerous purchasers, most of them ladies; the men were but three or four and the disposal of the wares all committed to neat young women attired in black dresses with long trains. It struck him at first that the young woman he sought was even here not within sight, and he was turning away to look elsewhere when he suddenly noted a tall gentleman who stood in the middle of the room and who was none other than Captain Sholto. It next became plain to him that the person standing upright before the Captain, as still as a lay-figure and with her back turned to himself, was the object of his own quest. In spite of her averted face he instantly "spotted" Millicent; he knew her shop-attitude, the dressing of her hair behind and the long grand lines of her figure draped in the last new thing. She was showing off this treasure to the Captain, who was lost in contemplation. He had been beforehand with Hyacinth as a false purchaser, but he imitated a real one better than our young man, as, with his eyes travelling up and down the front of their beautiful friend's person, he frowned consideringly and rubbed his lower lip slowly with his walking-stick. Millicent stood admirably still—the back 376 view of the garment she displayed was magnificent. Hyacinth stood for a minute as still as she. By the end of that minute he was convinced Sholto saw him, and for an instant he thought him about to make Milly do as much. But Sholto only looked at him very hard a few seconds, not telling her he was there; to enjoy that satisfaction he would wait till the interloper had gone. Hyacinth gazed back at him for the same length of time—what these two pairs of eyes said to each other requires perhaps no definite mention—and then turned away.

That evening about nine o'clock the Princess Casamassima drove in a hansom to Hyacinth's lodgings in Westminster. The door of the house was a little open and a man stood on the step, smoking his big pipe and looking up and down. The Princess, seeing him while she was still at some distance, had hoped he was Hyacinth, but he proved a different figure indeed from her devoted young friend. He had not a forbidding countenance, but he faced her very directly as she descended from her hansom and approached the door. She was used to the last vulgarity of stare and didn't mind it; she supposed him one of the lodgers in the house. He edged away to let her pass and watched her while she tried to twist life into the limp bell-pull beside the door. It gave no audible response, so that she said to him: "I wish to ask for Mr. Hyacinth Robinson. Perhaps you can tell me——"

"Yes, I too," the man strangely smirked. "I've come also for that."

She seemed to wonder about him. "I think you must be Mr. Schinkel. I've heard of you."

"You know me by my bad English," her interlocutor said with a shade of benevolent coquetry.

"Your English is remarkably good—I wish I 377 spoke German as well. Only just a hint of an accent, and evidently an excellent vocabulary."

"I think I've heard also of you," Schinkel returned with freedom.

"Yes, we know each other in our circle, don't we? We're all brothers and sisters." The Princess was anxious, was in a fever; but she could still relish the romance of standing in a species of back slum and fraternising with a personage so like a very tame horse whose collar galled him. "Then he's at home, I hope; he's coming down to you?" she went on.

"That's what I don't know. I'm waiting."

"Have they gone to call him?"

Schinkel looked at her while he puffed his pipe. "I've galled him myself, but he won't zay."

"How do you mean he won't say?"

"His door's locked. I've knocked many times."

"I suppose he is out," said the Princess.

"Yes, he may be out," Schinkel remarked judicially.

They stood a moment face to face, after which she asked: "Have you any doubt of it?"

"Oh *es kann sein*. Only the woman of the house told me five minutes ago that he came in."

"Well then he probably went out again."

"Yes, but she didn't hear him."

The Princess reflected and was conscious she was flushing. She knew what Schinkel knew about their young friend's actual situation and she wished to be very clear with him and to induce him to be the same with her. She was rather baffled, however, by the sense that he was cautious—justly cautious. He was polite and inscrutable, quite like some of the high personages—ambassadors and cabinet ministers—whom she used to meet in the great world. "Has the woman been here in the house ever since?" she asked in a moment. 378

"No, she went out for ten minutes half an hour ago."

"Surely then he may have gone out again in that time," the Princess argued.

"That's what I've thought. It's also why I've waited here," said Schinkel. "I've nothing to do," he added serenely.

"Neither have I," she returned. "We can wait together."

"It's a pity you haven't some nice room," the German suggested with sympathy.

"No indeed; this will do very well. We shall see him the sooner when he comes back."

"Yes, but perhaps it won't be for long."

"I don't care for that; I'll wait. I hope you don't object to my company," she smiled.

"It's good, it's good," Schinkel responded through his smoke.

"Then I'll send away my cab." She returned to the vehicle and paid the driver, who said with expression "Thank you, my lady" and drove off.

"You gave him too much," observed Schinkel when she came back.

"Oh he looked like a nice man. I'm sure he deserved it."

"It's very expensive," Schinkel went on sociably.

"Yes, and I've no money—but it's done. Was there no one else in the house while the woman was away?" the Princess resumed.

"No, the people are out; she only has single men. I asked her that. She has a daughter, but the daughter has gone to see her cousin. The mother went only a hundred yards, round the corner there, to buy a pennyworth of milk. She locked this door and put the key in her pocket; she stayed at the grocer's, where she got the milk, to have a little conversation with a friend she met there. You <u>379</u> know ladies always stop like that—*nicht wahr?* It was half an hour later that I came. She told me he was at home, and I went up to his room. I got no sound, as I have told you. I came down and spoke to her again, and she told me what I say."

"Then you determined to wait, as I've done," said the Princess.

"Oh yes, I want to see him."

"So do I, very much." She said nothing more for a minute, but then added: "I think we want to see him for the same reason."

"*Das kann sein—das kann sein.*"

The two continued to stand there in the brown evening, and they had some further conversation of a desultory and irrelevant kind. At the end of ten minutes the Princess broke out in a low tone, laying her hand on her companion's arm: "Mr. Schinkel, this won't do. I'm intolerably worried."

"Yes, that's the nature of ladies," the German sagely answered.

"I want to go up to his room," the Princess said. "You'll be so good as to show me where it is."

"It will do you no good if he's not there."

"I'm not sure he's not there."

"Well, if he won't speak it shows he likes better not to have visitors."

"Oh he may like to have *me* better than he does you!" she frankly suggested.

"*Das kann sein—das kann sein.*" But Schinkel made no movement to introduce her into the house.

"There's nothing to-night—you know what I mean," she remarked with a deep look at him.

"Nothing to-night?"

"At the Duke's. The first party's on Thursday, the other next Tuesday."

"*Schön.* I never go to parties," said Schinkel. <u>380</u>

"Neither do I."

"Except that *this* is a kind of party—you and me," he dreadfully grinned.

"Yes, and the woman of the house doesn't approve of it." The footstep of a jealous landlady had become audible in the passage, through the open door, which was presently closed from within with a little reprehensive bang. Something in this touch appeared to quicken exceedingly the Princess's impatience and fear; the danger of being warned off made her wish still more uncontrollably to arrive at the satisfaction she had come for. "For God's sake, Mr. Schinkel, take me up there. If you won't I'll go alone," she pleaded.

Her face was white now and, it need hardly be added, all beautiful with anxiety. The German took in this impression and then, with no further word, turned and reopened the door and went forward, followed closely by his companion.

There was a light in the lower region which tempered the gloom of the staircase—as high, that is, as the first floor; the ascent the rest of the way was so dark that the pair went slowly and Schinkel led his companion by the hand. She gave a suppressed exclamation as she rounded a sharp turn in the second flight. "Good God, is that his door—with the light?"

"Yes, you can see under it. There was a light before," he said without confusion.

"And why in heaven's name didn't you tell me?"

"Because I thought it would worry you."

"And doesn't it worry *you?*"

"A little, but I don't mind," Schinkel professed. "Very likely he may have left it."

"He doesn't leave candles!" she returned with vehemence. She hurried up the few remaining steps to the door and paused there with her ear against it. <u>381</u> Her hand grasped the handle and turned it, but the door resisted. Then she panted to her companion: "We must go in—we must go in!"

"But what will you do when it's locked?" he contended.

"You must break it down."

"It's very expensive," said Schinkel.

"Don't be abject!" cried the Princess. "In a house like this the fastenings are worth nothing; they'll easily yield."

"And if he's not there—if he comes back and finds what we've done?"

She looked at him a moment through the darkness, which was mitigated only by the small glow proceeding from the chink. "He *is* there! Before God he's there!"

"*Schön, schön,*" said her friend as if he felt the contagion of her own dread but was deliberating and meant to remain calm. She assured him that one or two vigorous thrusts with his shoulder would burst the bolt—certain to be some wretched morsel of tin—and she made way for him to come close. He did so, he even leaned against the door, but he gave no violent push, and the Princess waited with her hand against her heart. Schinkel apparently was still deliberating. At last he gave a low sigh. "I know they find him the pistol, it's only for that," he mumbled; and the next moment she saw him sway sharply to and fro in the gloom. She heard a crack and saw the lock had yielded. The door collapsed: they were in the light; they were in a small room which looked full of things. The light was that of a single candle on the mantel; it was so poor that for a moment she made out nothing definite. Before that moment was over, however, her eyes had attached themselves to the small bed. There was something on it—something black, something ambiguous, something 382 outstretched. Schinkel held her back, but only an instant; she saw everything and with the very vision flung herself, beside the bed, upon her knees. Hyacinth lay there as if asleep, but there was a horrible thing, a mess of blood, on the counterpane, in his side, in his heart. His arm hung limp beside him, downwards, off the narrow couch; his face was white and his eyes were closed. So much Schinkel saw, but only for an instant; a convulsive movement of the Princess, bending over the body while a strange low cry came from her lips, covered it up. He looked about him for the weapon, for the pistol, but in her rush at the bed she had pushed it out of sight with her knees. "It's a pity they found it—if he hadn't had it here!" he wailed to her under his breath. He had determined to remain calm, so that, on turning round at the quick advent of the little woman of the house, who had hurried up, white, staring, scared by the sound of the smashed door, he was able to say very quietly and gravely: "Mr. Robinson has shot himself through the heart. He must have done it while you were fetching the milk." The Princess rose, hearing another person in the room, and then Schinkel caught sight of the small revolver lying just under the bed. He picked it up and carefully placed it on the mantel-shelf—keeping all to himself, with an equal prudence, the reflexion that it would certainly have served much better for the Duke.

THE END

Milton Keynes UK
Ingram Content Group UK Ltd.
UKHW040817051024
449151UK00004B/301